Also by Janie Hibler

Easy and Elegant Seafood (1984)
Fair Game: A Hunter's Cookbook (1983)

Dungeness Crabs
and Blackberry Cobblers

Dungeness Crabs
and Blackberry Cobblers

The Northwest Heritage Cookbook

by Janie Hibler

Alfred A. Knopf   New York   1996

This Is a Borzoi Book
Published by Alfred A. Knopf, Inc.

ISBN 0-394-57745-0
ISBN 0-679-76576-X (pbk.)
LC 91-52733

Manufactured in the United States of America

Published November 6, 1991
First Paperback Edition, February 1996

This book is dedicated to the memory of my father,
James F. Franke

There should be no need to argue that the kitchen window is a good observatory from which to watch the course of history.

—Leonard N. Beck, *Two "Loaf-Givers"*

Cultivators of the earth are the most valuable citizens. They are the most vigorous, the most independent, the most virtuous, and they are tied to their country, and wedded to its liberty and interests, by the most lasting bonds.

—Thomas Jefferson

CONTENTS

ACKNOWLEDGMENTS

My lasting appreciation to:
Judith Jones, Barbara Durbin, and Gary Hibler

Also to:
Judith Weber
Ginger Johnston
Dorothy Johansen
Jerry Larson
Esther Nelson
Joe Easley
Floyd W. Bodyfelt
Ignacio Vella
Kassie Franke
Kelly Hibler
Kristin Hibler
Oregon Historical Society
Japanese American Citizens League, Seattle
Nordic Heritage Museum, Seattle
Oregon Department of Agriculture

I also wish to express my deep gratitude to the
hundreds of people who took their time to offer me
information and assistance during the three years it took
to write this book. It would be impossible to name
them all, but without their help, this book could
not have been written.

INTRODUCTION

The Pacific Northwest is physically isolated from the rest of the nation but because it is so rich in agriculture, game, and seafood, it has long been self-sufficient when it comes to providing food. I was born and raised there, in a tiny town in northern California, and as a child always took the bounty of the region for granted. It was not until I ran the Kitchen Kaboodle Cooking School in Portland in the late 1970s that I realized how exceptional this part of the world is. Professionals who came to teach were thrilled with the amazing selection of fresh seafood, fish, vegetables, and fruit. Once, a chef from La Varenne in Paris arrived for several classes. I had spent the morning racing all over town searching for the best and the freshest and was quite nervous as he rummaged through the boxes of food I had assembled. Finally, he looked up and beamed. "Ahhh, Portland is a little Paris. Just look at this beautiful food!"

I grew up in a small community called Bayside, just outside of Arcata on the foggy California coast, 300 miles north of San Francisco and 120 miles south of the Oregon border. The area was, and still is, heavily populated by ranchers, dairy farmers, loggers, and fishermen. Our house sat in a clearing near a redwood forest with a small creek winding through the back of the property. There were huckleberry bushes and wild sorrel growing near the barn, and in summer, we hunted for wild blackberries in the meadow and fished for trout in the creek. We used jarred salmon eggs for bait, and when we ran out, would take off our shoes and socks and wade into the icy creek water to find the caddis fly larvae, tiny wormlike creatures housed in tubular shells, to bait our hooks. We gathered clams—big, juicy razor clams when possible—at Clam Beach and bought fresh Dungeness crabs as soon as the crabbing boats returned to the docks with their crab pots full. My father enjoyed nothing more than our Friday night suppers of fresh crab, or, when the crabs were not in season, just-caught sand dabs.

My godparents have a ranch ten miles inland from the coast toward Redding, where my brother and I helped out each year during haying. I fondly remember my job of running to the milking barn to skim the cream from the top of the milk cans for the morning cereal. My godmother made enormous breakfasts for the crew: eggs, bacon, fried potatoes, toast, jam, and, of course, hot oatmeal with real cream and loads of brown sugar. I loved those meals.

My father and brother duck-hunted on a large pond at the ranch whenever they could get away, for like many people in the Pacific Northwest, they were avid hunters. Nowhere is the sport better; the entire region is covered by the Pacific Flyway, the migratory route for waterfowl. My mother would stuff the ducks with sticks of celery and onion wedges and bake them in a hot oven until they were just done, so that their juices ran free and clear and the skin was crackling good.

My mother and German grandmother were both good cooks and I grew up knowing the difference between good food and mediocre food—although, again, did not realize this until much later. Everything I remember either woman making was given great care. When my grandmother lived in Oakland, California, she thought nothing of searching out the best, which might mean going all the way into San Francisco for a certain kind of pork. Occasionally my father took us with him to San Francisco when he went on business. What a treat to eat at Ernie's or the exotic Trader Vic's! Back home we ate out at the local Italian restaurants, delighting in homemade ravioli, roast squab, and apple fritters. And so I grew up knowing sophisticated and more down-home fare—and loving both.

This duality seems to be a characteristic of the region. As I researched old cookbooks and histories for this book, I discovered dishes as refined as crème brûlée next to others as homespun as blackberry cobbler. I read about how loggers, who have always played an important role in the area, made their own bread and butter at remote logging camps, and when the supper bell sounded, loaded huge plates with enormous quantities of food, spooning dessert right onto the same plate. And yet, just a few hundred miles away in the cities, elegant dinner parties were the rule.

Portland, especially, has a long history of a cosmopolitan lifestyle that many people might not immediately associate with the Pacific Northwest. The city was populated with families who had made their fortunes in canning and lumber and who were anxious to be considered enlightened in every way. Well into the twentieth century they maintained an aura of sophistication by staging grand events and formal dinner parties to which the ladies would wear imported Parisian fashions. Records of some of the parties as well as records of simpler cooking indicate that the food eaten a hundred years ago might easily be found on today's menus. I discovered recipes for curries from the large British population as well as recipes for blueberry catsup (concocted, no doubt, to make good use of the plentiful blueberry crop rather than in any attempt at culinary whimsy), lentil fritters, and alder-smoked salmon. By the late 1800s, Portland's finer hotels offered extensive menus that might include choices between roast duck or fricandeau of lamb with mushroom puree, spring onions and mangoes, fresh tomatoes and foie gras Strasbourg, blackberry pie and imperial blancmange with cream.

The Pacific Northwest has long been known for its tiny Olympia oyster, fresh Chinook salmon, fried razor clams, Dungeness crab, blackberry cobbler, and huckleberry pie. I include recipes for these in the book. Some are from old cookbooks and I have barely altered them; others I have updated; and still others are my own creation.

I learned to cook from my mother but it was not until I was grown and had my own family that I began to cook seriously. After I got married and moved to Eugene for graduate studies, my husband and I spent five years as relatively poor students. Fortunately he liked to hunt as much as my father and brother had, and I stocked our freezer with venison and ducks. I often say I learned to cook game in self-defense: The sheer quantity laid away in the freezer presented a delightful challenge. As often as possible, we supplemented the game with seafood and fish. The days we gathered clams and mussels or fished for salmon, smelt, and steelhead turned into exhilarating outings that always ended with a marvelous feast. The long growing season allowed us to set the table with fresh vegetables from our own garden and ripe berries plucked from a nearby blackberry patch. We frequently had other students around the table, and, as is characteristic of the region, everyone contributed something from the garden, the sea, or the woods. Ever since I can remember, friends and neighbors have shared food. If someone had extra salmon, he would share it. Women exchanged jars of "put-ups" such as blackberry jam and pear butter. People who gathered wild mushrooms from the forest floor happily supplied others with these pungent delicacies.

I am sure the generous spirit of the region evolves from pioneer days, when survival depended on cooperation in all things. The vast Pacific Northwest, which covers more than a third of the United States, was first explored by trappers as they pushed ever westward in search mainly of beaver. The formidable Hudson's Bay Company financed many of the expeditions into the wilderness in its quest to establish posts and trading routes for its far-flung empire. The British-run company sought to practice conservation in the fur fields, maintain stable prices, and integrate the Native Americans into its operation with relative justice and tranquillity. Eventually trapping gave way to lumbering and farming as more and more settlers made their way to the virgin territory.

In 1825 the Hudson's Bay Company built Fort Vancouver on the plain above the mighty Columbia River. An outpost for the increasing trading and trapping in the area, the fort was about 115 miles from the coast and 6 miles from the juncture of the Willamette and Columbia rivers. Dr. John McLoughlin oversaw the operation of the fort, which today is in Vancouver, Washington, and still maintained as an historic site.

McLoughlin welcomed adventurers, scientists, and scholars who traveled to Fort Vancouver from England and eastern North America to taste life in the wilderness and test various theories and ideas. For instance, David Douglas, the famed botanist, spent time there. Under McLoughlin's tutelage, fine meals were prepared at the fort, wrought from the bounty of the land as well as the lush and extensive vegetable gardens and orchards and 1,500 acres of wheat fields he had surrounding the compound. Dr. McLoughlin had long before decided he preferred the frontier to medicine, but nevertheless made certain he enjoyed a good life. To this end, he set his table with Spode china and fine stemware into which he poured wines and brandy imported from Europe, dressed for dinner nightly, and insisted that elk roast and bear steak be served with the same ceremony as more refined dishes handed around by liveried Indian servants.

In a journal she kept during her trip westward, missionary Narcissa Whitman described meals she had at Fort Vancouver with Dr. McLoughlin in September 1836. Married to Presbyterian missionary Marcus Whitman, Narcissa was a golden-haired beauty who, by all reports, relished the excitement and wonders of life in the untamed West. Her spirit and enthusiasm infuse several firsthand accounts written by people who knew her, and although she was brutally killed by a Cayuse Indian in 1844, she was, eight years earlier, one of the first of two white women to enter the territory. Her daughter, Alice Clarissa, born in 1837, was the first white child born west of the Continental Divide.

I have not given you a description of our eatable here [wrote Narcissa]. There is such a variety I know not where to begin. For breakfast we have coffee or coaco, Salt Salmon & roast duck wild & potatoes. When we have eaten our supply of them our plates are changed & we made a finish on bread & butter. For dinner we have a greater variety. First we are always treated to a dish of soup, which is very good. Every kind of vegitable in use is taken & choped fine & put into water with a little rice & boiled to a soup. The taumatoes are a promanant article. Usually some fowl meat duck or any kind, is cut fine & added if it has been roasted once it is just as good, (so the cook says) they spiced to the taste. After our soup dishes are removed, then comes a variety of meats, to prove our tastes. After selecting & tasting, changes plates & try another if we choose, so at every new dish, have a clean plate. Roast duck is an every day dish, boiled pork, tripe, & sometimes trotters, fresh

*Salmon or Sturgeon, yea to numerous to mention. When
these are set aside A rice pudding or an apple pie is next
introduced. After this melons next make their appearance,
some times grapes & last of all cheese, bread or biscuit &
butter is produced to complet the whole.*

As the days of the beaver trappers and the dominance of the
Hudson's Bay Company drew to a close, first-generation Americans
from the South and Midwest found their way to the fertile Willamette
Valley and environs. New Englanders arrived by boat by sailing around
Cape Horn, bringing household goods and books not much seen on
the frontier. They settled inland, naming newly founded cities after
their East Coast homes of Portland and Salem. British and Scandinavians settled along the coast, feeling at home in the damp climate and
along the rocky shore, and made their living fishing, logging, and
working in dairies. The first Asians to arrive were the Chinese, who
came in the 1850s to work in the gold mines but frequently took jobs
building the railroads and working in logging camps and canneries.
The Japanese followed, lured by high pay and numerous jobs.

The pioneers and immigrants brought more than their recipes and
cooking styles with them. Many were experienced farmers, sheepherders, brewers, and bakers. The French Canadians constructed a boat
fashioned after the St. Lawrence skiff and the bateaux of their home-
land that quickly became the prototype for the Rogue River and the
McKenzie River drift boats; Mediterranean fishing boats were the
model for the Pacific Northwest salmon trollers.

Salmon, more than any other food, is associated with the region.
Long before the white settlers arrived, Native Americans had learned to
catch, smoke, and revere the fish. Tribes such as the Multnomah,
Clackamas, Wishram, Tillamook, and Skagit patterned their lives and
many of their religious ceremonies around the spawning cycles of the
salmon. The Indian method for smoking salmon is, I feel, their greatest contribution to the food of the area, although they also taught the
pioneers much about the edible wild berries, mushrooms, and plants
available for the picking in the forests and fields.

The Native American desire to live in harmony with nature was evident to me when I was growing up and knew the Hoopa and Yurok Indians who lived nearby. Because we grew up side by side and because my sister-in-law is a Yurok, I have a very special place in my heart for them. While some of them attended our high school, many went to school on the Hoopa Indian Reservation and we played against them in basketball and football. I recently went to the annual Root Festival on the Warm Springs Reservation in central Oregon and witnessed, as I knew I would, the deep devotion of the Indians as they celebrated the yearly renewal of the earth.

The number of tribes of Native Americans in the Pacific Northwest attests to its amazing geographical diversity. The region is most easily understood if divided north to south by the magnificent Cascade Mountain range. West of the mountains lie the coastal strip and the fertile western lowlands. East of the mountains is the arid and semi-arid Intermontane region. The mountains themselves receive 200 to 600 inches of snowfall a year at their highest elevations, where the alpine summer lasts barely thirty days. The deep Pacific extends inland through the Strait of Juan de Fuca for more than 200 miles, and where the land and sea meet, begin majestic conifer forests with some of the world's tallest and oldest trees. Here, in damp and shady fern-lined groves, thrives an enormous variety of wild mushrooms as well as wildlife and birds. Bays and estuaries all along the coastline are natural nurseries for many species of fish and shellfish and refuges for migratory game birds. Deer and elk roam the misty coastal hillsides, often coming down into towns to forage through backyards.

The western lowlands extend from the Rogue Valley in southern Oregon to the Puget Sound lowlands in the north. Rainfall in this largely landlocked region averages thirty-five to forty-five inches a year and the rich alluvial soil is fed by a vast network of rivers and creeks that contain a variety of trout and seasonal runs of salmon, steelhead, and shad. Lakes and ponds provide nesting grounds for ducks and geese, and deer inhabit the lower foothills of the Cascades. Both Portland and Seattle are situated in the lowlands, as is the fertile Willamette Valley. The valley, well known for its bountiful agriculture, is precisely halfway between the equator and the north pole, and the long summer days and mild weather make it ideal for growing a large number of diversified crops. The gentle temperate climate and rolling countryside are perfect, too, for berries of every description and have made the Pacific Northwest the berry capital of the world.

East of the Cascades the dense Douglas fir forests give way to flat fields of waving wheat that punctuate the Intermontane region. Much of the land has been irrigated, making valleys such as the Wenatchee and Okanogan well known for agriculture. Oregon's high desert lies in the southeastern part of the state, its 24,000 square miles making it approximately the size of West Virginia and the Pacific Northwest's primary cattle-grazing country. Throughout the Intermontane region live mule deer, Rocky Mountain elk, antelope, mountain sheep, and many species of upland game.

From such topographic and climatic variety and so many cultural and ethnic roots—Native American, pioneer, and immigrant—the cuisine of the Pacific Northwest has blossomed into an exciting and innovative one. Today the most influential and fastest-growing population is Asian. East-meets-West or Pacific Rim cooking is exploding up and down the entire West Coast, with Vancouver, Seattle, and Portland as much in the forefront of this culinary movement as Los Angeles and San Francisco. Throughout the book you will find recipes reflecting the Asian influence as I see it.

I hope *Dungeness Crabs and Blackberry Cobblers* brings you closer to the variety and joys of the cooking from this rich, abundant region. Some of the recipes will probably read like old friends, others will quickly become new and intriguing acquaintances. As you read through the book, you will discover how we, from the region, have always prepared game, seafood, fish, vegetables, and fruit. You will also find new ways to cook with the indigenous ingredients, mingling them with more exotic, imported foodstuffs to create dishes unlike any prepared elsewhere in the world. And as you go along, you will, I trust, recall the many men and women who, through hard work and an admirable sense of adventure, settled the area we know as the Pacific Northwest.

Dungeness Crabs
and Blackberry Cobblers

A Sharp Carousel II, 700 watt microwave/convection oven
was used for all the microwave recipes in this book.

How the Coyote Brought Fire
to the People

*At the beginning of the world, people had no fire. The only fire anywhere
was on top of a high mountain, guarded by evil spirits, or skookums. The
skookums would not give any of their fire to the animal people. They were
afraid that if people should become comfortable, they might become
powerful—as powerful as the spirits.*

*So the people had no heat in their lodges, and they had to eat their
salmon raw. When Coyote came among them, he found them cold and
miserable. "Coyote," they begged, "bring us fire from the mountains, or we
will die from the cold."*

"I will see what I can do for you," Coyote promised.

*When the new sun came up, Coyote began the long climb to the
snow-covered top of the mountain. There he found that three old,
wrinkled skookums watched the fire all day and all night, one at a time.
While one guarded, the others stayed in a lodge near by. When it became
another's turn to watch, the one at the fire would come to the door and say,
"Sister, sister, get up and guard the fire."*

*At dawn, when the air was chilly, the new guard was slow in coming
from the lodge. "This is my time to steal a brand of fire," Coyote said to
himself. But he knew that he would be chased by the three skookums. They
were old, but they were very swift runners. How could he get away from them?*

*Though Coyote was very wise, he could not think of a good plan. So
he decided to ask his three sisters who lived in his stomach in the form of
huckleberries. They were very wise. They could tell him what to do.*

But at first his sisters in the form of huckleberries would not help him.

3

"If we tell you," they said to Coyote, "you will say that you knew that yourself."

Coyote remembered that his sisters did not like hail. So he looked up into the sky and called out, "Hail! Hail! Fall down from the sky."

His sisters were afraid and cried, "Stop! Stop! Don't bring the hail. Don't bring the hail. We will tell you whatever you need to know."

Then his three sisters told him how he could get a brand of fire from the three skookums and how he could bring it down the mountain to the people.

When they had finished talking, Coyote said, "Yes, my sisters. That is what I thought. That was my plan all the time."

When Coyote had come down from the skookums' fire, he called all the animals together, just as his sisters had directed. He told each animal— Cougar and Fox and Squirrel and others—to take a certain place along the mountainside. Each place was in a line between the people's lodges and the fire guarded by the skookums.

Then he climbed the mountain again and waited for the sun to come up. The skookum guarding the fire saw him, but she thought him just an ordinary animal skulking around the lodge.

At dawn, Coyote saw the skookum leave the fire and heard her call, "Sister, sister, get up and guard the fire."

As she went inside the lodge, Coyote sprang forth and seized a burning brand from the fire. Down across the snow fields he ran. In an instant the three skookums were following him, showering ice and snow upon him as they ran. He leaped across the huge cracks in the ice, but soon he could hear the skookums behind him. Their hot breath scorched the fur on his flanks. One of them seized the tip of his tail in her claw, and it turned black. Ever since then, coyote tails have been tipped with black.

Panting and hot, Coyote reached the tree line and sank to the ground, tired and out of breath. There Cougar jumped from his hiding place behind some little fir trees. He seized the burning brand and ran down through the scrubby trees and the rocks. When he came to the taller trees, Cougar passed the fire to Fox. Fox ran with it until he came to the thick underbrush.

Then Squirrel seized the hot brand and leaped from tree to tree. The fire was still so hot that it burned a black spot on the back of Squirrel's neck and made his tail curl up. You can see the black spot and the curled tail on squirrels, even today. The skookums, still chasing the fire, hoped to catch Squirrel at the edge of the forest.

But under the last tree, Antelope was waiting to run with the brand across the meadow. Antelope was the fastest of all the animals. One after another, the animals carried the fire. All hoped the skookums would soon be tired out.

At last, when only a coal was left, it was given to squatty little Frog. Squatty little Frog swallowed the hot coal and hopped away as fast as he could hop. The youngest skookum, though she was very tired, was sure she could catch Frog. She seized his tail, and held tight. But Frog did not stop. He made the biggest jump he had ever made. And he left his tail behind him in the skookum's claws. Ever since, frogs have had no tails.

Still Frog did not stop. He made a long, deep dive into a river and came up on the other side. But the skookum leaped across. A second time she caught up with Frog. He was too tired to jump again. To save the fire, he spat it out of his mouth on Wood, and Wood swallowed it. The other two skookums joined their sister. All three stood by, helpless, not knowing how to take the fire away from Wood. Slowly they went back to their lodge on top of the mountain.

Then Coyote came to the place where the fire was, and the people came close, too. Coyote was very wise. He knew how to bring fire out of Wood. He showed the people how to rub the two dry sticks together until sparks came. He showed them how to make a bigger fire from the burning chips and pine needles.

Ever after that, the people knew how to use fire. With fire they cooked their food and with fire they heated their homes.

—*Ella E. Clark,* Indian Legends of the Pacific Northwest
(Berkeley, California: University of California Press, 1953).

This story was told all the way from the Karok along the Klamath River in northern California to the Plateau tribes of northern Washington.

Appetizing Bites of the Northwest

When I entertain, I often don't serve appetizers before a meal, but when I do, I like them to be simple, fresh, and not overly filling. The abundance of local fresh foods in the Pacific Northwest provides a wide selection of exciting offerings from which to choose.

Many of my favorite appetizers are seafood. Oysters on the half shell, freshly shucked and floating in a sea of sweet oyster liquor, were often served at the beginning of a meal before the turn of the century. Today, fresh oysters are still in demand and there's an even greater variety to choose from. When I serve them at home, I simply sprinkle the shucked oysters with freshly cracked pepper and lemon juice.

Other local shellfish, such as crab, shrimp, and crawfish, can also be served just as they are—straight from the shell—accompanied by an herb mayonnaise, a lettuce-lined basket filled with crisp vegetable slices, or both. Delicious chunks of alder-smoked salmon, available through-out the year, can be paired with fresh local bread or crackers for another simple seafood appetizer that tastes great and takes little effort.

Fresh fruit and locally made cheese can pass as either an appetizer or a dessert. Fresh pears are in the markets most of the year, but they need to be purchased several days in advance to ripen, and there's a wide variety of apples to choose from. Apples that are slightly tart, such as Gravenstein or Newton, are delicious served sliced with crackers and local sharp cheddar cheese. Recently I was in Portland at the home of good friends, Doug and Trudi Walta. For an appetizer they offered bunches of tiny champagne grapes sprinkled with sweet fresh black-berries on a large white porcelain platter. Accompanied by a basket of crackers and a wedge of locally made cheese, it was simple and elegant.

When I have a more formal dinner party, I serve appetizers as a first course. Steamed Oysters with Champagne Mayonnaise, Pan-Fried Curried Oysters with Sour Cream and Caviar, and Smoked Rainbow Trout with Gin and Capers all make spectacular hors d'oeuvres— and they're simple to prepare. They offer guests a few savory bites of Northwest bounty to whet the appetite for the meal to come.

KIMMAI'S VIETNAMESE SHRIMP AND PORK ROLLS

PHYLLO PURSES FILLED WITH WILD MUSHROOMS AND GOAT CHEESE

WILD MUSHROOM PIZZA

VEGETABLE PLATTER WITH WARM BLUE CHEESE DIP AND SMOKED EGGS

PEAR SLICES WITH OREGON BLUE CHEESE AND PROSCIUTTO

WINTER PEARS WITH GOUDA CHEESE AND SMOKED HAZELNUTS

SMOKED HAZELNUTS

POLENTA TOAST WITH CAVIAR AND SOUR CREAM

SMOKED RAINBOW TROUT WITH GIN AND CAPERS

BELGIUM ENDIVE STUFFED WITH HERB-FLAVORED CRAB

DUNGENESS CRAB AND SPINACH RAVIOLIS

WILD CRAWFISH WITH FRESH DILL

SMOKED STURGEON PÂTÉ

RUSSIAN RYE WITH SMOKED SALMON AND SORREL MAYONNAISE

COCKTAIL RYE BREAD WITH SMOKED STURGEON BUTTER

PACIFIC NORTHWEST SALMON-CAPER SPREAD

FOCACCIA WITH SMOKED SALMON AND BASIL MAYONNAISE

SMOKED SALMON IN TOASTED NORI WRAPPERS

BALLARD GRAVLAX WITH FRESH DILL

SMOKED SABLEFISH (BLACK COD) WITH MUSTARD DIPPING SAUCE

OYSTERS ON THE HALF SHELL WITH CRACKED PEPPER AND LEMON

STEAMED OYSTERS WITH CHAMPAGNE MAYONNAISE

PAN-FRIED CURRIED OYSTERS WITH SOUR CREAM AND CAVIAR

ASPARAGUS ROLLS WITH PROSCIUTTO AND FRESH ROSEMARY

BAGUETTE SLICES WITH SHRIMP, AVOCADO, AND GOAT CHEESE

LENTIL PÂTÉ

Kimmai's Vietnamese Shrimp and Pork Rolls

A Vietnamese Survivor Catering in Portland

Kimmai, a native of Ho Chi Minh City (formerly Saigon), barely escaped from Vietnam after the Communist takeover in 1975. She and her four children crawled all night through a forest to reach the boat that was to take them to freedom. When she tried to pay the boat owner with diamonds and jewels she had hidden inside her daughter's backpack, she discovered her daughter had thrown the back-pack away—it had gotten too heavy on the long trip through the woods. She pleaded with the boat owner and was eventually allowed to get on the

~~~~→

The recent influx of Asians into the Pacific Northwest has made them our fastest-growing ethnic group. Like other immigrant groups before them, they have introduced the cuisine of their homeland to the public in small family-owned restaurants. I first ate these scrumptious shrimp and pork rolls in Kimmai Hong's Vietnamese restaurant, The Saigon Express, in Portland. Kimmai fills rice paper (sold dried at most oriental grocery stores) with fresh shrimp, cilantro, mint, slivers of carrot, lettuce, and rice noodles, then rolls them like a typical Chinese egg roll. She doesn't deep-fry them, though, but serves them just as they are, crisp and fresh, with a tasty peanut dipping sauce that will keep in the refrigerator for weeks. These rolls have been voted the best shrimp rolls in the Pacific Northwest by both the *Downtowner* and *Pacific Northwest* magazine.

Makes 10 shrimp rolls

1	10-ounce boneless pork tenderloin*
5	ounces rice noodles
10	rice papers, 8½ inches in diameter
1½	pounds medium shrimp, cooked and peeled
1	cup fresh mint leaves
2	cups cilantro leaves
1	small carrot, peeled and cut into 2-inch slivers
4	ounces bean sprouts
5	green leaf lettuce leaves, shredded
1	bunch cilantro
	Peanut Dipping Sauce (recipe follows)

* I sometimes make these rolls omitting the pork.

Boil the pork tenderloin in enough water to cover until cooked (about 20 minutes). Let cool to room temperature, then cut into thin slices. Set aside.

Soak the rice noodles in water to cover for 30 minutes. Bring the water to a boil and cook for 5 minutes. Drain.

To assemble the rolls, dampen one side of a piece of rice paper and lay it, damp side down, on a flat surface. Put 2 shrimp in the center of the paper, 2 slices of pork over the shrimp, followed by 4 leaves each of mint and cilantro and 5 slivers of carrot. Arrange a tablespoon each of bean sprouts and rice noodles over the herbs, followed by ¼ cup shredded lettuce.

Fold one end of the rice paper over the top of the filling, tuck in both sides, and roll it over. Dip your finger in water and rub it along the edge to seal it closed. Place it, seam side down, on a plate. Repeat for the other 9 pieces of rice paper. Serve the spring rolls on a bed of cilantro leaves with the following Peanut Dipping Sauce.

boat with her children. After an almost fatal boat trip, they arrived in Malaysia and lived in a refugee camp for six months before finally coming to the United States. Kimmai first settled in Salem, but eventually came to Portland, where she currently works as a caterer and markets her spring rolls and sauces.

Peanut Dipping Sauce
Makes about 2 cups

- ½ cup black bean sauce or hoisin sauce
- ¼ teaspoon crushed garlic
- ¼ cup sugar
- ½ teaspoon salt
- 1 cup water
- 1 teaspoon corn oil
- ¼ cup creamy peanut butter
- 4 tablespoons crushed, roasted peanuts

Cook the black bean sauce, garlic, sugar, salt, water, and oil for 3 minutes over medium heat. Stir in the peanut butter and cook, stirring constantly, for 2 more minutes.

Let the sauce cool. Serve it at room temperature garnished with the chopped peanuts.

Well-Guarded Secrets

*Asians and Europeans
have used wild mush-
rooms in their cooking
for centuries and they
have gradually intro-
duced them to Amer-
icans. The moist climate
of the Pacific Northwest
makes it one of the
nation's most prolific
wild mushroom-grow-
ing regions, and today
favorite mushroom
patches are well-
guarded secrets. The
legendary University
of Seattle professor and
author Angelo M.
Pellegrini wrote in his
book,* Wine and the
Good Life *(New York:
Knopf, 1965):*

   *"Oh, these mush-
rooms! I have never
tasted any so delicious!"*
   *"I went ninety miles
into the Cascade Moun-
tains to get them for you."*
   *"Where in the
Cascades?"*
   *"North of Mount
Rainier and south of
Mount Baker."*
   *"Some two hundred
miles of mountains sep-
arate the two."*
   *"Right. And some-
where on that rocky,
timbered patch of*

Phyllo Purses Filled with Wild Mushrooms and Goat Cheese

The mild and moist climate of the Puget Sound low-lands surrounding Seattle produces lush grasses that livestock graze on nine months of the year. Dairy products from this region are exceptional, and Caprial Pence, chef at Fullers restaurant in the Seattle Sheraton Hotel and Towers, combines rich local goat cheese with several Northwest wild mushrooms in this delicious appetizer. I have decreased the amount of butter and thyme from the original recipe.

Makes 1 dozen

Filling

1	tablespoon unsalted butter
3	shallots, peeled and chopped
3	garlic cloves, peeled and chopped
2	cups sliced wild mushrooms, such as chanterelle, shiitake, and oyster mushrooms
¼	cup mild goat cheese
½	teaspoon whole dried thyme, crushed*
⅛	teaspoon salt
⅛	teaspoon freshly ground pepper
4	sheets phyllo dough, 12 x 17 inches
3–4	tablespoons unsalted butter, melted

   * *I buy dried thyme leaves and crush them in the palm of
   my hand. This tastes much fresher than ground thyme.*

Preheat the oven to 350°F. and lightly grease a baking sheet.

Heat the butter in a sauté pan and sauté the shallots and garlic for 3 or 4 minutes. Add the mushrooms and sauté until tender. Remove them from the heat and stir in the goat cheese and thyme. Season with salt and pepper and let cool.

Stack the sheets of phyllo and cut them into 12 stacks of squares (approximately 4 x 4 inches). Take one stack of squares and brush two 4 x 4-inch sheets of phyllo with butter. Place 2 more sheets on top of the buttered phyllo. Put 1 tablespoon of the mushroom mixture in the middle of the dough. Bring the corners up to form a packet and seal ends by brushing with butter. Repeat until all the filling is used. Tightly wrap any extra pastry dough and store in the refrigerator.

Bake on a cookie sheet for 20 minutes, or until the phyllo is golden brown. Serve immediately.

ground there is a tiny spot whence these mushrooms came. To ask a mushroom hunter to take you to the patch, or to tell you exactly where it is, is to ask for that which is not in his nature to give. He may be generous and honest to the core in all else; but where mushrooms are in question, he is the embodiment of greed and deceit. Ask him, as you asked me, where he found his mushrooms, and he will point vaguely toward a convenient horizon, or send you miles to the north if he gathered them to the south. Well, I am myself a mushroom hunter with decades of experience, seasoned in deceit; but since you are my friends, I will tell you this much: The genus is Boletus; the species, edulis. It is the undisputed Monarch of edible mushrooms. In this state it thrives at certain altitudes in the Cascade Mountains; in some places in the spring; in others, in the fall. I can say no more; I have been more explicit than the code of Brotherhood permits. Go now and search for them and find them if you can...."

Wild Mushroom Pizza

This showy pizza recipe was given to me by my good friend Betty Shenberger, who uses two types of mushrooms being cultivated in the Pacific Northwest, the shiitake and the oyster, and a mixture of cheeses and fresh herbs, for a savory filling. She makes it on a rectangular baking sheet and arranges the strips of bright red peppers in neat rows over the white cheese filling. You can substitute with whatever kinds of wild mushrooms you find in your part of the country. Firmer mushrooms, such as morels and chanterelles, will need to be slowly sautéed in a small amount of butter before being added to the pizza.

8 servings

1½ *tablespoons cornmeal*
1½ *tablespoons dry yeast*
1 *cup warm water*
4 *tablespoons olive oil (¼ cup)*
3 *cups all-purpose flour*
1 *teaspoon salt*
2 *ounces Montrachet cheese*
2 *ounces cream cheese*
2 *tablespoons sour cream*
8 *ounces shredded mozzarella cheese (2 cups)*
1 *pound fresh or canned plum tomatoes, sliced and drained (approximately 6 medium-size)*
½ *cup thinly sliced onion*
3–4 *thinly sliced sun-dried tomatoes*
3 *tablespoons each chopped fresh parsley and basil*
2 *tablespoons chopped fresh rosemary*
2 *ounces shiitake mushrooms, thinly sliced*
2 *ounces oyster mushrooms, thinly sliced*
½ *peeled, roasted red pepper, thinly sliced (see page 202)*
½ *cup shredded Parmesan cheese*

Preheat the oven to 350°F. and dust a 13-inch pizza pan or a 10 x 15-inch baking sheet with cornmeal.

Dissolve the yeast in ¼ cup of the warm water. Stir in the remaining ¾ cup water and 2 tablespoons of the olive oil and set aside. (Or mix in the food processor. See method below.) This dough requires no rising.

Blend the flour and salt together and stir in the liquid. Form the dough into a ball and knead 10–12 times on a floured surface.

Roll out the dough and arrange it on the pan. Bake for 10 minutes. Remove it from the oven and brush it with 1 tablespoon olive oil and set aside.

Raise the oven temperature to 425°F.

Blend the Montrachet, cream cheese, and sour cream together and set aside.

Sprinkle the crust with the mozzarella cheese and cover with a layer of plum tomatoes and onions. Add the sun-dried tomatoes and chopped herbs. Dot with the Montrachet mixture and bake 10 minutes.

Heat the remaining 1 tablespoon olive oil and sauté the wild mushrooms for 3–4 minutes. Spread the mushrooms over the pizza and arrange the red pepper strips over all. Sprinkle with Parmesan cheese and return to the oven for another 10 minutes, or until the cheese melts. Let stand 5–10 minutes before cutting.

Food Processor Method for Crust:

Dissolve the yeast in ¼ cup warm water and stir in the remaining water and 2 tablespoons olive oil. Measure the flour and salt into a food processor workbowl with a steel blade. Turn the machine on and slowly add the liquid until the dough forms a ball. Add 1 or 2 more tablespoons of water if necessary.

Vegetable Platter with Warm Blue Cheese Dip and Smoked Eggs

Oregon Blue Cheese

Oregon Blue Cheese has a wonderful creamy interior marbled with deep blue veins. It's made from raw cow's milk at the Rogue River Valley Creamery in Central Point, Oregon, and aged ninety days. The owner, ninety-two-year-old Thomas G. Vella (whose son Ignacio manages the Vella Cheese Factory in Sonoma, California), is a native of Sicily who returned to his home-land after fighting in World War I. One day shortly thereafter, he met with a band of peasants on the baron's property (who was not in residence) to initiate land reform. They went to the dining-room parapet overlooking the surrounding countryside to divvy up the baron's property. Two of the men immediately began to quarrel over the same piece of land, pulled knives, and fought each other to the death. According to Ignacio, his father said: "The hell with this. We haven't even done what

~~~~>

I like to serve this dip on cold wintry nights when the fir trees are covered with snow. The smoked eggs can easily be prepared inside by marinating them in soy sauce flavored with liquid smoke. When the dip is warmed, the heat not only thins it, but intensifies its flavor.

4–6 servings

4 ounces Oregon Blue Cheese
½ cup mayonnaise
½ cup sour cream
1 garlic clove, peeled and crushed
   Pinch of salt, if necessary
   Smoked Eggs, halved or quartered (recipe follows)
   Crudités
6 lettuce leaves

Blend the blue cheese, mayonnaise, sour cream, garlic, and salt together until the mixture is smooth. Heat it in a saucepan until it is warm or microwave on Medium for 90 seconds.

Arrange Smoked Eggs and crudités on lettuce leaves with cheese dip in the center.

Smoked Eggs

Peel 4 hard-boiled eggs and smoke for 1 hour, using alder or hickory chips and a cold (less than 200°F.) smoke. If you don't have a smoker, gently crack the hard-cooked eggs and soak them in a mixture of ½ cup soy sauce and ½ teaspoon liquid smoke for 1–2 hours. Peel before serving.

Crudités

Use an assortment of crudités, such as asparagus spears, carrots, celery, endive leaves, broccoli florets, scallions or green onions, jìcama, sugar snap peas, red bell peppers, and cherry tomatoes.

Pear Slices with Oregon Blue Cheese and Prosciutto

The major winter pear varieties include the Anjou, Bosc, Comice, Nelis, Forelle, and Seckel pears and, of the national harvest, ninety-five percent are grown in Oregon and Washington. Pears have a sweet, buttery flesh which makes them a perfect counterbalance to the saltiness of the prosciutto and cheese used in this recipe.

4 servings

4   *butter lettuce leaves*
6   *ounces thinly sliced prosciutto*
1   *ripe pear, cored and sliced into ½-inch-thick wedges*
½   *pound Oregon Blue Cheese, broken into bite-size pieces*

Line a plate with lettuce leaves.

Separate the pieces of prosciutto and lay them on a cutting board. Cut each piece in half, lengthwise, into approximately twelve 3 x 5-inch pieces. Slice each wedge of pear in half, or into a bite-size piece, and put each piece in the center of a piece of prosciutto. Put ½–1 teaspoon of blue cheese on top of the pear and wrap the prosciutto over the pear and cheese. Place, seam side down, on the lettuce-lined serving plate and chill until served.

we're going to do and you're already killing each other." He threw their weapons on the table and immediately went down to Palermo to apply for a visa. He sailed for New York and eventually settled in Sonoma, California, where he started the Vella Cheese Factory in 1931 and the Rogue River Valley Creamery in 1935. Tom eventually brought Danish cheese maker Leon Warming to the Rogue River Valley Creamery and he developed Oregon Blue Cheese. According to Floyd Bodyfelt, one of the country's top cheese experts and extension dairy-processing specialist at Oregon State University, the Danish-style Oregon Blue Cheese is "the most underrated blue cheese in North America." I think it's one of America's best blue cheeses and I particularly like its mild flavor and creamy texture. As you can see by the recipes in this book, I use it in everything from appetizers to desserts.

Winter Pears with Gouda Cheese and Smoked Hazelnuts

Yakima Gouda Cheese

I was first introduced to Yakima Gouda cheese at a local deli in Portland. I was waiting for my order at the counter when a tall, blond man strolled up and ordered a pound of Yakima Gouda cheese in a strong accent. He commented that he had driven all the way from eastern Oregon to buy this cheese that tasted just like the Gouda from his native Holland. And it's not surprising that it should be the genuine article—the cheese is

~~~~>

A Danish dairy farm

I use locally produced Yakima Valley (Washington) Gouda cheese for this recipe. It has a deep, rich flavor and smooth texture that is wonderfully compatible with a slice of pear.

6–8 servings

1   pound Gouda cheese
2   ripe winter pears
1   pound Smoked Hazelnuts (see page 17)

Remove the rind from the cheese and put the cheese in the center of a serving dish. Vertically cut the pears into quarters and remove the cores. Cut each quarter into ¼-inch slices and arrange them on the plate around the cheese. Put a cheese knife on the plate and serve accompanied by the smoked nuts.

Smoked Hazelnuts

I have included two different techniques for smoking hazelnuts and either way it's a simple process. The nuts are first roasted in the oven, which not only intensifies the flavor but makes it easier to remove their skins.

Makes 1¾ cups

½   *pound shelled hazelnuts (1¾ cups)*
1½ *tablespoons butter or corn oil margarine, melted*
¼   *teaspoon kosher salt*
½   *teaspoon liquid smoke*
¾   *teaspoon chili powder*
    Dash of cayenne pepper

Preheat the oven to 275°F.

Spread the shelled hazelnuts in a shallow pan and roast for 20–30 minutes, until their skins crack. Remove the skins by rubbing the nuts while warm with a rough cloth or between your hands.

Oven Method:

Mix the butter, salt, liquid smoke, chili powder, and cayenne pepper together. Toss the nuts in the mixture and wipe out the pan they were baked in. Put the nuts back in the pan and bake them for an additional 10 minutes at 275°F.

Using a Smoker:

To smoke the nuts in a smoker, toss them with the butter, salt, chili powder, and cayenne pepper. Place them on a screen or in a small wire basket and smoke them for 1 hour with cold smoke using alder chips.

made by the Yakima Cheese Company in Sunnyside, Washington. Dave Newhouse, one of the owners, is the son of Dutch immigrants. He and his partner brought an expert Dutch cheese maker to the United States several years ago to teach them how to make authentic Gouda. It is a semisoft, brine-ripened cheese that's made from the milk of Holsteins. "We like to moderate the butterfat content—the closer we can get the butterfat content to the protein level, the better the cheese."

Polenta Toast with Caviar and Sour Cream

Pacific Northwest Caviar

Another Pacific North-west caviar processor is Marko Petrich, owner of Tony's Smokehouse and Cannery, Inc., in Oregon City, Oregon. He learned the tech-nique from his late grandfather Tony Petrich, a Yugoslavian fisherman who emi-grated to the United States in 1923. Marko buys skeins of sturgeon eggs from local fisher-men when the short sturgeon season is open in the Columbia River. "There's a lot of waste when you make caviar. The eggs are salted, then left to sit on a screen and you must repeat that process over and over again until every individual egg is broken away from the skein. It's in very limited supply but I sell it for $120 a pound wholesale when I have it."

The first year his grandfather was in the United States, he worked as a fisherman in San Francisco and made $1,800. His boss asked him if he wanted to be paid in paper or

Michael Josephson's family came to the Oregon coast in 1850 from a Swedish settlement in Finland, and repre-sents four generations of fishermen on the Columbia River. His grandfather Anton Josephson founded Josephson's Smoke House in Astoria, Oregon, in 1920 and today Michael processes smoked foods and caviar in the ways passed down from previous generations. According to Michael, "The best of our caviar is from the white sturgeon and it is on a par with imported Beluga but it's better. For one thing, it's fresher and the eggs are always in excellent condition."

A simple way to serve inexpensive caviar is with thin slices of polenta toast, topped with a dollop of sour cream and a pea-size mound of caviar. I usually make the toast several days in advance and store it in an airtight container. High-quality caviar should be served right out of the containers.

Makes 2½ dozen

1¾   cups water or homemade chicken stock
      or reduced-sodium canned chicken broth
 ½   teaspoon salt (omit if using canned broth)
 ¾   cup cornmeal
 4   tablespoons butter (¼ cup)
 ½   cup sour cream
 2   ounces caviar or lumpfish roe
 1   bunch Italian parsley

Grease an 8¾ x 2½-inch loaf pan.

Heat ¾ cup water or chicken broth with the salt. Stir the remaining 1 cup of liquid into the dry cornmeal and when it is smooth, gradually stir the mixture into the boiling salted water. Add the butter and cook over low heat for 5 minutes, stirring constantly. Pour the polenta into a greased loaf pan and allow to cool for 3–4 hours or in the refrigerator overnight.

Preheat the oven to 350°F.

Remove the loaf of polenta from the pan and slice into rectangles ¼ inch thick. Cut each rectangle in half. Place them on a cookie sheet and bake them for 10 minutes, turning once. Remove the toast to a cookie rack to cool.

Spread each piece with sour cream and put ⅛ teaspoon of caviar or lumpfish roe in the center. Arrange the polenta toast on a serving dish and garnish with sprigs of Italian parsley.

gold. Not understanding any English, he chose gold and Marko remembers his grandfather telling him the gold coins were so heavy he could barely get on the streetcar.

*Arriving flat broke in mid-winter,
I found it* [Puget Sound] *enveloped in fog,
and covered all over with timber,
As thick as the hair on a dog…*

—From the song
"The Old Settler,"
by Francis Henry, 1874

Smoked Rainbow Trout with Gin and Capers

*Farming
Rainbow Trout*

*The Hagerman Valley,
also called "Thousand
Springs," is located in
south central Idaho and
this lovely area has
made Idaho famous for
its rainbow trout.
Seventy-five percent of
the nation's farmed
rainbows are raised here
in springs that lie
between the Snake
River and the canyon
wall. When I asked Leo
Ray, owner of Fish
Breeders of Idaho, why
the Idaho trout are so
good, he said it was
because of the water.
"Hagerman Valley has
the largest volume of
spring water in the
United States, maybe in
the world. We have
springs bigger than most
rivers that pour out of
the canyon walls and
flow down towards the
river." All of the trout
are reared in 55°F.
spring water, and cat-
fish and talapia are
farmed in 90°F. ther-
mal springs nearby.*

One fall several years ago, a well-known Portland chef from Denmark, Willie Madsen, prepared a memorable game dinner for members of the Portland Culinary Alliance. It was held at the Edelweiss, a rustic German restaurant on the outskirts of Vancouver, Washington. He served the dinner in a large room with a "game table," an old European tradition. In the center of the room he created a typical fall scene, including several stuffed pheasants with their striking gold-and-bronze-colored plumage. Four long tables, exquisitely set and decorated with golden oak leaves, were placed in a connecting square framing the scene, providing a charming atmosphere for the meal. He started the evening by serving smoked rainbow trout, accompanied by tomatoes stuffed with horseradish cream.

4 servings

    4   *smoked rainbow trout fillets,
        approximately 6 ounces total weight*
    4   *teaspoons gin*
    1   *teaspoon capers, drained*
    4   *tomato slices
        Horseradish Cream (see page 178)*

Arrange the trout fillets on 4 salad plates and sprinkle each with 1 teaspoon gin and ¼ teaspoon capers. Garnish each plate with a tomato slice topped with a dollop of Horseradish Cream.

Belgian Endive Stuffed with Herb-Flavored Crab

The slightly bitter leaves of the Belgian endive make handy edible utensils for cocktail parties. In this recipe, I stuff the slender, canoe-shaped leaves with mounds of crab, bound together with homemade herb mayonnaise. Once they are prepared they can be kept covered in the refrigerator up to two hours in advance of serving.

8 servings

- 4 *lettuce leaves*
- ½ *pound Belgian endive (2 endives)*
- ½ *pound picked crabmeat, bay shrimp, or smoked salmon*
- ⅓ *cup Basil Mayonnaise (page 31)*
  Pinch of salt

Arrange the lettuce leaves on a serving dish and set aside. Trim ⅛ inch off the stem end of the endive and separate the leaves. Discard any that are brown and rinse the remaining leaves under cold water. Lay them on a paper towel to dry.

Stir the crabmeat, mayonnaise, and salt together in a bowl. Stuff each endive leaf with a heaping teaspoon of the crab mixture and arrange them on the serving dish.

A day's catch in the lush redwood country of northern California

Dungeness Crab
and Spinach Raviolis

Dungeness Crab

Several years ago, when I was visiting Washington's Olympic Peninsula with a friend, we stopped for lunch at a restaurant perched above scenic Dungeness Bay, the namesake of the Dungeness crab. Once we were seated, I asked the waitress if they were serving fresh local crab. In response she replied: "Honey, they're so fresh one just crawled in the kitchen!" She promptly delivered a cooked crab, two bibs, two nutcrackers, and a bowl of herb mayonnaise to our table. The crabmeat was just as she had promised—sweet, moist, and perfectly flavorful—and we ate until nothing was left but a heap of empty orange shells. This tasty crab, a favorite among crab connoisseurs, is harvested all the way from northern California to the Aleutian Islands.

These unique crab raviolis were created by Kaspar Donier, a Swiss-trained chef who recently opened Kaspar's by the Bay overlooking Elliott Bay in Seattle. He wraps ready-made wonton wrappers, available at many Pacific Northwest grocery stores, around the colorful spinach and crab filling, making the assembly of these tasty appetizers a simple task. They can be made up to a day ahead of time if they are kept tightly covered in the refrigerator.

4 appetizer servings

12   *wonton wrappers*
 2   *tablespoons butter (⅛ cup)*
 5   *ounces crabmeat, preferably Dungeness,*
     or small pink (bay) shrimp
 4   *ounces blanched spinach (1 bunch)*
 ½   *shallot, chopped*
 1   *sprig tarragon, chopped*
     Dash of Pernod (optional)
     Pinch of salt and pepper

Sauce

 ⅓   *cup white wine, such as Riesling*
 1   *shallot, chopped*
 1   *cup homemade chicken stock or reduced-sodium canned*
     chicken broth
 ¾   *cup heavy cream*
 1   *bunch fresh chives, chopped*

Boil wonton wrappers, 6 at a time, in a large pot of boiling water for 2–3 minutes. Let cool in the water. Melt butter in a frying pan and sauté crabmeat and spinach with the shallot, tarragon, and Pernod. Simmer about 2 minutes until all the liquid has evaporated. Remove the mixture from the pan, season with salt and pepper, and let cool.

Drain wontons and lay them on a flat surface. Place a tablespoon of the crab mixture in the middle of each and fold all sides of the wrapper into the middle to close the ravioli.

Steam wontons on a rack over simmering water in a covered pan or wok for about 3 minutes.

To make the sauce, simmer the wine and shallot in a saucepan until it is reduced by half. Add the chicken stock and cream and continue reducing until the desired consistency is achieved. Add the chives at the last minute.

Arrange 3 raviolis on a plate and cover with the sauce.

Ernest Ceccanti hand-making traditional raviolis at the Monte Carlo restaurant in Portland, which he founded in 1926

Wild Crawfish with Fresh Dill

Wild Crawfish

Just mention crawfish in the Pacific Northwest, and Jake's Famous Crawfish Restaurant (established in Portland in the late 1800s) always comes up. This old Portland landmark still features wild crawfish, which live in almost every stream in the Pacific Northwest that reaches a temperature over 40°F. The local commercial wild harvest is second in the nation, and, unlike the warm-water crawfish caught

Removing the Sand Vein

The sand vein can be removed from the craw-fish after it is cooked by twisting back and forth on the middle of the three tail flippers until it pulls loose. Or purge the crawfish by putting them in cold, salted water for 15 minutes before cooking.

The crystal-clear streams of the Northwest are loaded with wild crawfish. They are not difficult to catch if you know how: just grasp the crawfish body between your thumb and forefinger, right behind the claws, and pull it out of the water. They're feisty creatures with powerful claws that can give a painful pinch, so be careful and wear leather gloves if you have them. Another method of catching them is to use a crawfish trap, available at outdoor stores. Crawfish can also be special-ordered at the fish market. For a casual party I enjoy serving these bright orange crustaceans whole, in a large glass crock with slices of fresh lemon and a head of dill. If they are the main course, I serve a dozen per person, since only the tail and claw meat are eaten.

4 servings

1   bottle dry white wine
2   lemons, sliced
3   tablespoons kosher salt
4   shallots, chopped
2   heads fresh dill (as for pickles)
5   pounds live crawfish (see second note in margin)

Put the wine, 1 sliced lemon, salt, shallots, and 1 head of fresh dill in a large pot and bring to a bowl. Add the crawfish and boil for 5 minutes or until they turn a bright red color. Turn off the heat and let stand for 5 more minutes.

With a strainer remove the crawfish from the stock and put them in an uncovered glass crock or large glass bowl. When the stock is cool, pour it through a strainer over the crawfish and use just enough liquid to cover them. Poke the remaining slices of lemon and remaining head of fresh dill in among the crawfish.

Smoked Sturgeon Pâté

Sturgeon were a favorite of the Native Americans who smoked them as a means of preservation. These prehistoric fish are still caught in the Columbia River, ten minutes from downtown Portland, and in Neah Bay in Puget Sound. During the short sturgeon-fishing season, smoked sturgeon is available locally. If you want to smoke your own, follow the Master Recipe for Smoking Fish on page 160. I make the pâté a day ahead of time to allow the flavors to intensify. It has the consistency of a thick dip and can also be served accompanied by a bowl of veggies for dunking.

6 servings

¼	*pound smoked sturgeon or smoked salmon*
2	*green onions or scallions, trimmed*
1	*teaspoon fresh lemon juice*
½	*cup mayonnaise*
2	*teaspoons soft butter*

Place all the ingredients in a blender or food processor and process until well blended, about 1 minute. Spoon into a small crock and chill for 1–2 hours before serving. Serve on melba toast or any nonsalted cracker.

in the gulf states, this is a cold-water crustacean with exceptionally sweet meat that's preferred by the Scandinavians. Twenty-five percent of the harvest is sold to Scandinavian countries, and the remainder goes to Europe or stays in the United States. Most of the commercial catch comes from tributaries of the Columbia River in Oregon, although Washington, Idaho, and British Columbia all have small commercial catches.

Crawfishing party, Tualatin River, Oregon, about 1895

Russian Rye with Smoked Salmon and Sorrel Mayonnaise

Wild Sorrel

Wood sorrel, a forest herb found in the damp forests of the Pacific Northwest, tastes like cultivated sorrel, but they are not related. There are several varieties of wild sorrel, which resembles a four-leaf clover with three leaves. While some is edible and has a sharp bite, care should be taken not to consume too much, since it contains oxalic acid, which is mildly toxic.

I first enjoyed the French tradition of pairing the rich flavor of salmon with the sharp taste of sorrel at a cooking class taught by Henri Pujo-Perissere, a French chef who left his native land to settle in the Pacific Northwest. He made a sorrel soup which was served over a piece of poached salmon. In this recipe I make home-made Sorrel Mayonnaise and spread a thin layer of it on rye bread. I serve it with a thin slice of smoked salmon for a simple hors d'oeuvre. If you're having a casual party, it's not necessary to assemble this appetizer ahead of time. Serve the bread in a basket with a crock of Sorrel Mayonnaise and pass the salmon on a platter lined with lettuce leaves.

8–10 servings

1　8-ounce loaf Russian rye cocktail bread, sliced
½　cup Sorrel Mayonnaise (recipe follows)
½　pound smoked salmon fillet, sliced into bite-size pieces to fit the bread (see page 160 for smoked salmon instructions)

Spread each piece of bread with a generous amount of Sorrel Mayonnaise. Top with a slice of smoked salmon. Place on a serving platter and serve immediately.

Sorrel Mayonnaise

Cultivated sorrel is a perennial herb resembling spinach that flourishes in the mild climate of the western Pacific Northwest. When the tender first leaves appear in April, I have to race to harvest them before the entourage of local slugs beats me to it. Its unique sour taste provides a pleasing contrast to the rich smoked salmon.

Makes approximately 2 cups

⅓	cup sorrel
¼–½	teaspoon salt
1	teaspoon lemon juice
1	garlic clove
1	whole scallion or green onion, cut into thirds
1	egg
1	cup corn oil
½	cup olive oil

Put the sorrel, salt, lemon juice, garlic, scallion, and egg in the bowl of a food processor or blender and process for 30 seconds. Blend the oils and, with the machine still running, add the oil mixture drop by drop until the mixture thickens. Season with more salt if necessary.

Store-Bought Mayonnaise Flavored with Sorrel
Makes 2½ cups

2	cups commercial mayonnaise
⅓	cup sorrel
1	garlic clove
1	scallion, greens included
	Salt (optional)

Put all the ingredients in a blender or food processor and process until smooth. Season with salt if necessary.

A Warning about Salmonella

Due to a current outbreak of salmonellosis on the East Coast, the U.S. Department of Agriculture and the federal Food and Drug Administration recommend avoiding food containing raw eggs.

Trading Fairs

The Pacific Northwest Native Americans were nomadic, following available food sources during the changing seasons. During the summer the Indians who annually gathered along the Columbia River to fish would host huge trading fairs near The Dalles, a small town on the Columbia River eighty-five miles north of Portland. Their reliable food source, dried salmon, and the control of transportation on the river gave them great bartering power with other Indian tribes. The Dalles was a trade center for centuries, with tribes coming from as far away as the plains, Spokane, and northern California.

Cocktail Rye Bread
with Smoked Sturgeon Butter

While this recipe is similar to Smoked Sturgeon Pâté, it does have a different flavor and texture. Serve it as an appetizer or use a teaspoon on grilled steaks of albacore, halibut, or swordfish just as they come off the grill to embellish their flavor.

8 appetizer servings

¼ pound smoked sturgeon or smoked salmon, broken into small pieces
8 tablespoons soft butter (½ cup)
   Salt and pepper (optional)
1 small loaf of thinly sliced cocktail rye bread

Put the sturgeon and butter in a blender or food processor and process for 1 minute, or until the mixture is well blended. (If you are using a blender you may have to stop the machine several times and push the mixture off the sides with a spatula.) Season with salt and pepper if necessary. Serve at room temperature on thin slices of cocktail rye bread or as a flavoring for grilled fish.

Pacific Northwest
Salmon-Caper Spread

I like to pack this savory appetizer into small crocks and give them as gifts during the holidays. I make it by simply blending grated cheddar cheese and cream cheese and embellishing it with capers, smoked salmon, beer, paprika, and olive oil. It makes a versatile appetizer that can be used as a spread on cocktail bread, a topping for baked potatoes, or served hot on English muffins. I split and toast the muffins in advance—they're crisper that way. Then I completely cover the rounds with a generous layer before heating the muffins under the broiler (or in the microwave) until they are bubbly hot.

Makes 3 cups

8   *ounces sharp cheddar cheese, shredded*
4   *ounces softened low-fat cream cheese*
2   *tablespoons extra-virgin olive oil*
½   *teaspoon sweet paprika*
2   *heaping teaspoons capers, drained*
½   *pound smoked salmon fillet, crumbled*
¼   *cup beer*

Blend all the ingredients together and pack in a small crock. Store in the refrigerator for several days before using (it will keep up to 2 weeks). Bring to room temperature before serving.

Drying Fish in the Wind and Sun

Any smoked fish that has the word "Indian" in it, such as "Indian squaw candy" and "Indian hard-smoked sides" refers to the ancient Native American method of drying fish in the natural elements, and it's often cold-smoked as well. Salmon jerky, similar to squaw candy, is made from narrow strips of cold-smoked salmon.

Warm Springs Indians fishing dipnets at Sherars Bridge on the Deschutes River in central Oregon

Wild Salmon

The largest river empty-ing into Puget Sound is the Skagit River, named after the Native Amer-icans who have lived along its banks for cen-turies. This glacier-fed river flows down the western banks of the rugged northern Cascade Mountains and into the sound near Mt. Vernon, Washington. It produces one-third of all the wild salmon in Puget Sound and is one of the only rivers in the Pacific Northwest still to have runs of steelhead, a rain-bow trout that spends part of its life in the ocean, as well as all five of the salmon species.

Of the five varieties of salmon in the eastern Pacific Ocean, the most prized is the Chinook (also called king), which includes the white king —a rare strain that has white meat instead of the characteristic red-dish-orange. This strain of Chinook is unable to absorb the pigment astaxanthin that is found in the diet of crus-taceans they eat. The Chinook salmon has the highest fat content and the most intense flavor of

Focaccia with Smoked Salmon and Basil Mayonnaise

Focaccia is a disk-shaped Italian bread that has recently become available commercially in the Pacific Northwest. This flavorful bread is brushed with olive oil and sprinkled with salt and fresh rosemary before it is baked. I have omitted the rosemary and flavor the baked slices of bread with Basil Mayonnaise before topping with pieces of smoked salmon.

8–10 servings

1	*pound smoked salmon*
1	*loaf Focaccia (recipe follows) or ¼ commercial loaf, cut into small, 2 x 3-inch pieces, ⅓ inch thick*
½	*cup Basil Mayonnaise (recipe follows)*

Remove any skin from the smoked salmon and cut the fish into bite-size pieces. Spread a piece of bread with the Basil Mayonnaise and cover with the smoked salmon. Repeat for the remaining pieces of bread and serve on a large platter.

Focaccia
Makes one 8-inch Focaccia

1½	*teaspoons active dry yeast (half a ¼-ounce package)*
½	*cup warm water*
1¼	*cups flour*
¾	*teaspoon salt*
3	*tablespoons olive oil*

Preheat the oven to 400°F.

Sprinkle the yeast over the water and stir until the yeast dissolves. Combine the flour and ½ teaspoon salt together in a bowl. Whisk 2 tablespoons olive oil into the dissolved yeast and stir the mixture into the flour. Add more flour if necessary to make a dough that is soft but doesn't stick to your fingers.

Knead the dough on a floured board until it is smooth and elastic, about 3–4 minutes. Cover and let the dough rest for 20 minutes. Shape the dough into a disk-shaped round, approximately 8 inches in diameter and 1 inch thick.

Brush the surface of the bread with the remaining tablespoon of olive oil. Make indentations in the bread 2 inches apart with the end of a wooden spoon. Sprinkle the bread with the remaining ¼ teaspoon salt and bake for 15 minutes.

Transfer the bread to a rack to cool.

Basil Mayonnaise
Makes 1¾ cups

- ½ cup torn basil leaves
- 1 teaspoon lemon juice
- 1 egg
- ½ teaspoon salt
- 1 garlic clove, peeled
- ¾ cup mild olive oil
- ¾ cup corn oil

Put the basil, lemon juice, egg, and salt into a blender or food processor and turn the machine on. Drop in the garlic clove and process for 30 seconds. Combine the oils and, with the machine still running, slowly add the oils until the mixture gradually thickens. Store any leftover mayonnaise in a covered jar in the refrigerator.

Store-Bought Mayonnaise Flavored with Basil
Makes 1¼ cups

- 1 cup commercial mayonnaise
- ¼ cup chopped basil
- ½ teaspoon lemon juice
- 1 garlic clove, minced

Put the mayonnaise, basil, and lemon juice in blender or food processor and turn the machine on. Drop in the garlic clove and process until the mayonnaise is smooth.

any of the salmon species. The silver salmon has about half the fat content of the Chinook—the same as the Atlantic/Norwegian salmon—and it can be substituted in any recipe that calls for Chinook salmon. The sockeye salmon has a bright reddish-orange flesh and a fat content slightly less than the Chinook. Its high fat content makes it, along with the Chinook, my favorite salmon species to smoke and, because of the bright color of their flesh, to poach. The sockeye also has a landlocked cousin called the kokanee. The chum and pink salmon have the lowest fat content and the least amount of flavor; they are most often canned.

A Warning about Salmonella

Due to a current outbreak of salmonellosis on the East Coast, the U.S. Department of Agriculture and the federal Food and Drug Administration recommend avoiding food containing raw eggs.

Smoked Salmon in Toasted Nori Wrappers

Local Indian ceremonies and religious practices were closely related and often centered around the harvest of indigenous foods. The Root Feast, the Huckleberry Festival, and the First-Salmon Ceremony were carefully timed, coinciding with the changing seasons. Many tribes still hold these ceremonies, reaffirming their culture and teaching their children traditions of past generations. Here, first-caught salmon are being prepared for a Thanksgiving festival.

Nori is a type of roasted seaweed familiar to most people as the deep green wrapper around slices of sushi. Dried, it resembles thick green tissue paper and it's flexible enough to be filled and folded without breaking. Sheets of it can be purchased at stores that carry Japanese ingredients. Ten sheets come in a one-ounce package and each piece can be cut in half. Store leftover sheets in a plastic bag.

4 servings

5	sheets nori, cut in half
1	pound smoked salmon fillet, skin and gray fatty flesh removed
¼	pound enoki mushrooms
10	sprigs watercress
10	sprigs fresh dill

Lay the 10 pieces of nori on a flat surface and arrange a piece of salmon, a few mushrooms, and a sprig of watercress and fresh dill on each piece. Starting at one pointed end, roll each piece around its filling and place on a serving plate, seam side down. Serve immediately.

Ballard Gravlax with Fresh Dill

Ballard, the Scandinavian neighborhood of Seattle, is nestled on a hillside overlooking the ship canal and Shilshole Bay ten minutes north of downtown. It's not difficult to understand how Norwegian and Swedish fishermen were drawn to this picturesque area that greatly resembles their homeland. One of the traditional Norwegian dishes prepared from salmon is gravlax, or pickled salmon. I like to serve it thinly sliced, accompanied by a basket of dark bread and small dishes filled with chopped onion, capers, and lemon wedges. Eric Benson is a retired chef who emigrated to the United States from Norway with his family in the 1950s. He sometimes makes gravlax by layering the salmon between pine boughs to give it a slightly different flavor.

Eating Raw Fish

To minimize the risk of illness from eating raw fish or marinated fish, freeze the fish at 0°F. for 24–48 hours, large fish for 48 hours or more.

Makes 2 pounds

1   cup chopped fresh dill (be sure to use the green herb, not dill seed)
⅓   cup kosher salt
⅓   cup sugar
2   pounds Chinook or silver salmon fillets, skinned

Put ½ cup of the fresh dill in the bottom of a shallow bowl.
   Rub the salt and sugar on both sides of the fillets and place them on top of the chopped dill. Sprinkle the remaining dill over the salmon and cover the top of the salmon with plastic wrap. Put a brick or something heavy on top of the salmon and put it in the refrigerator. Cure the salmon for 48 hours, turning it several times. Pour off any liquid as it accumulates.

Smoked Sablefish (Black Cod) with Mustard Dipping Sauce

I first tasted smoked sablefish at the Royal Chinook Inn, a quaint tavern overlooking the Columbia River east of Portland. It was served to us in thick chunks, smoked to a deep golden brown. The meat itself was creamy white, with rich buttery flakes, and we washed it down with beer from a local microbrewery. Sablefish, also known as black cod, though it's not a member of the codfish family, has the same oil content as the Chinook salmon and consequently remains exceptionally moist when it is smoked.

4 servings

　　Mustard Dipping Sauce (recipe follows)
　6　butter lettuce leaves
　1½　pounds smoked sablefish or smoked albacore*
　1　baguette, thinly sliced

　　* If you want to smoke your own, follow the Master Recipe
　　for Smoking Fish on page 160.

Make the mustard sauce in a small bowl and put it in the center of a serving dish lined with lettuce leaves. Remove the skin and any visible bones from the fish and cut it into bite-size pieces. Lay the smoked fish pieces in a circle around the mustard sauce and serve with a basket of the baguette slices.

Mustard Dipping Sauce

　¼　cup sour cream
　¼　cup low-fat yogurt
　1　teaspoon Dijon mustard
　1　small garlic clove, pressed

Blend the sour cream, yogurt, mustard, and garlic together at least 1 hour before serving.

Oysters on the Half Shell with Cracked Pepper and Lemon

Diana Kennedy, renowned authority on Mexican cookery, introduced me to this simple method of eating fresh oysters with freshly cracked pepper. I like to serve them nestled in seaweed in a shallow basket. The seaweed can be ordered ahead of time at the fish market.

6–8 servings

> Seaweed
> 2 dozen very fresh oysters on the half shell
> Freshly ground pepper
> 1 lemon, cut into wedges

Arrange the seaweed in a basket and gently push the oysters on the half shell down into it so they stay upright and do not lose their liquor. Sprinkle each with a twist of freshly ground pepper. Garnish with the lemon wedges and serve immediately.

Bill Webb, of Westcott Bay Sea Farms, downing a fresh oyster

Steamed Oysters with Champagne Mayonnaise

Pacific Oysters

The Olympia, or native Pacific oyster, is the only oyster indigenous to the West Coast. It used to be found all along the Pacific Coast from Alaska to Baja (in California it was called the California oyster), but overharvesting, pollution, and several detrimental pests have drastically reduced its population. It's now being cultivated primarily in south Puget Sound near Shelton, Washington. These diminutive oysters are unbelievably sweet with a slight coppery aftertaste and, because they are dime-size, it takes 200 of them to make a pint! The Pacific oyster was introduced from Japan in the 1920s and today it is the main oyster cultivated on the West Coast. This bivalve is often marketed under the name of the

Steamed oysters are delicious when napped with this simple sauce that tastes as though it took hours to make. I use store-bought mayonnaise as a convenient base and embellish it with champagne and balsamic vinegar, an unlikely combination that works amazingly well (you can, of course, use dry white wine). The champagne mayonnaise forms a rich, buttery-smooth glaze when it is spooned over the hot oysters.

4 servings

1	*pound rock salt*
2	*pounds raw oysters in the shell (approximately 10–12)*
½	*cup mayonnaise*
2	*tablespoons dry champagne or dry white wine*
1	*teaspoon balsamic vinegar*
2	*tablespoons chopped chives*

Put a ½-inch layer of rock salt in a shallow serving dish and set aside.

Pour a small amount of water in the bottom half of a steamer and bring it to a boil.

Scrub the oyster shells under cold running water. Discard any that are not closed. Arrange the oysters in layers, as flat as possible, in the top half of the steamer. Steam the oysters over boiling water, covered, until their shells pop open, about 15 minutes.

Using a towel, remove the top shell of each oyster and discard. Nestle the remaining oysters on the half shell in the rock salt.

Stir together mayonnaise, champagne, and vinegar. Place ½–1 teaspoon of champagne mayonnaise on each oyster and garnish with a few chopped chives. Repeat for the remaining oysters and serve immediately.

Pan-Fried Curried Oysters with Sour Cream and Caviar

The late Enoteca Restaurant and Wine Bar in Seattle used to serve these. The fiery-flavored oysters are balanced by the sour cream and the salty caviar.

6 servings

1	cup flour
5	teaspoons ground cumin
5	teaspoons paprika
5	teaspoons curry powder
5	teaspoons turmeric
¼	teaspoon ground coriander
½	teaspoon ground ginger
¼	teaspoon cayenne pepper
1	teaspoon kosher salt
24	small oysters
2–3	tablespoons butter or corn oil
6	sprigs parsley or equivalent amount of chives
6	lemon wedges
½	cup sour cream
1	teaspoon caviar or lumpfish roe

Blend the flour, cumin, paprika, curry powder, turmeric, coriander, ginger, cayenne pepper, and salt together. Just before serving, dredge the oysters in the flour mixture. (Don't do this ahead of time or they will become gummy.)

Melt the butter in a skillet and sauté the oysters 30 seconds on each side. Garnish each plate with a sprig of parsley, a lemon wedge, and a heaping tablespoon of sour cream topped with a dab of caviar. Place 4 oysters on each plate and serve immediately.

bay where it is harvested, such as the Quilcene oyster from Quilcene Bay in Washington, the Penn Cove select from Penn Cove, Washington, the Wescott Bay from Wescott Bay, Washington, the Willapa Bay from Willapa Bay, Oregon, and the Yaquina Bay from Yaquina Bay, Oregon. Two recent additions to Pacific Northwest oyster farms are the mild-tasting European flats and the sweet Kumamotos, two of my favorite oysters. Local oyster bars are also selling the "triploid," or neutered oyster. Because the chromosomes in the oyster have been changed from two to three, the triploid no longer goes through a sex cycle (at which time an oyster's meat is of poor eating quality).

Asparagus Rolls with Prosciutto and Fresh Rosemary

For the pioneers of the West, a common language and culture were the threads that wove together large ethnic groups within a city's boundaries. Each neighborhood had its own grocery stores stocked with ingredients not available in American markets. As time passed, the neighborhoods were gradually absorbed into the American mainstream (except in the larger cities where many of them still exist); simultaneously, the delicatessen became a melting pot for ethnic and specialty foods. Today supermarkets carry all kinds of imported goods and many have their own delicatessens. The current availability of prosciutto is a good example of this change: In the sixties, I bought it at my favorite Italian market, in the seventies and eighties a local delicatessen in Portland carried it, and now I can buy prosciutto in many grocery stores, already sliced and sealed in plastic bags.

4 servings

1	*pound asparagus*
2–3	*ounces prosciutto (4 pieces)*
2–3	*ounces light cream cheese*
½	*teaspoon fresh rosemary, chopped*
	Freshly ground pepper
1	*tablespoon extra-virgin olive oil*

Preheat the oven to 350°F.

Prepare the asparagus by holding the base firmly and bending the stalk until it breaks off. Discard the ends. Fill the bottom half of a steamer with an inch of water and lay the asparagus in the top half. Cover and bring the water to a boil. Steam 8–10 minutes, or until almost tender.

Lay the 4 pieces of prosciutto out on a flat surface. Spread with equal amounts of cream cheese and sprinkle with the chopped rosemary. Put 4 asparagus spears in each and roll up. Put, seam side down, on a baking sheet. Season with freshly ground pepper and drizzle the olive oil over all. Bake, uncovered, for 10–12 minutes.

Microwave Instructions:

Prepare the asparagus by holding the base firmly and bending the stalk. It will break where it is too tough to eat. Put the spears in a shallow microwave-safe dish and add 2 tablespoons water. Microwave on High 3–4 minutes. Drain. Lay the 4 pieces of prosciutto on a flat surface. Spread with equal amounts of cream cheese and sprinkle with the chopped rosemary. Put 4 asparagus spears in each and roll up. Place, seam side down, on a baking sheet. Season with freshly ground pepper and drizzle with olive oil. Cover with microwave-safe plastic wrap and cook on High for 3 minutes.

Italian delicatessen and delivery truck, Portland, Oregon, 1915

Baguette Slices with Shrimp, Avocado, and Goat Cheese

One of the sweetest and tastiest West Coast shellfish is the tiny pink shrimp known as bay shrimp. They're available fresh in local fish markets from the first of April until the end of October. Only the cooked and shelled tail section is sold; it takes 150–180 of them to make a pound. In this recipe, I combine the shrimp with avocado, sweet onion, cilantro, and goat cheese to create a light and simple appetizer. It can also be served as a salad on a bed of lettuce or as a sandwich filling.

Makes 3 cups

1	*pound bay shrimp (approximately 2 cups)*
1	*diced avocado (¾–1 cup)*
¼	*cup chopped sweet Italian onion*
¼	*cup fresh cilantro leaves*
2	*ounces mild, crumbled goat cheese, such as Montrachet*
1	*tablespoon lemon juice*
2	*tablespoons mild olive oil*
¼	*teaspoon salt*
	Scant ¼ teaspoon freshly ground pepper
1	*baguette cut into thin, silver dollar–size slices or 1 bag tortilla chips*

Put the shrimp, avocado, onion, cilantro leaves, and goat cheese in a medium-size bowl. Whisk the lemon juice, olive oil, and salt and pepper together and pour over the shrimp mixture. Toss and serve surrounded by slices of bread or tortilla chips.

Lentil Pâté

Pureed lentils make a delicious pâté when they are cooked in chicken stock and seasoned with garlic and cumin to enhance their flavor. Bright green chopped parsley is stirred in to give a bit of color and texture but I prefer the additional dynamic flavor of cilantro. I never add it, though, unless I know my guests like it as much as I do.

Makes 1½ cups

 1   cup lentils
1¾ cup homemade chicken stock
     or reduced-sodium canned chicken broth
 1   clove garlic
 ¾ teaspoon ground cumin
 ½ teaspoon salt
 2   tablespoons chopped Italian flat-leaf parsley or cilantro
     (reserve several whole leaves for garnish)
     Crackers

Rinse the lentils and put them in a small pot with the chicken stock. Bring the stock to a boil and cover the pan. Reduce the heat to simmer, and cook the lentils until they are tender (about 25 minutes). Drain, if necessary, and transfer the lentils to a blender or food processor bowl. Add the garlic, cumin, and salt to the lentils and puree until the pâté is smooth. Stir in the parsley or cilantro. Scoop the mixture into a small crock or bowl and garnish with the reserved parsley or cilantro leaves. Serve with crackers.

Savory Soups

Soups have long been an integral part of the diet during the long, cold winters in the Pacific Northwest. The Native Americans heated rocks and dropped them into watertight baskets filled with water and pieces of dried salmon and berries. The pioneers made simple soups with ingredients from their gardens—potatoes, tomatoes, onions, beans—and staples from the pantry. Barley and rice soups were commonplace in the early days.

As new ethnic groups swelled the population, they adapted and changed their Old World recipes, incorporating ingredients they found in the new land. Crab cioppino, an American version of an Italian stew, was created by West Coast Italian fishermen, for instance. German noodle soup, Scotch mutton broth, and Vietnamese bouillabaisse are other examples.

At the turn of the century, it became fashionable to serve consommé at the beginning of a formal meal. *The Alpha Cookbook*, printed in Baker, Oregon, in 1904, gives the following advice for planning a menu: "After the oysters, come the soups. If two soups are to be served, select one clear and one thick: but if one is to be used, give the preference to the clear soup."

Today, in restaurants and homes alike, there's a variety of soups reflecting both the past and the present—black beans with venison sausage, wild mushroom soup, or a simple soup such as cream of potato.

I have selected fifteen soup recipes for this chapter, all based on indigenous foods of the Pacific Northwest: lentils, fresh vegetables, seafood, and beef. Most of the soups are so hearty that I prefer to serve them as a main course accompanied by a tossed green salad, a loaf of crusty bread, and a glass of wine.

Over the years, soups in general have remained popular in the cool Pacific Northwest climate, and perhaps it's because they also nourish and warm the soul.

SEPTEMBER HARVEST CHOWDER

FRESH TOMATO SOUP WITH BASIL

CREAM OF CAULIFLOWER SOUP WITH HAZELNUT BUTTER

FRESH MUSHROOM SOUP WITH CHIVE DUMPLINGS

SMOKY PUMPKIN SOUP

ROAST GARLIC SOUP WITH HALIBUT, POTATOES, AND FRESH CORN

SKID ROAD LENTIL SOUP WITH ITALIAN SAUSAGE

BASQUE RED BEAN SOUP WITH CHORIZO

GERMAN BEEF SOUP WITH SAUERKRAUT

CHEDDAR CHEESE SOUP WITH PEPPERED BACON AND ALE

CLASSIC ITALIAN CRAB CIOPPINO

CAPTAIN BILL WEBB'S OYSTER STEW

EMERALD CITY SPINACH AND OYSTER SOUP

NORTHWEST VIETNAMESE BOUILLABAISSE

GEODUCK CLAM CHOWDER

September Harvest Chowder

September is the ideal month of the year to make a fresh vegetable chowder. There is so much available in the garden, at country stands, and at farmers' markets. I vary this recipe depending on what is available.

4–6 servings

3 ears of corn, shucked
3 tablespoons butter or corn oil margarine
½ cup chopped onion
1 stalk celery, thinly sliced
1 carrot, peeled and thinly sliced
2 tomatoes, seeded and chopped
2 medium potatoes, peeled and diced
½ red pepper, seeded and diced
1 teaspoon salt (omit if using canned broth)
3 cups homemade chicken stock
    or reduced-sodium canned chicken broth
1 cup milk (2% fat)
½ cup fresh basil, chopped

Two Japanese gardeners sell their vegetables at Seattle's Pike Place Market.

Cut the corn off the cob and set aside. Melt the butter in a 5-quart pot and sauté the onion, celery, and carrot. Add the tomatoes, potatoes, red pepper, salt, stock, and corn to the pan. Simmer for 25 minutes, or until the potatoes are tender. Don't overcook them or they will be mushy.

Add the milk and chopped basil and heat for 2–3 more minutes. Serve immediately.

Fresh Tomato Soup with Basil

The following recipe is from Pat Struckman, a well-known Portland cooking teacher. I like to make it in the summer with the large, sun-ripened beefsteak tomatoes that are sweet and juicy. They're pureed with fresh basil leaves and this wonderfully pungent herb adds a depth of flavor that can't be found when dried basil is used.

4 servings

    3   *tablespoons butter or corn oil margarine*
    ½   *cup chopped onion*
    ¼   *cup shredded carrot*
    4   *large tomatoes, peeled (about 2 pounds)*
    ⅓   *cup packed fresh basil leaves*
    1   *teaspoon salt (omit if using canned broth)*
  1½   *cups homemade chicken stock or*
        reduced-sodium canned chicken broth
    2   *tablespoons alphabet pasta*
        (or any small pasta, such as orzo)

In a 3 quart soup pot heat the butter and sauté the onion and carrot until the onion is soft. Put the tomatoes, basil, salt, and chicken stock in the pot and bring it to a boil. Cover, reduce the heat to simmer, and cook for 10 minutes.

Put the soup in a blender or food processor in small batches and process until smooth. Pour it back into the pot and add the pasta. Cook over medium heat until the pasta is tender.

Cream of Cauliflower Soup with Hazelnut Butter

Hazelnut versus Filbert

There are two theories on how the filbert, also known as the hazelnut, got its name. One suggests that it was named after the husk which completely covers some of the varieties, resembling a "full beard," while the other relates it to its ripening date around August 22, which is also St. Philibert's Day and the time when the hazelnut is ripe in England. Locally, it is generally accepted that "hazel' referred to the native wild nut (Corylus cornuta) *and "filbert" to the cultivated variety* (Corylus avellana). *Waverley Root wrote in his book* Food *(New York: Simon & Schuster, Inc., 1980): "In 1942 the American Joint Committee on Horticultural Nomenclature decided to call all members of the genus* Corylus *filberts, and to hell with it." Unfortunately it didn't work and the industry is currently marketing them as hazelnuts.*

I don't use flour in this soup since the pureed cauliflower thickens itself. I make it in large batches and freeze it in plastic containers without the hazelnut butter. Just before it's served, when the soup's piping hot, I put a dab of butter in the center of each bowl. The golden brown butter adds a rich flavor to supplement the mildness of cauliflower, but the soup's good without it, too.

2–3 servings

4 cups homemade chicken stock
   or reduced-sodium canned chicken broth
1 pound cauliflower, broken into florets
1 carrot, cut into 2-inch pieces
1 stalk celery, cut into 2-inch pieces
¼ cup chopped onion
1 cup half-and-half or milk
½ teaspoon salt
¼ teaspoon white pepper
   Hazelnut Butter (recipe follows)

Heat the chicken stock and drop the cauliflower, carrot, celery, and onion into the pot. Cook until the vegetables are tender. With a slotted spoon, transfer the vegetables to the bowl of a food processor or blender. Add a small amount of stock and puree until smooth. Pour the pureed vegetables back into the stock and add the remaining ingredients. Serve hot with ½ teaspoon Hazelnut Butter floating on top of each serving.

Hazelnut Butter

  2 tablespoons butter or corn oil margarine
  1 tablespoon chopped, roasted hazelnuts

Blend the butter and hazelnuts together. Hazelnuts can be roasted in a regular oven or microwave.

To Oven-Roast Hazelnuts:

Spread shelled hazelnuts in a shallow pan and roast in a 275°F. oven for 20–30 minutes, until the skins crack. Remove the skins by rubbing the nuts while warm with a rough cloth or between your hands. Chop the hazelnuts in a blender or food processor.

To Microwave-Roast Hazelnuts:

Place the hazelnuts in a single layer in a microwave-safe dish and microwave on High for 3–4 minutes. Remove the skins by rubbing the nuts while warm with a rough cloth or between your hands. Chop the hazelnuts in a blender or food processor.

A familiar 1930s sight at the Pike Place Market in Seattle was Theresa De Maritini, "the lady of the wheelbarrow."

47

Fresh Mushroom Soup
with Chive Dumplings

Fresh mushroom soup is so simple to make and it can be varied depending on the variety of mushrooms available. I like to leave the broth just as it is, full of the delicate flavor of the mushrooms. The only additional seasoning is the chives in the chive dumplings.

4 servings

2	tablespoons butter
4	ounces commercial meadow mushrooms, sliced into vertical ¼-inch slices
2	ounces shiitake mushrooms, sliced into vertical ¼-inch slices
2	ounces oyster mushrooms, sliced into vertical ¼-inch slices
2	tablespoons plus 1 cup flour
4½	cups plus 3 tablespoons homemade chicken stock or reduced-sodium canned chicken broth
½	teaspoon salt (omit salt if using canned broth)
1	tablespoon baking powder
3	tablespoons chopped fresh chives

In a 2-quart pot, heat the butter until it melts. Add the mushrooms and sauté over medium-low heat until they are soft. Sprinkle with 2 tablespoons flour and cook them for 3 more minutes, tossing the mushrooms as they cook. Pour in 4 cups chicken stock and season with ¼ teaspoon salt. (If canned chicken broth is used, it will already be salty enough.) Gently simmer for 10 minutes.

To make the dumplings, blend the remaining 1 cup flour, baking powder, remaining ¼ teaspoon salt, and chives together. Add the remaining ½ cup plus 3 table-spoons chicken stock and stir until well mixed. Spoon golf ball–size mounds of dough into the simmering mushroom soup. Cook uncovered for 5 minutes. Cover and cook for 5 more minutes, or until the dumplings are cooked.

Smoky Pumpkin Soup

Pumpkin patches brighten up fall fields all over the Pacific Northwest, adding one last splash of color before the gray of winter. When the weather starts to turn cold I automatically get out my collection of soup recipes. The following hearty pumpkin soup is creamy smooth with a slightly smoky flavor, perfect for a chilly fall evening.

3–4 servings

⅓   *cup diced leek*
2   *strips bacon, diced*
1   *carrot, cut into quarters*
2½   *cups homemade chicken stock*
     or reduced-sodium canned chicken broth
1   *cup cooked, fresh or solid-pack pumpkin*
½   *teaspoon liquid smoke*
1   *tablespoon butter*
½   *teaspoon flour*
⅓   *cup plain yogurt*
1   *teaspoon salt*
¼   *teaspoon white pepper*
2   *sprigs fresh parsley, chopped*

Sauté the leek, bacon, and carrot together over medium-high heat for 5–8 minutes, or until the bacon starts to brown. Discard any grease that may have accumulated. Add 1 cup chicken stock and continue cooking until the carrots are tender.

Transfer the soup to a food processor or blender and add the pumpkin. Process until it is smooth, about 20 seconds. Remove the puree to a heavy pot and add the remaining stock, liquid smoke, and butter.

Stir the flour into the yogurt. Just before serving, stir the yogurt-flour mixture into the soup. Season with salt and pepper and garnish with a sprinkling of chopped parsley.

How to Bake a Pumpkin

Bake a small, whole pumpkin in a 350°F. oven until it can be pierced easily with a fork. Remove the pumpkin from the oven and, when it is cool enough to handle, cut it in half and remove the seeds and pulp. Cut the skin away from the meat and pack enough meat in a measuring cup to equal 1 cup. Measure the remaining meat and store it in the freezer in 1-quart bags for pumpkin pie.

Roast Garlic Soup with Halibut, Potatoes, and Fresh Corn

Erikson's

Erikson's was a legendary 1800s Portland saloon that occupied an entire block (see "Skid Road," page 52).

"…A ghostlike place now is Erikson's, teeming with memories. What stories those bars could tell. Here men related wonderful tales of prowess on land and sea; many a perilous voyage was sailed around those mahogany counters, many a hazardous trail traveled over again, many a daring feat of valor here re-enacted! Safe to say more logging was done within those walls than in all the woods of the northwest since logging began! Free from the greatest of faults, commonplaceness, it breathed the tang of the sea, the scent of the forests, the smell of the sagebrush desert. Here was the flavor of the wilds, the spirit of untamed things. Erikson's belongs to Portland's youth, its period of wild oats sowing. It but expressed the

I steam the potatoes separately in this recipe to keep them from overpowering the subtle sweetness of the garlic broth. Once the potatoes are steamed and the cayenne pepper toast is made, the remaining ingredients are all cooked in the same pot. I put it on the table and serve the seafood stew family-style.

4 servings

1	whole head garlic
1	teaspoon olive oil
1	quart homemade chicken stock or reduced-sodium canned chicken broth Salt
2	pounds halibut, boned, skinned, and cut in 1-inch cubes
2	ears corn, shucked and cut into thirds
1	pound steamed red new potatoes
½	cup fresh basil, chopped Cayenne Pepper Toast (recipe follows) or garlic bread

Preheat the oven to 325°F.

Cut ½ inch off the top of the garlic head, exposing the cloves. Put the garlic head in a small baking dish and drizzle olive oil over it. Bake for 45 minutes or until the garlic cloves inside the papery skin are soft.

Pour the chicken stock into a 2-quart pot. Squeeze the cooked garlic out of the garlic head into the stock and discard the skin. Whip with a wire whisk or fork to disperse the cooked garlic.

Heat the garlic stock to simmer and salt to taste.

Gently drop the halibut, corn, and potatoes into the hot stock and cook for 3–4 minutes, just until the halibut is cooked. It will turn snow white when it's done; don't overcook it or it will be dry. Stir in the chopped basil and ladle the soup into individual warmed shallow soup bowls. Serve with Cayenne Pepper Toast or garlic bread.

Cayenne Pepper Toast

  4   *tablespoons butter or corn oil margarine*
  8   *slices sourdough bread*
      Scant ⅛ teaspoon cayenne pepper

Preheat the oven to 325°F.
   Butter one side of the bread and sprinkle on a smidgen of cayenne pepper. Place the bread on a baking sheet, buttered side up, and bake for 12–15 minutes, or until the bread is crisp and lightly golden brown. Serve the bread warm in a bread basket.

times. It was a reckless age, a prodigal age, a mad age, if you will, but who will deny that it was an age worth while!…"

—*Charles Oluf Olsen,*
The Oregon Journal,
June 27, 1926

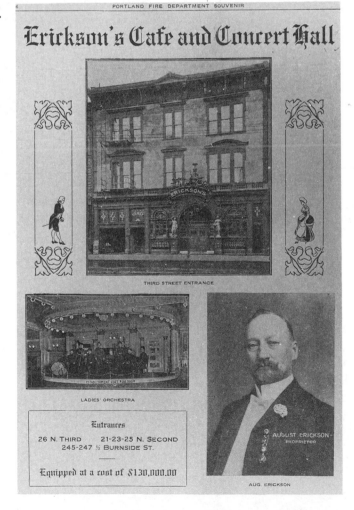

PORTLAND FIRE DEPARTMENT SOUVENIR

Erickson's Cafe and Concert Hall

THIRD STREET ENTRANCE

LADIES' ORCHESTRA

Entrances

26 N. THIRD   21-23-25 N. SECOND
    245-247 ½ BURNSIDE ST.

Equipped at a cost of $130,000.00

AUGUST ERICKSON
PROPRIETOR

AUG. ERICKSON

51

Skid Road Lentil Soup
with Italian Sausage

Skid Road

A "skid road" is a term carried over from the wild logging days of the West. Originally it referred to a road built by half burying a row of limbless trees which was used to skid fallen trees down to the lumber mill or water's edge. Eventually it came to refer to that part of town where loggers, sailors, prospectors, Indians, and soldiers came to spend their money. A legendary Portland skid road saloon was Erickson's, built by August Erickson, a Russian Finn, in the early 1800s. It filled almost an entire city block and had five different entrances. The bar, 684 linear feet long, wrapped around the interior of the building, and if you needed a bite to eat, there was a free lunch. Stewart H. Holbrook aptly described the lunch scene in his book, Holy Old Mackinaw *(New York: Macmillan, 1938):*

"The free lunch was prodigious, one of its many standard items

This lentil soup is thick and filling, with a subtle spicy flavor from the toasted cumin seeds. I garnish it with a dollop of sour cream and a few sprigs of cilantro or parsley just for color.

Makes about 2 quarts

2   cups lentils, rinsed
2½   quarts homemade chicken stock or reduced-sodium canned chicken broth
1   pound fresh Italian sausage
1   cup water or enough water to cover the sausage
½   teaspoon ground cumin
½   teaspoon toasted cumin seeds*
½   teaspoon salt
½   cup light sour cream or yogurt (optional)
¼   cup fresh cilantro or parsley (optional)

   * Toast cumin seeds over medium-high heat in an ungreased cast-iron skillet until they start to turn dark brown.

Bring the lentils and chicken stock to a boil. Reduce the heat to simmer and cook until the lentils are tender, about 1 hour. Puree the lentils and the chicken stock in a blender or food processor. It may have to be done in several small batches if you have a small workbowl or blender. Put the puree back in the pot and set aside.

Prick the sausage with a fork, cover with water, and simmer for 5 minutes. Discard the water, prick the sausage again, and sauté until it is lightly brown on all sides. Cut the sausage into ¼-inch slices and add to the lentil puree. Season with ground cumin, toasted cumin seeds, and salt.

Reheat and serve in heated soup bowls with a dollop of sour cream or yogurt and a sprinkling of cilantro leaves.

Basque Red Bean Soup with Chorizo

Clarine Villeneuve works for the Idaho Bean Commission and she sent me this recipe from their headquarters in Boise, Idaho. Clarine, who is writing a cookbook on Basque recipes, suggests serving this hearty soup with a salad, Basque Sheepherder's Bread (page 82), and a favorite bottle of wine.

10 servings

2 cups red beans
1 large onion, chopped
1 pound Basque chorizo, cut into thirds
1 8-ounce can tomato sauce
2–3 potatoes, peeled and quartered
2 tablespoons corn oil
1 teaspoon salt
½ teaspoon pepper

Soak the beans overnight in cold water. Drain and cover with 2 quarts of water. Bring the water to a boil, then reduce the heat to simmer and cook until the beans are tender. Add the remaining ingredients and cook slowly for 3–4 hours.

being the half of a roast ox. Soft bread for sandwiches was cut exactly one and one-half inches thick; the Swedish hardtack bread, round and large as grindstones and almost as hard, stood in stacks. The mustard pot held a quart. Round logs of sliced sausages filled huge platters. Pickled herring swam in a large bucket of brine. Beer was five cents, hard liquor two for a quarter."

(See "Erickson's," page 50.)

German Beef Soup with Sauerkraut

Wild Celery

Wild celery, or Indian celery, grows throughout much of the Pacific Northwest. Once the stem is picked, it's necessary to peel back the top layers to reveal the tender and intensely celery-flavored center.

German immigrants who settled in the Pacific Northwest might have used a German sausage in this full-bodied soup that borders on being a stew. Either way, hearty soups are a must in the cold wet winters of the Pacific Northwest and this recipe makes enough for a large crowd. It doesn't freeze particularly well, so you might want to cut the recipe down to meet your needs.

Makes a generous 4½ quarts

2	tablespoons olive oil
2	pounds beef stew meat
3	cups homemade beef stock or reduced-sodium canned beef broth
1	28-ounce can peeled tomatoes, with juice, diced
1	can beer (12 ounces)
¼	cup red wine
1	cup sauerkraut, with juice
2	garlic cloves, minced
¼	cup Italian flat-leaf parsley, chopped
1	bay leaf
¼	teaspoon whole dried thyme, crushed
1	teaspoon salt (omit if using canned broth)
½	teaspoon freshly ground pepper
4	cups potatoes, peeled and diced
2	cups onions, chopped
1	cup shredded carrot
2	stalks celery, chopped
2	tablespoons butter or corn oil margarine
2	tablespoons flour

Heat the oil and brown the meat on all sides. Add the broth, tomatoes, beer, red wine, sauerkraut and its liquid, garlic, parsley, bay leaf, thyme, salt, pepper, potatoes, onions, carrots, and celery and bring to a boil. Reduce the heat, skim the broth, and cover. Simmer until the beef is tender when pierced with a fork, about 2 hours.

When the meat is done, heat the butter in a saucepan and stir in the flour. Cook until well browned, stirring constantly, about 3 minutes. Remove from the heat and spoon in enough broth from the soup to make a thin paste, then blend the paste into the soup and simmer uncovered, another 10 minutes.

Portland's Blitz Weinhard Brewing Company has grown up with Portland. The brewery, founded by German immigrant Henry Weinhard in the 1850s, sold its beer at many bars in Portland, including the Columbia Saloon.

Cheddar Cheese Soup with Peppered Bacon and Ale

Peppered Bacon

Peppered bacon is lightly covered with freshly cracked pepper. I buy it thickly sliced at a local butcher shop or I make my own following the recipe on page 232.

Tillamook, a Chinook Indian word meaning "land of many waters," is the name of both a county and a town on the northern Oregon coast. This fertile valley is blessed with lush pasture homesteaded by Swiss and German immigrants. Their descendants are still living in the area, and a quick tour of the county shows rural mailboxes with names such as Schid, Naegil, Becker, Awald, Hurliman, Gienger, Lagler, Baumgartner, Tohl, Boquist, Leuthold, and so on. Many of the immigrants became dairy farmers and they pioneered the manufacture of hard cheese by forming a co-op that for many years shipped both butter and cheese out of Tillamook Bay to San Francisco and Portland on *The Morningstar,* a locally made schooner. This recipe uses the full-flavored Tillamook cheddar cheese that's still being produced by the local Tillamook County Creamery Association.

4 servings

4 strips meaty peppered or plain bacon, chopped (see margin)
2 tablespoons butter or corn oil margarine
½ cup diced onion
¼ cup all-purpose flour
1 quart homemade chicken stock
    or reduced-sodium canned chicken broth
1 bottle ale (12 ounces)
6 ounces grated medium cheddar cheese
    Salt (optional)
½ teaspoon white pepper

Brown the bacon in a soup pot and pour off any grease. Put the butter and onions in the pot with the bacon and cook for 5 more minutes over medium heat. Sprinkle with the flour and cook, stirring, for 3 minutes. Stir in the stock, ale, and cheese and season with salt and pepper.

Classic Italian Crab Cioppino

Cioppino, a tomato-based hot crab soup, has been popular on the West Coast since the Italian immigrants arrived in San Francisco in the 1800s. Many of the Italian families moved farther north up the coast and settled in small fishing communities. In the town where I grew up near Humboldt Bay, five hours north of San Francisco, there were many good Italian restaurants, and cioppino was often featured on their menus. It should be eaten with plenty of sourdough French bread for dunking into the spicy soup, and bibs should be provided.

4 servings

- 2   *tablespoons mild olive oil*
- 1   *cup onion, chopped*
- 1   *28-ounce can peeled tomatoes, chopped, with juice*
- ½   *teaspoon ground oregano*
- ¼   *cup fresh chopped basil*
- 1   *bay or myrtle leaf (optional)*
- 1   *cup dry white wine*
- 3   *garlic cloves, minced*
- 2   *cooked Dungeness crabs, cleaned, jointed, and cracked (see page 150)*
- ½   *teaspoon salt*

Heat the olive oil in a deep, nonaluminum pot and sauté the onion until it starts to soften. Stir in the chopped tomatoes, oregano, basil, bay leaf, white wine, and half of the garlic and simmer for 30 minutes. Add the remaining garlic, crab, and salt and cook until the crab is hot. Remove the bay leaf and serve in warmed soup bowls with crusty sourdough bread.

Using Myrtle Leaves

The Oregon myrtle tree, also known in northern California as pepperwood, California laurel, and California bay, has aromatic leaves that can be added to dishes as a substitute for true bay leaves. A little bit goes a long way, so use this wild herb judiciously. These fragrant leaves, if they are tucked into the corners of dark pantry shelves, will also keep away pesky kitchen moths.

A crab hawker in Eureka, California, at the turn of the century

Captain Bill Webb's Oyster Stew

Sea Farming

The pioneers who followed the Oregon Trail and headed south into California went in pursuit of gold. Those who rolled on westward were seeking gold, too, but a different kind—theirs was in the soil. They settled in the fertile valleys of the Oregon Territory and farms sprang up like weeds after a spring rain. Agriculture laid the economic framework of the new frontier.

Today, over 150 years later, there's a new kind of farm in the West, and the ocean is its gold. For example, Bill Webb is a sea farmer who lives with his wife on picturesque Westcott Bay, nestled in the San Juan Islands of Washington, a peaceful inlet that provides moderate weather

When Bill Webb, of Westcott Bay Sea Farms in the San Juan Islands, sent me his favorite oyster stew recipe, he added this postscript: "This stew seems to taste even better the next day after having been in the refrigerator overnight." I've made it several times but it's so good I never have any left over.

6 servings

2–3   pounds peeled potatoes (about 6 medium)
  2   dozen large oysters in their shells (2 cups oyster meat)
  4   tablespoons corn oil margarine, butter, or olive oil
1½   cups chopped onions (about 2 large)
  3   large garlic cloves, finely chopped
  1   quart low-fat buttermilk
    Salt to taste
    Freshly ground pepper
    Fresh parsley for garnish

Cook the potatoes in 2 quarts boiling water. Remove the potatoes to cool and measure 6 cups of the cooking liquid and pour it into the bottom of a steamer. Discard the remaining water.

Put the oysters in the top of the steamer and steam until their shells open, about 15 minutes. Discard any that do not open. Set the oysters aside to cool.

Melt the margarine, butter, or olive oil in a stew pot and gently sauté the onions and garlic until soft.

Shuck the oysters, saving any oyster juice remaining in the shells, and chop the meat into bite-size pieces. Measure 2 cups or more of meat, firmly packed, and add to the garlic and onions.

Pour any remaining liquid from the bottom of the steamer through a sieve and into the stew pot. Stir in the buttermilk and slowly heat the stew over low heat.

Chop the potatoes into bite-size pieces and add them to the stew. Season with salt and pepper. Serve in hot soup bowls garnished with a few fresh parsley leaves.

Emerald City Spinach and Oyster Soup

I learned how to make this soup from my good friend the French chef Henri Pujo-Perissere. He left the Pyrenees to relocate in Seattle, known to locals as the Emerald City because it is so green.

8 servings

1	quart milk (2% fat)
1	quart half-and-half
1	pound shucked oysters and their liquor
10	ounces rinsed spinach with water still on the leaves (approximately 7 cups)
2	teaspoons salt
	Freshly ground pepper to taste

Bring the milk and half-and-half to a boil in a 3-quart pot.

Put the oysters and their liquor in a sauté pan and poach for 2–3 minutes. Lay the spinach over the oysters and cook down until the spinach is just wilted—before it turns khaki colored.

Puree the spinach and oysters in a food processor or blender and add to the hot milk mixture. Season with salt and pepper and serve in warmed soup bowls.

and a nutrient-rich bay that not only feeds but protects his crops. He starts his crops by genetically selecting the brood stock and keeps them in the shellfish nursery until they're large enough to make it on

Captain Bill Webb and a stack of lantern nets

Northwest Vietnamese Bouillabaisse

Sea Farming, continued

~~~~~>

their own outdoors. The young shellfish are then transferred into nets called lantern nets, which resemble stacks of crab pots held together with rope. The lanterns are suspended deep in the crystal-clear water of Puget Sound with the spat, or young oysters, inside. Wild mussel larvae from the sound attach themselves to the outside of the nets. Along the bank and just below the water's edge grow the Manila (Japanese littleneck) clams. The native littleneck, although uninvited, has moved in on its own and is thriving lower down on the same bank, preferring a cooler location.

Kimmai Hong calls this recipe Seafood Delight and it surely is just that. The light broth is seasoned with seven fresh herbs before the shellfish is added, creating a hauntingly aromatic seafood soup. She learned how to cook by watching French and Vietnamese chefs who came to her home in Saigon (now Ho Chi Minh City) to cook on special occasions. In this recipe Kimmai uses the French technique for making a light fish soup and combines Vietnamese seasonings with fresh Pacific Northwest shellfish.

8 servings

4	cilantro sprigs
1	bay leaf
6	basil leaves
2	sprigs fresh dill
6	fresh mint leaves
2	scallions or green onions
2	tablespoons olive oil
½	cup chopped onion
4	garlic cloves, crushed
½	pound ripe tomatoes, peeled, seeded, and chopped, or ¾ cup canned tomatoes, seeded, drained, and chopped
1	cup fresh pineapple, sliced into bite-size pieces (not canned—it's too sweet)
2½	quarts water
1	stalk fresh lemon grass (see margin, page 119), cut into 3 pieces
3	tablespoons fish sauce (nuoc nam)*
2	tablespoons sugar
½	teaspoon chili garlic sauce (sambal oelek), * optional
½	teaspoon salt
2	tablespoons lemon or lime juice

These Indonesian condiments are available at most large grocery stores and oriental markets.

15 medium-size steamer clams, scrubbed
1 cooked Dungeness crab, cleaned, jointed,
   and cracked (see page 150)
15 medium-size shrimp, peeled and deveined, with tails on
1 pinch saffron (optional)

Chop the cilantro, bay leaf, basil, dill, mint, and scallions, including the green tops, and set aside.

Heat the olive oil in a soup pot and cook the chopped onion for 5 minutes or until tender but not browned. Stir in the garlic and tomatoes and cook over high heat for 5 more minutes. Add the pineapple, water, and lemon grass and simmer for an additional 20 minutes.

Stir in the fish sauce, sugar, chili garlic sauce, salt, and lemon juice and bring to a boil. Drop in the clams and crab and cook for 5 minutes, or until the clams open and the crab is warm. Add the shrimp, saffron, and chopped herbs and cook 1 more minute. Remove the pot from the heat and season with more salt if necessary. Discard the lemon grass stalks and serve immediately with noodles or plain rice.

Chinese New Year, 1933, Portland, Oregon

Geoduck Clam Chowder

Clam Chowder, à la "Old Settler"

"First 'Catch your clams an' peel 'em.' (The best way to accomplish this is to provide yourself with a pair of gum boots, a gunny sack and a spade, and go after 'em. They bite best when the tide is low.)

"Second: Prepare and chop separately 3 or 4 good sized potatoes, 1 large onion, and 1 pint of raw clams. Chop, or cut in small squares what would make a small cup of ham or bacon, and fry it brown in an iron kettle; then pour in boiling water, dump in your potatoes and onions, and cook until onions are done, and then, add the

"Five defendants in a million-dollar geoduck theft case [in Seattle] pleaded no contest Wednesday to reduced charges, leaving only the man accused of being the 'Clamscam' kingpin still on trial." This is a true story that could only have taken place in the Pacific Northwest, where the world's largest digging clam resides. It averages three pounds and the delicate, sweet meat can be prepared innumerable ways from ceviche to fried clam steaks, depending on the part of the clam used. In this recipe I use the minced neck (siphon) meat.

6 servings

1	cup ground or minced geoduck (substitute other minced clams if geoduck are not available)
¼	pound chopped bacon
1	cup chopped onion
¼	cup chopped celery
¼	cup all-purpose flour
1	quart half-and-half
1	pound cooked and cubed Yukon Gold or red new potatoes
	Salt to taste
	Freshly ground pepper

Before running the neck through the meat grinder, or grinding in a food processor, remove the geoduck from the shell by slipping a knife between the shell and the body. Cut the neck off at the base and dip it into boiling water to loosen the skin. Remove the skin by pulling it away with your fingers. The minced body meat can also be used.

Fry the bacon in a soup pot until it just starts to brown. Discard any grease that has accumulated. Add the onion and celery and cook for 5 more minutes. Add the clams and sprinkle the flour over all. Stir and cook over medium heat for 3 more minutes. Pour in the half-and-half and continue stirring until the soup thickens. Gently drop the potatoes into the soup and season with salt and pepper. Serve immediately.

clams, and stir well and boil about 5 minutes. Add 1 quart of milk, butter and creackers [sic], season and serve. N.B. Don't salt until ready to serve."—"Old Settler" (Theodore Brown)

—From The Capital City Cook Book, compiled by the Ladies of the Congregational Church (Olympia, Washington: Recorder Press, 1914).

Japanese family digging clams in Puget Sound

Wholesome Breads, Muffins, and Cereals

Wheat was one of the first crops planted by the settlers in the Pacific Northwest. It was sown, harvested, and threshed by hand and often ground in a coffee mill. This coarse whole wheat flour adequately served the needs of the pioneers until the gristmills were built to refine the flour. (Corn was treated in a similar manner and the coarsely ground cornmeal was used to make corn bread and cereal.) Over the years wheat has become a major crop in the Pacific Northwest. In spite of the fact that all kinds of breads are available commercially, bread is still being baked at home and automatic bread machines and food processors have made it easier than ever to whip up a loaf in no time at all.

The bread shelf at the grocery is a good place to observe the culinary influence of the Northwest's diverse ethnic heritage. There are British crumpets, Danish pastries, Greek bread, pita bread, and French bread. Some of the baked goods, such as English muffins and bread, are still made from sourdough.

A sourdough starter was a staple in early pioneer homes and it's still used extensively in Alaska and by local sheepherders. Natural wild yeast has been used as a leavening agent for thousands of years throughout the world.

Today you see dozens of new kinds of bread on local bakery shelves, such as focaccia, a disk-shaped Italian bread that is sold partially baked. The top of the bread is brushed with olive oil and sprinkled with salt and chopped rosemary at home, before you pop it in the oven. I like it so much I keep several loaves of it in my freezer.

Small local bakeries, no longer owned by Danish or German families, are producing a good assortment of dense whole wheat breads, sourdough baguettes, and hearty muffins, as well as more refined pastries, popular in previous years. It's the best of the past joining forces with the present, and the beginning of new Pacific Northwest traditions.

Hazelnut Buttermilk Pancakes with Blackberry Butter

These wonderfully dense pancakes, loaded with bits of roasted hazelnuts, are served with warm blackberry butter. The blackberry butter can be made days ahead and the pancake batter the night before.

4 servings

How to Seed Blackberries

Seed the berries by running them through a food mill or puree them in a food processor and push the crushed berries through a sieve. Or you could use an old-fashioned device such as the one above.

1   *package active dry yeast*
½   *cup warm water*
2½   *cups buttermilk (may need a little more if the batter needs thinning in the morning)*
3   *eggs*
2   *cups all-purpose flour*
3   *tablespoons sugar*
1   *tablespoon baking soda*
1   *teaspoon salt*
¼   *cup finely ground toasted hazelnuts*
    Blackberry Butter (recipe follows)

In a large bowl dissolve the yeast in warm water. Add the buttermilk and the remaining ingredients and mix well. Cover and place in the refrigerator overnight. In the morning stir in more buttermilk if the batter seems too thick.

Heat a lightly greased griddle and cook pancakes on one side until bubbles rise to the surface and pop. Turn the pancakes over and cook for 2–3 more minutes.

Blackberry Butter

I like to serve this intensely flavorful butter warmed and drizzled over hazelnut pancakes or French toast. It's not as sweet as syrup and it elevates an ordinary breakfast into a special occasion. Blackberry butter makes a great gift, too, tucked into a basket of homemade biscuits.

Makes 2 cups

8   tablespoons unsalted butter (½ cup)
2   cups fresh blackberries (substitute raspberries or strawberries) or 1 pound frozen and thawed, pureed and seeded (see margin, opposite page)
1   cup sugar

Melt the butter and stir in the blackberries and sugar. Remove from the heat and stir until the sugar is dissolved. Taste for sweetness. More sugar may need to be added depending on the sugar content of the blackberries. Store in the refrigerator (good for up to 2 weeks).

Microwave Instructions:

Put the butter, blackberries, and sugar in a microwave-safe bowl and microwave on High for 2 minutes. Stir and microwave for 2 more minutes.

Portland's Eastern Restaurant served "breakfast" throughout the day.

EASTERN RESTAURANT,
104 First Street, opp. Odd Fellows' Temple,
LEE & McLOUD, - - - - - - PROPRIETORS.

BREAKFAST BILL.

Steaks.		Eggs.	
Porter House	25	Boiled	15
Sirloin	25	Fried	15
Rump	15	Scrambled	15
Pork	15	Omelette	15
Veal	15		
Lamb Steak	15		
Lamb Chop	15	Toast.	
Ham	15	Dry	10
		Dipped	10
Fish, Fresh.		Milk	10
Salmon	15	Steak Toast	25
Trout	15		
Fish, Salt.		Bread.	
Salmon	15	White	
Mackerel	15	Corn	
Codfish	15	Graham	
Fish Balls	15	Rolls	
		Griddle Cakes	10
Fowl.		Bread and Milk	10
Spring Chickens	50		
Spring Duck	50		
Game.		Tea.	
Grouse	50	Green	10
Pheasant	50	Japan	10
Quail	50	Black	10
Squirrel	50		
Vegetables.		Coffee.	
Baked and Mashed Potatoes		Java	10
Sweet Potatoes		Chocolate	15

Breakfast from 6 A. M. to 11 P. M.

1870

67

Blueberry-Yogurt Coffee Cake

Homemade Yogurt

Homemade yogurt is simple to make and uses only three ingredients— a quart of whole milk, ⅓ cup instant nonfat dry milk, and 1 table- spoon plain yogurt. Just scald the whole milk and stir in the pow- dered milk. Let this cool to 90–120°F., then whisk in the yogurt, pour into a small bowl or a number of small bowls, and cover with plastic wrap. Incubate in a gas oven with a pilot light, or heat an electric oven to 150°F. and turn the oven off but leave the oven light on (yogurt thickens in a warm—but not too warm—environment). The yogurt will take 4–5 hours, but can be left overnight; the longer you leave it the tangier it gets.

This coffee cake is a summer favorite at our house which I often make a day in advance. I reheat it covered with foil in a 300°F. oven for 20 minutes. It can be warmed faster in the microwave, but I enjoy smelling the sweet, lingering aroma that drifts out of the oven as it reheats. Don't let its unusually thick batter worry you. It will push the sugar-cinnamon topping up as it bakes, and will sink down when it is removed from the oven. This is one of the few coffee cakes that improve with age.

8–10 servings

Topping

  1   cup sugar
  2   teaspoons cinnamon
  2   tablespoons butter, chilled and cut up

Coffee Cake

  8   tablespoons butter or corn oil margarine (½ cup)
1½ cups packed brown sugar
  1   egg
  1   teaspoon baking soda
  2   cups all-purpose flour
  1   cup plain yogurt (8 ounces)
  1   teaspoon vanilla
  2   cups blueberries, fresh or frozen

Preheat oven to 350°F. and butter a 9 x 13-inch baking dish.

Using a fork, blend the topping ingredients together in a small bowl. Set aside.

In the bowl of an electric mixer, cream together the butter, brown sugar, and egg. Add the baking soda, flour, yogurt, and vanilla and mix on medium speed for 2–3 minutes.

Pour the cake batter into the buttered baking dish and sprinkle the berries over the top. Gently press them into the batter. Sprinkle the cinnamon-sugar topping over all.

Bake for 45–50 minutes. If frozen blueberries are used, increase the baking time to 1 hour.

Food Processor Method:

Put the sugar, cinnamon, and 2 tablespoons butter in the workbowl and pulse 8–10 times. Place the mixture in a small bowl and set aside. To the same workbowl add ½ cup butter, the brown sugar, and the egg. Process for 30 seconds. Blend the baking soda and flour together in a small bowl and sprinkle it over the creamed mixture. Add the yogurt and vanilla and process for 1 minute. Pour the batter into the baking dish and sprinkle the berries over the top, pushing them down into the batter with your finger. Sprinkle with the cinnamon-sugar topping and bake for 40–50 minutes. If frozen blueberries are used, increase the cooking time to 1 hour.

Class picnic, Ballard, Washington, 1914

Cookhouse Buttermilk Biscuits

*The Logging Camp
Cookhouse*

*At the turn of the twen-
tieth century, loggers
still lived at the logging
site, and the center of
all social activity was
the cookhouse. Henry
Yesler, who operated
one of the first sawmills
in Seattle, built a cook-
house in 1853 which
remains legendary to
this day. It was open
twenty-four hours a day
and "no man nor beast
was ever turned away."*

Before the turn of the century, when loggers ate all their
meals at the cookhouse, buttermilk biscuits were made
the same day butter was churned, using the leftover buttermilk. Most buttermilk today is made from cultured
skim milk, but it still provides a pleasing tangy bite to
baked products.

Makes approximately 1 dozen

2	*cups flour*
1	*tablespoon baking powder*
½	*teaspoon baking soda*
½	*teaspoon salt*
1	*tablespoon sugar*
¼	*cup corn oil*
1	*cup buttermilk*

Preheat the oven to 450°F.

Stir the dry ingredients together. Whisk together the
oil and buttermilk and stir it into the flour mixture. Turn
out onto a floured board or pastry cloth and knead 3–4
times until smooth. Roll out to ½-inch thickness and
cut with a 2½-inch biscuit cutter. Place on an ungreased
cookie sheet and bake for 10 minutes.

Food Processor Method:

Preheat the oven to 450°F.

In a food processor workbowl pulse the dry ingredients 4 times. Blend the corn oil and buttermilk together
and, with the machine running, slowly pour the liquids
into the dry ingredients. Turn out onto a floured board
or pastry cloth and knead 3–4 times until smooth. Roll
out to ½-inch thickness and cut with a 2½-inch biscuit
cutter. Place on an ungreased cookie sheet and bake for
10 minutes, or until the tops are lightly golden brown.

James Beard's Cream Biscuits

I sampled the following recipe for cream biscuits one year when James Beard was in Portland teaching a cooking class. He grew up in Portland, and this wonderfully light and tender biscuit was a specialty of his family's Chinese cook. The recipe is also in James Beard's collection of bread recipes, *Beard on Bread* (New York: Alfred A. Knopf, 1974).

Makes about 12 biscuits

> 2 cups all-purpose flour
> 1 teaspoon salt
> 1 tablespoon double-acting baking powder
> 2 teaspoons granulated sugar
> ¾–1 cup cream
>   Melted butter

Preheat the oven to 425°F. and grease a baking sheet.

Sift together the dry ingredients. Stir in the cream until the dough is smooth. Knead the dough on a floured surface for 1 minute and roll out to ½–¾ inch thick. Cut into rounds or squares, dip in butter, and arrange on the baking sheet.

Bake for 15–18 minutes.

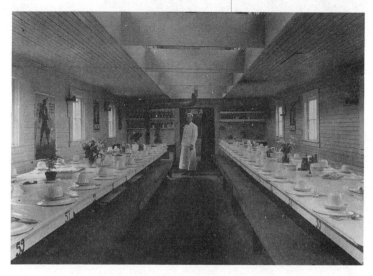

A Chinese cook in a typical logging camp cookhouse waiting for the arrival of hungry loggers

Old-Fashioned Breakfast Bread Pudding

A large British population settled along the Pacific Northwest coast. Bread pudding was standard fare for dessert, but I like to serve it for breakfast. This simple recipe actually tastes more like baked French toast. I make it with sourdough French bread but any bread will do. It puffs up as it bakes and will be a rich golden brown when done.

4 servings

4 teaspoons butter or corn oil margarine
7 thick slices of bread with crust (round sourdough bread slices, ¾–1 inch thick, just to fit in the bread pan)
3 tablespoons toasted and coarsely chopped hazelnuts
¾ cup maple syrup
3 eggs
1½ cups milk

Preheat oven to 350°F. and grease the bottom and sides of an 8 x 5½ x 3-inch loaf pan.

Butter one side of each piece of bread and arrange 2 slices, buttered side up, in the bottom of the pan. If the bottom is not covered, cut a third of a piece of bread in half and arrange it next to the other 2 slices. Sprinkle the bread with 1 tablespoon hazelnuts. Repeat for 2 more layers of buttered bread with hazelnuts.

Whisk the syrup, eggs, and milk together and pour over the bread.

Bake at 350°F. for 50 minutes, or until the top is golden brown. Let the pudding set for 10 minutes before serving.

Serve from the pan accompanied by blackberry jam.

Grandma Skinner's Scottish Scones

The late Grandma Skinner, a native of Stoneyburn, Scotland, was the grandmother of Jan Roberts-Dominguez, who writes a syndicated newspaper column called "Green Cuisine." This is Grandma's original recipe. The scones are cooked the old-fashioned way, on a griddle, whereas contemporary versions are usually baked. I serve the scones warm with butter and homemade jam for breakfast.

Makes 16 scones

3	cups all-purpose flour
1½	teaspoons salt
1½	teaspoons baking soda
1½	teaspoons cream of tartar
1	teaspoon granulated sugar
1	tablespoon butter
1½	cups buttermilk

Sift the flour, salt, baking soda, cream of tartar, and sugar together into a bowl. By hand, rub the butter into the flour, making small cornmeal-like granules. Add the buttermilk all at once; then working quickly but gently, mix with a dinner knife until the dough is just barely mixed. Add a little more buttermilk if necessary, but don't make the dough sticky.

Divide the dough into quarters. On a floured board, roll out each quarter into a circle ¼ inch thick. Cut each circle into quarters.

Heat a lightly greased griddle to medium-hot and fry the scones in batches until they turn a light golden color. Turn the scones over and cook on the other side. Now brown all of the edges by standing the triangles up and leaning against each other for about 30 seconds. As the scones come off the griddle, cool in a tea towel until ready to use.

Variation with Salmon

Add ½ pound smoked skinless salmon fillet, diced, to the dough when the buttermilk is added.

Peanut Butter Granola

Variation

Dried fruits and toasted nuts can be added to this recipe to enhance its flavor and nutritional value.

This recipe was given to me during the granola years of the mid-seventies. We always take the granola, sealed in plastic bags, on summer float trips down the Deschutes River in central Oregon. I serve it topped with low-fat yogurt and fresh blueberries. The fresh blueberries keep surprisingly well on camping trips if they are stored chilled in a sturdy plastic container.

Makes 11 cups

1	cup creamy peanut butter
1	cup corn oil
½	cup honey
9	cups rolled oats
1	cup toasted wheat bran
1	cup wheat germ

Preheat the oven to 300°F.

In a small saucepan gently heat the peanut butter, oil, and honey until it is smooth and homogeneous.

Blend the oats, bran, and wheat germ together in a 9 x 13-inch baking dish. Drizzle the peanut butter mixture over all and stir with a wooden spoon to distribute the liquid. Bake, uncovered, for 20–25 minutes, stirring once or twice. The granola should be golden brown. Do not overcook.

Betty's Cucumber-Dill Muffins

Betty Shenberger, a good friend and my "right arm" for many years when I ran several cooking schools in Portland, teaches food-processor classes and this is one of her terrific recipes. These muffins are perfectly moist and go particularly well with seafood.

Makes 1 dozen

Local Herb Farms

2   cups all-purpose flour
3   tablespoons sugar
½   teaspoon salt
½   teaspoon baking soda
1   tablespoon baking powder
½   cup shredded English cucumber (or plain, peeled and seeded)
1   heaping tablespoon finely chopped fresh dill or 1 teaspoon dried
1⅓ cups buttermilk
2   eggs
5   tablespoons plus 1 teaspoon butter, melted (⅓ cup)

Preheat the oven to 400°F. and grease muffin tins.

Combine the dry ingredients in a bowl. Add the cucumber, dill, buttermilk, eggs, and butter and stir just until blended.

Spoon the mixture into the muffin tins, filling each cup ⅔ full. Bake for 20–25 minutes. Remove from muffin tins and serve warm.

Food Processor Method:

Combine the dry ingredients in the workbowl, and pulse about 10 seconds. Add the cucumber and dill. In a 2-cup measure, lightly mix together the buttermilk, eggs, and melted butter; pour over the dry ingredients. Pulse, just to blend, about 4 times. Do not overmix.

Spoon the mixture into greased muffin tins, filling each cup ⅔ full. Bake for 20–25 minutes. Remove from muffin tins and serve warm.

When I first ran the Kitchen Kaboodle Cooking School in Portland during the late 1970s, I always looked forward to the annual visit of Perla Meyers. Not only were her classes great, but she always brought fresh dill with her from New York because it wasn't available locally. Today, there is an abundance of herb farms throughout the western lowlands from northern California all the way to British Columbia.

Fresh Raspberry Tea Bread

Pacific Northwest Wheat

Ninety percent of the soft white winter wheat grown in the United States comes from Washington, Oregon, and Idaho. In fact, wheat is the principal agricultural crop for Washington State and a major crop in both Idaho and Oregon. There are two primary wheat-growing regions and both of them are east of the Cascades: the arid land of north central Oregon and central Washington; and the Palouse in southeastern Washington and north-western Idaho, where wheat is alternated with crops of peas, lentils, and barley. Small quantities of wheat are

Many of the wagon trains that rolled over the Oregon Trail brought families from the Midwest and South who settled outside Portland. The county names in Oregon, such as Polk, Jefferson, Jackson, and Lincoln, reflect their influence. Portland itself was settled by New Englanders who arrived on boats. (The name "Portland" came from the flip of a coin: Was the new city to be named Portland, after Portland, Maine, or Boston, after Boston, Massachusetts?) English Yankees loved their afternoon tea, and in the nineteenth century the serving of afternoon tea was common in Portland. Today, Portland's Heathman Hotel has revived the tradition. The following recipe for raspberry tea bread produces a moist bread with a lovely sweet cardamom aftertaste. It could easily be served as a dessert with a Pacific Northwest late-harvest Riesling.

Makes 1 loaf

¾	cup fresh raspberries
⅓	cup raspberry liqueur (see page 278)
1	cup plus 1 tablespoon sugar
8	tablespoons corn oil margarine or butter (½ cup)
1	egg
1½	cups all-purpose flour
1	teaspoon ground cardamom
2	teaspoons baking soda
⅓	cup buttermilk

Preheat the oven to 350°F. and grease an 8 x 3¾ x 2½-inch loaf pan.

Macerate the raspberries in the raspberry liqueur for 30 minutes.

Cream 1 cup sugar with the butter. Add the egg and beat well. Stir in the flour, cardamom, baking soda, and buttermilk. Drain the raspberries, reserving the liqueur, and carefully fold them into the batter. Pour the batter into the prepared pan and drizzle with the liqueur. Sprinkle with the remaining tablespoon of sugar and bake for 45 minutes.

Food Processor Method:

Preheat the oven to 350°F. and grease a loaf pan.

Macerate the raspberries in the raspberry liqueur for 30 minutes.

Put 1 cup of sugar and the butter in the workbowl and pulse 8–10 times. Add the egg and process for 30 seconds. In a small bowl stir the flour, cardamom, and baking soda together. Sprinkle the dry ingredients over the creamed sugar and process for 30 seconds. With the machine still running, gradually pour in the buttermilk.

Pour the batter into the prepared pan. Drain the berries, reserving the liqueur, and carefully fold in the berries. Drizzle the liqueur over the batter and sprinkle with the reserved tablespoon of sugar.

Bake for 45 minutes.

also grown west of the Cascades in the Willamette Valley.

Most of the crop is sold internationally (about twenty percent stays in the Pacific Northwest), and it's transported down the Columbia/Snake river system by barge to the port of Portland or

Harvesting and enjoying food in the outdoors has always been a special part of living in the Pacific Northwest.

Three-Grain Freezer Bread

*Pacific Northwest
Wheat, continued*

Kalama, or shipped by
rail to the port of
Seattle. Ships from
Japan, Korea, Taiwan,
India, and Egypt can
regularly be seen loading
wheat at the port termi-
nal wheat elevators.*

*Soft white winter
wheat has a low protein
level (and consequently
low gluten level) and it's
used primarily for pastry
products—cakes, cook-
ies, etc.—flatbreads,
oriental noodles, and
cereals. According to
Bon Lee, the chemist at
the Pendleton Flour
Mills in Pendleton,
Oregon, the company
sells over a hundred dif-
ferent blends of flours
that are used for every-
thing from cake flour to
premixed batters. Even
all-purpose flour is a
blend of hard and soft
winter wheat.*

**Kalama, named after a
Hawaiian, is a port on the
Columbia River in Wash-
ington, twenty miles down-
stream from Portland.*

When I make this bread I bake only one of the loaves.
The other one I cover with plastic wrap and foil, and
store in the freezer. It takes only two hours for the frozen
bread to thaw and rise before it is ready to be baked.
I buy the wheat germ, millet, and sunflower seeds at a
health food store. Both the sunflower seeds and millet
are toasted to enhance their flavor. This bread makes
incredible toast.

Makes 2 loaves

1	package active dry yeast
2–2½	cups warm water
6	cups all-purpose flour
¼	cup sugar
¾	cup wheat germ
¼	cup toasted sunflower seeds (see margin, next page)
½	cup toasted millet
1	tablespoon salt
4	tablespoons corn oil margarine or butter, softened (¼ cup)

Grease a large bowl and two 8 x 3¾ x 2½-inch loaf pans.

Dissolve the yeast in ½ cup warm water and set aside.

Measure the flour, sugar, wheat germ, sunflower seeds,
millet, and salt into a large bowl. Stir in the butter,
dissolved yeast, and 1½ cups of water. Add more water
if necessary.

Knead the bread on a lightly floured board until
smooth. Put the dough in a greased bowl, cover, and let
rise until doubled. Punch the dough down and shape
into 2 loaves.

Put the unbaked loaves in 2 greased, 8 x 3¾ x 2½-
inch loaf pans. Cover one loaf of dough with a layer of
plastic wrap, followed by foil, and store in the freezer.
Cover the other loaf with plastic wrap and let rise in a
warm spot until doubled.

Preheat the oven to 400°F. Bake the bread dough for
10 minutes, then reduce the heat to 350°F. and bake for

another 20 minutes. Remove the bread from the pan and bake it on the oven rack an additional 5 minutes.

To Cook the Frozen Dough:

Take the bread from the freezer and remove the foil. Keep the loaf covered with plastic wrap and let it rise in a warm place until doubled, about 2 hours.

Preheat the oven to 400°F. Bake the bread dough for 10 minutes, then reduce the heat to 350°F. and bake for another 20 minutes. Remove the bread from the pan and bake it on the oven rack an additional 5 minutes.

Food Processor Method:

Dissolve the yeast in ½ cup warm water and set aside. Measure the flour, sugar, wheat germ, and salt into the workbowl with 4 tablespoons (¼ cup) butter cut into pieces. Turn the machine on and slowly add all the dissolved yeast and 2 cups of water. Process until the dough forms a mass. If the dough seems dry and doesn't ball up, add a little more water. Continue to process for 60 more seconds to knead the bread. Knead the sunflower seeds and millet in by hand. Put the dough in a greased bowl, cover, and let rise until doubled. Punch down and shape into 2 loaves. Put the dough into the two 8 x 3¾ x 2½-inch loaf pans.

Cover each loaf with a layer of plastic wrap, followed by foil, and store in the freezer. Take the bread from the freezer and remove the foil. Keep the loaf covered with plastic wrap and let it rise in a warm place until doubled, about 2 hours.

Preheat the oven to 400°F.

Bake the loaves for 10 minutes, then reduce the heat to 350°F. and bake for another 20 minutes. Remove the bread from the pan and bake it on the oven rack the last 5 minutes of baking time.

Toasting Sunflower Seeds

To toast sunflower seeds put them in an ungreased cast-iron skillet over medium-high heat. Constantly shake the pan back and forth across the heat until the seeds turn golden brown.

Homemade Bread with Black Sesame Seeds and Kosher Salt

A Pioneer Woman's Reminiscence

"*Mother was baking some bread when some of these savage-looking Indians came into our camp. While she looked up to watch them one of them came near the fire. When Mother looked back to see how her bread was coming along the bread was gone. The Indian had stolen the hot bread. Mother hoped it has burned him well, but if it did he made no sign.*"

—From Fred Lockley, Conversations with Pioneer Women, "*Lucy Ann Henderson Deady,*" *compiled and edited by Mike Helm (Eugene, Oregon: Rainy Day Press, 1981).*

I like to make this recipe for company since it can be prepared ahead of time and requires little last-minute attention. Put it in the oven thirty minutes before the guests arrive. When the doorbell rings they will be greeted by the wonderful aroma of homemade bread and it will be warm and perfect for slicing when dinner is served.

Makes one 9-inch round loaf

1	package active dry yeast
1	cup plus 2 tablespoons warm water
¼	cup nonfat dry milk
1	tablespoon sugar
1	teaspoon salt
2	tablespoons olive oil
3½	cups flour
1	egg, beaten
1	tablespoon black sesame seeds, toasted
1	teaspoon kosher salt

Grease a 10 x 15-inch baking sheet.

Sprinkle the yeast over the warm water until it dissolves. Blend in the nonfat dry milk, sugar, salt, and olive oil. Stir the flour into the yeast mixture until most of the lumps are gone. Knead the dough on a lightly floured surface until smooth. Add more flour if necessary. Shape into a 9-inch round loaf and place on a greased baking sheet.

Cover it with plastic wrap and let it rise in the refrigerator at least 2 hours and up to 6 hours.

Preheat the oven to 400°F.

Remove from the refrigerator and take off the plastic wrap. Let stand at room temperature for 10–15 minutes. Brush with the beaten egg and sprinkle with the sesame seeds and salt. Bake for 30 minutes, or until done. Remove to wire rack and cool.

Food Processor Method:

Grease a 10 x 15-inch baking sheet.

Sprinkle the yeast over the warm water until it dissolves. Put the nonfat dry milk, sugar, salt, olive oil, and flour in the bowl of a food processor and pulse 2 or 3 times to blend. With the machine running, slowly add the water and yeast and process until the dough forms a mass. Add more water if necessary. Continue to process for 1 more minute to knead the bread. Transfer the dough to a lightly floured surface and knead until smooth. Add more flour if necessary. Shape into a 9-inch round loaf and place on a greased baking sheet.

Cover it with plastic wrap and let it rise in the refrigerator for 2–6 hours.

Preheat the oven to 400°F.

Remove from the refrigerator and take off the plastic wrap. Let stand at room temperature for 10–15 minutes. Brush with the beaten egg and sprinkle with the sesame seeds and salt. Bake for 30 minutes, or until done.

A Klamath Indian woman grinds wokas, the seeds of the water lily, on a metate (a flat mortar) using a two-horned grinder. The ground seeds and local freshwater fish were the main staples of the diet.

Basque Sheepherder's Bread

The following recipe from Anita Mitchell won the bread-baking contest at the National Basque Festival several years ago. It was an old Basque custom for the sheepherder to slash the sign of the cross on top of the loaf and then to serve the first piece to his invaluable dog.

A Basque sheepherder in Idaho following the flock with his chuck wagon

Makes 1 huge loaf (4½ pounds)

     3   cups very hot tap water
     ½   cup butter, margarine, or shortening
     ½   cup sugar
    2½   teaspoons salt
     2   packages dry yeast
         About 8½–9 cups all-purpose flour
         Corn oil

In a bowl combine the hot water, butter, sugar, and salt. Stir until the butter melts; let cool to warm (110–115°F.). Stir in yeast, cover, and set in a warm place until bubbly, about 15 minutes.

Add 5 cups of the flour and beat with a heavy-duty mixer or wooden spoon to form a thick batter. With a spoon, stir in enough of the remaining flour (about 3½ cups) to form a stiff dough. Turn dough out onto a floured board and knead until smooth, about 10 minutes, adding more flour as necessary.

Place the dough in a very large greased bowl and let rise, covered, until doubled in volume.

Punch down dough and knead a few minutes on a floured board, then form into a smooth ball. Cut a circle of foil to cover the bottom of a 5-quart cast-iron Dutch oven. Grease the inside of the Dutch oven and the underside of the lid with corn oil.

Place the dough in the pot and cover with the lid. Let rise in a warm place until the dough pushes up the lid by about ½ inch, about 1 hour (watch closely). Preheat the oven to 375°F.

Bake, covered, for 12 minutes. Remove the lid and bake for another 40–50 minutes, or until the loaf is golden brown and sounds hollow when tapped. Remove from the oven and turn the loaf out (you'll need a helper) onto a rack to cool.

Basque Traditions

Basque sheepherders traditionally baked their bread in large cast-iron kettles buried in a bed of hot coals. This recipe has been adapted to the oven but nothing has been lost in the process. It makes a robust-looking loaf that is deliciously yeasty-flavored with an even-textured crumb. It is essential, though, to thoroughly grease the inside of the pot and lid so the bread can be turned out easily when done. The bread can also be baked in a 5½-quart round French oven.

Basic Sourdough Starter

Feeding the Starter

To feed the starter, put 1 cup of the starter in a large bowl and discard the rest. Stir in 1 cup warm water and 1 cup flour and cover with plastic wrap. Let it set in a warm spot for 8 hours. Put 1 cup of the revived starter back in the jar, discarding any left over, and store in the refrigerator. If the starter has not been used for several months, repeat this entire process again, using 1 cup revived starter, 1 cup flour, and 1 cup warm water.

There's really no flavor comparable to the intense taste of foods made with sourdough. Pancakes, waffles, breads, and pastries take on a flavor all their own that's difficult to reproduce using any other method. All the sourdough recipes in this book have been made using a recipe for starter developed by the Oregon Wheat Commission. It will keep for years if it is fed monthly and kept properly covered in the refrigerator.

Makes 7–8 cups

½   cup lukewarm water (105–115°F.)
1   package dry yeast
2   cups all-purpose flour
1   tablespoon salt
1   tablespoon sugar
1½   cups cold water

Pour the warm water into a bowl and stir in the yeast until dissolved.

Measure the dry ingredients into a large bowl and stir in the yeast mixture and the cold water. Cover with plastic wrap and place in a warm place, 80–90°F., for 3–4 days. Stir the starter down daily.

Pour the starter into a jar, allowing room for expansion, and cover with plastic wrap or wax paper before closing the lid. Store in the refrigerator.

Sourdough English Muffins

A basket of these intensely flavored English muffins along with a jar of homemade blackberry jam makes a gift that rivals anything money can buy. The recipe comes from a small cookbook, *Sourdough Jack's Cookery & Other Things*, by Jack Mabee (San Francisco: Jack Mabee, 1970).

Makes 2 dozen

- 1 cup sourdough starter
- 2 cups milk
- 5 cups all-purpose flour
- 2 tablespoons sugar
- 1 teaspoon salt
- 1 teaspoon baking soda
- 6 tablespoons cornmeal

The night before, beat the starter, milk, and 4 cups of flour together in a large bowl.

In the morning, stir into the batter ½ cup flour, the sugar, salt, and baking soda. Add more flour if it is too sticky. Use some of the remaining flour to lightly dust a pastry board. Turn the dough out onto the board and knead until smooth. Add more of the remaining flour if necessary.

Roll the dough to a ¾-inch thickness and cut into biscuits with a 3-inch cutter. Sprinkle the cornmeal on 2 baking sheets, transfer the biscuits to the baking sheet, and let rise, covered with a dish towel, for 45 minutes.

Heat a lightly greased skillet to medium-low and slowly cook the English muffins 7 minutes on each side. Let the muffins cool on a rack for 5 minutes before serving. These also freeze well tightly sealed in plastic bags.

Whole Wheat Sourdough Biscuits

An Oregon Homesteader's Biscuits

The late Jessie Wright was a lovely, soft-spoken woman who homesteaded in the western Cascades. Before her death at age ninety-two, she told me how she used to make her own starter:

"My husband liked sourdough biscuits every morning for breakfast and I had to learn how to make those blasted things. He showed me once, then it was my job to fix them. I would make baking powder pancakes without eggs and would just add a little bit of sugar. I'd leave it until it started to bubble, then I'd add flour and milk. When this started to bubble again, I'd add more milk and flour. The bubbling meant it was souring—starting its own yeast. Before I made biscuits I added some baking powder."

This recipe was given to me by a Native American friend, Sandy French. She and her husband used to live in Portland and every year they gathered the native wild plum in southern Oregon to make jam for these wonderful biscuits. I have fond memories of sitting at her kitchen table on rainy afternoons, eating these absolutely delicious biscuits hot from the oven.

Makes 2½ dozen

- 8 tablespoons butter (½ cup)
- 1 cup whole wheat flour
- ¾–1 cup all-purpose flour
- 1 tablespoon sugar
- 2 teaspoons baking powder
- ½ teaspoon salt
- 2 cups sourdough starter (prepared the night before, page 84)

Cut the butter into the dry ingredients with two knives or a pastry blender. Stir in the sourdough starter until smooth.

Turn the dough out onto a floured board and knead until smooth. Roll out to ½-inch thickness and cut into biscuits using a 2½-inch biscuit cutter. Cover and let rise on a greased baking sheet for 1 hour.

Preheat the oven to 425°F.

Bake the biscuits for 15–20 minutes. Serve with butter and homemade jam.

Food Processor Method:

Place all the ingredients except the starter in the work-bowl. Pulse 8–10 times until the butter is cut into the dry ingredients. Pour in the starter and process for 30–45 seconds.

Turn out onto a floured board and knead until smooth. Roll out to ½-inch thickness and cut into biscuits using a 2½-inch biscuit cutter. Cover and let rise on a greased baking sheet for 1 hour.

Bake for 15–20 minutes. Serve with butter and wild plum or blackberry jam.

An Old Formula for Yeast

Wash and cut up one-half gallon potatoes (without peeling), boil, add tablespoonful pressed hops. In another dish put one-half potato water. Mix thoroughly by hand, mashing the potatoes. Put through colander and then add one pint China yeast.* Fill one-half gallon jar within two inches of top and stand in warm place to rise 6 hours, stirring in a couple of hours. Put away in cool place. Will keep one moon.—Lou Wee

*China yeast is a Chinese leavening agent in the shape of a hard, white ball that needs to be broken up before it's used. It's not unusual for the Chinese to use more than one leavening agent, as they did here, to give the sourdough starter more leavening power.

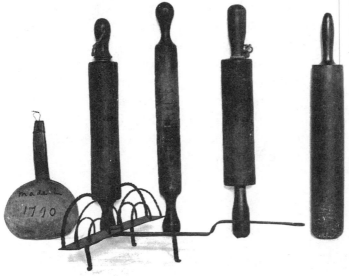

Blueberry-Sourdough Corn Bread

Reviving the Starter

The night before you make the corn bread put 1 cup sourdough starter in a large bowl and discard any remaining starter. Stir in 1 cup flour and 1 cup warm water until it's smooth. Cover the bowl with plastic wrap and let it sit overnight in a warm spot. The next day use 1 cup of this revived starter to make the bread and put the remaining cup in a jar for storage, leaving room for it to expand. Cover and store in refrigerator.

Fresh blueberries provide a refreshing kick to this dense and moist sourdough corn bread. The top of the bread will crack as it bakes, giving it a nice rustic appearance. Keep the cooled bread wrapped, airtight, in foil. It tastes better the second day.

6–8 servings

1	cup sourdough starter (prepared the night before, page 84)
1	cup all-purpose flour
1	cup yellow cornmeal
1	tablespoon baking powder
1	teaspoon baking soda
1	teaspoon salt
½	cup sugar
1	egg
1	cup milk
¼	cup corn oil
½	cup fresh blueberries

The night before prepare the sourdough starter (as on page 84) or revive it (as directed in the sidebar).

Preheat the oven to 375°F. and grease a 10-inch Bundt pan.

Put the flour, cornmeal, baking powder, baking soda, salt, and sugar in a large mixing bowl. Stir in the egg, sourdough starter, milk, and corn oil until well blended. Gently fold in the blueberries until they are evenly distributed.

Pour the batter into the Bundt pan and bake for 40 minutes, or until a toothpick stuck into the center comes out clean. Let the bread cool for 5 minutes before unmolding.

Sourdough Buttermilk Pancakes

My family loves these light and slightly sour pancakes for Sunday morning breakfast. In the summertime I serve them accompanied by bowls of fresh berries, sour cream, and powdered sugar.

4–6 servings

  1 cup sourdough starter (prepared the night before, page 84)
  1 cup buttermilk
  1 cup all-purpose flour
  2 beaten eggs
  2 tablespoons sugar
  1 teaspoon baking soda
  ¼ teaspoon salt

Stir all the ingredients together until the mixture is smooth. Heat a lightly greased griddle and cook the pancakes on one side until bubbles rise to the surface and pop. Turn the pancakes over and cook for 2–3 more minutes.

Variation:

To make waffles, add ¼ cup corn oil or melted butter to the batter.

An experienced outdoor cook flips a pancake over a campfire.

89

Sourdough Danish Pastry
Basic Recipe

Sourdough Danish Pastries are not difficult to make. I like to shape the dough into two different pastries, both using the same filling and glaze but looking entirely different. The Glazed Almond Packets are small squares, while the Pacific Northwest Sasquatch Claws are rectangular and resemble Danish bear claws. The claws are also sprinkled with coarse sugar and chopped walnuts before they're baked, giving them a completely different appearance.

Basic Sourdough Pastry for Glazed Almond Packets and Pacific Northwest Sasquatch Claws (recipes follow)

3½–4	*cups all-purpose flour*
½	*cup sugar*
1	*tablespoon baking powder*
1	*teaspoon baking soda*
1	*teaspoon salt*
1	*cup sourdough starter (prepared the night before, page 84)*
8	*tablespoons butter, melted and cooled (½ cup)*
1	*cup milk*

Almond Filling for Glazed Almond Packets and Pacific Northwest Sasquatch Claws

8	*tablespoons softened butter (½ cup)*
½	*cup powdered sugar*
½	*cup almond paste*

Almond Glaze for Glazed Almond Packets and Pacific Northwest Sasquatch Claws

1½	*cups powdered sugar*
2	*teaspoons almond extract*
⅓	*cup milk*

Preheat the oven to 400°F. and grease a baking sheet.

To Make the Pastry:

Place the flour, sugar, baking powder, baking soda, and salt in a large bowl. Stir in the sourdough starter, butter, and milk. Shape the dough into a ball and knead on a floured board for 3–4 minutes, or until smooth; add more flour if necessary. Cut the dough in half and set aside.

To Make the Filling:

Put the butter, powdered sugar, and almond paste in a mixing bowl and blend with a fork until smooth. Divide in half and set aside.

To Make the Glaze:

Put the powdered sugar, almond extract, and milk in a small bowl and stir until smooth. Divide in half and set aside.

A Danish bakery in Ballard, Washington

Glazed Almond Packets

Makes 9 packets

½   *dough recipe for Basic Sourdough Pastry**
½   *filling recipe for Almond Filling**
1   *egg, beaten*
½   *glaze recipe for Almond Glaze**

   * See page 90

Preheat the oven to 375°F. and grease a baking sheet.
   On a floured board roll half the dough into a
14 x 14-inch square. Cut dough into thirds, vertically
and horizontally, creating 9 squares. Place 1 tablespoon
of the filling in the middle of each square. Starting with
one square, fold the ends into the center and pinch together, gently pushing them down into the filling. Place
on a greased baking sheet. Repeat for the remaining
squares. Let rise in a warm place for 15 minutes.
   Brush the almond packets with beaten egg and bake
for 10–12 minutes, or until lightly brown on top. Remove the packets from the oven and set them on a wire
rack with wax paper underneath it. Drizzle each with
1 teaspoon of the almond glaze.

*Preparing Pastries
Ahead*

*Both of these pastries
can be made a day
ahead and can be
reheated in the micro-
wave. Place on a plate
and dot with a teaspoon
of butter. Microwave on
High for 45 seconds.*

Pacific Northwest Sasquatch Claws

Sasquatch, or Big Foot as he is sometimes called, is a large, manlike creature reputed to live deep in the woods of the Pacific Northwest. No one knows if he has claws or if he really exists, as far as that goes, but if he has been smart enough to elude mankind over the centuries he deserves to have a pastry named after him.

Makes 9 claws

- ½ *dough recipe for Basic Sourdough Pastry**
- ½ *filling recipe for Almond Filling**
- ½ *cup chopped walnuts*
- ½ *glaze recipe for Almond Glaze**
- 1 *egg, beaten*
- 2 *tablespoons coarse sugar (available at specialty food stores)*

  * See page 90

Heat oven to 375°F. and grease a baking sheet.

Roll half the dough on a floured board into a 7 x 18-inch rectangle. Spread half the dough, lengthwise, with the almond paste filling and sprinkle with ¼ cup nuts. Fold the other half (lengthwise) over the filling and gently press the edges of the dough together.

Cut the dough into 2-inch widths, making nine 2 x 3½-inch pieces. Cut 3 slits, ⅔ of the way into each pastry, on the folded edge.

Place on a greased baking sheet and spread the slits apart into a crescent or clawlike shape. Let rise in a warm place for 15 minutes. Brush with beaten egg and sprinkle with coarse sugar and the remaining ¼ cup chopped walnuts. Bake for 15 minutes.

Remove from the oven and place on a wire rack with a sheet of wax paper underneath it. Drizzle each pastry with 1 teaspoon of the almond glaze.

Master Polenta Recipe

Hupa Indian women in Northern California preparing corn meal. Mush was cooked by using two sticks to drop a hot rock into a basket filled with water and coarsely ground corn meal.

In northern California, Eureka Lodge 1274—Sons of Italy in America—regularly has polenta feeds to raise money for special projects. Polenta is a traditional dish from northern Italy, where most of these families come from. It is made from ground cornmeal, either fine-grained or coarsely ground, and can be served in place of potatoes, pasta, or rice. The following recipe uses fine-grained American yellow cornmeal available at most grocery stores. My preference is for imported Italian cornmeal but it's often difficult to find. Polenta is an ideal dish to accompany grilled meats, game dishes, or tomato-based stews, such as chicken cacciatore.

4 servings

1¾ cups water or homemade chicken stock or
     reduced-sodium canned chicken broth
½ teaspoon salt (omit if using canned broth)
¾ cup cornmeal
4 tablespoons butter (¼ cup)

Heat ¾ cup water with the salt. Stir the remaining 1 cup of water into the dry cornmeal and, when it is smooth, slowly stir the mixture into the boiling salted water with a wire whisk. Add the butter and cook over low heat, stirring, until it melts. Serve the polenta immediately, on a warm platter or in individual servings; it becomes quite firm when it cools. Leftover polenta can be cut up, fried in oil, and served with the same foods listed above.

Garlic-Flavored Polenta with Two Cheeses

1   *Master Polenta Recipe (see page 94)*
1   *pressed garlic clove*
½   *cup freshly grated Parmesan cheese (2 ounces)*
½   *cup grated sharp cheddar cheese (2 ounces)*

Follow the Master Polenta Recipe. Stir in the garlic, Parmesan cheese, and cheddar cheese with the butter. Continue stirring until the polenta is smooth.

Polenta with Cougar Gold Cheese

Cougar Gold is a white cheddar cheese made at Washington State University in Pullman and named after its inventor, Dr. Norman Golding, and WSU's mascot, the cougar. The idea to make cheese surfaced when administrators realized they had a surplus of milk from the university's Holsteins during school vacations. The deliciously smooth cheese, sold in green-and-white-striped cans, is nutty-flavored and dangerously addictive.

1   *Master Polenta Recipe (see page 94)*
1   *cup grated or crumbled Cougar Gold Cheese or any*
    flavorful hard cheese, such as white cheddar (4 ounces)

Follow the Master Polenta Recipe. Stir in the cheese with the butter and continue stirring until the polenta is smooth.

Huntsman Cheese Variation

Huntsman cheese, imported from England, is a combination of layers of Double Gloucester and Stilton. I crumble it with my fingers as I add it to the cooked polenta.

Add 4–6 ounces Huntsman cheese (1 cup) or substitute ½ cup grated cheddar and ½ cup crumbled blue cheese.

Meats and Poultry

The following meat and poultry entrées are a combination of old-fashioned recipes, such as stew and fried smoked pork chops, and more contemporary dishes with new flavors—Roast Chicken with Shiitake Mushrooms and Fresh Raspberries and Kimmai's Vietnamese Ginger Chicken. The success of any of these recipes lies in using good, fresh ingredients.

Cooks living in the Pacific Northwest have readily available an abundance of game and seafood, as well as locally raised livestock and poultry. Beef has been around in the Pacific Northwest ever since ranchers brought cattle of Spanish descent to the Oregon Territory from California in 1836.

Gradually the cattle business, along with farming, replaced the dwindling fur trade, and today it's one of the Pacific Northwest's thriving industries.

Merino sheep, also of Spanish descent, were also introduced from California about the same time but it wasn't until the turn of the century, when there was a decreased demand for wool, that sheep were bred for their meat instead of their wool. Today, lamb is raised on both sides of the Cascades and it's available in the markets most of the year.

The poultry industry is concentrated in both the Willamette Valley and the Puget lowlands surrounding Seattle. I enjoy experimenting with new ways of cooking these flavorful chickens that are available year-round.

GARLIC-BRAISED BEEF SHANKS WITH TOMATOES AND ANGEL-HAIR PASTA

GRILLED FLANK STEAK WITH THREE-MUSHROOM STUFFING

STUMPTOWN STEW

GRILLED LUMBERJACK STEAK WITH BLACK BEAN MARINADE

EAST SIDE BARBECUED RIBS

PORK TENDERLOIN STUFFED WITH GARLIC AND FENNEL SEED

SMOKED PORK CHOPS WITH POTATOES AND SAUTÉED APPLE SLICES

LENTILS WITH BRATWURST AND BEER

LEG OF LAMB WITH WHOLE CLOVES OF GARLIC AND YUKON GOLD POTATOES

GRILLED LAMB CHOPS WITH GARLIC PASTE

RACK OF LAMB WITH LENTIL FRITTERS

BASQUE LAMB SHANKS WITH GARBANZO BEANS

ROTISSERIE DUCK WITH PEACH-GINGER SAUCE

ROAST CHICKEN WITH SHIITAKE MUSHROOMS AND FRESH RASPBERRIES

CHICKEN CACCIATORE

ROAST CHICKEN WITH BARLEY-MUSHROOM STUFFING IN BLACKBERRY SAUCE

BUTTERFLIED GRILLED CHICKEN

KIMMAI'S VIETNAMESE GINGER CHICKEN (GA XAO GUNG)

Garlic-Braised Beef Shanks with Tomatoes and Angel-Hair Pasta

The Elusive Cow

It was Dr. John McLoughlin who stocked Fort Vancouver, the Hudson's Bay Company outpost, with thirty-one cattle and seventeen pigs (see Introduction). In 1933, Dean Collins, author of The Cheddar Box *(Portland, Oregon:* The Oregon Journal, *1933) wrote:*

"The Hudson's Bay cattle in the later years of the occupation had become as wild as deer so that settlers, Indians and employees of the company stalked them by moonlight and got almost as much sporting thrill out of bagging an elusive cow as one gets nowadays out of stalking and dropping a deer."

Beef shanks are sometimes difficult to find so it may be necessary to special-order them at your butcher shop.

4 servings

6	tablespoons mild olive oil
3	carrots, sliced into ½-inch pieces
1	large stalk celery, sliced into ½-inch pieces
2½–3	pounds beef shanks
1	cup white wine
1	28-ounce can peeled tomatoes, with juice
2	garlic cloves, peeled and chopped
2	teaspoons dried whole thyme, crushed
½	teaspoon salt
1	teaspoon freshly cracked pepper
1	pound fresh angel-hair pasta

Heat 2 tablespoons olive oil in a 5½-quart heavy pot with a lid and sauté the carrot and celery slices for 2–3 minutes before adding the beef shanks. Brown the meat on all sides and add the wine, tomatoes, garlic, 1½ teaspoons thyme, salt, and pepper to the pot. Cover and simmer 1¼ hours or until the meat can be pierced easily with a fork. (It can also be baked at 350°F. for 1 hour, 40 minutes.)

When the beef is tender, heat 4 quarts of salted water with 2 tablespoons olive oil to a boil. Add the pasta and boil for 2–3 minutes, or until done. Drain the noodles and place in a large pasta bowl. Sprinkle the remaining 2 tablespoons olive oil, remaining ½ teaspoon thyme, and a pinch of salt over the pasta and toss.

Ladle the shanks and all the cooking juices over the pasta and serve immediately.

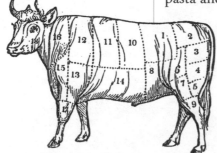

Grilled Flank Steak with Three-Mushroom Stuffing

The mild-tasting oyster mushroom is a native of the Pacific Northwest and grows in clusters on fallen alder or cottonwood trees. This fan-shaped mushroom and its stronger-tasting cousin the shiitake are both cultivated commercially in Oregon's Willamette Valley.

4 servings

 2 *tablespoons butter or corn oil margarine*
 2 *ounces shallots, peeled and chopped*
 2 *ounces fresh shiitake mushrooms, cut into*
    thin vertical slices
 4 *ounces oyster mushrooms, cut into thin vertical slices*
 4 *ounces commercial mushrooms, cut into*
    thin vertical slices
 ¼ *teaspoon salt*
 ½ *teaspoon pepper*
 ½ *cup soy sauce*
 ⅛ *cup dry sherry*
 ½ *teaspoon ground ginger*
1½ *pounds flank steak*

Melt the butter and sauté the shallots for 5–8 minutes, until they start to soften. Add the mushrooms and season with salt and ¼ teaspoon pepper. Cook them until they become tender. Let cool.

Blend the soy sauce, sherry, ground ginger, and remaining ¼ teaspoon pepper together and marinate the meat in it for 30 minutes on each side. Transfer the meat to a flat surface, reserving the marinade, and spread the cooked stuffing over the meat. Roll the meat, lengthwise, over the filling and tie it in place with string.

Brush the roll with the reserved marinade and grill on all sides over hot coals for approximately 30 minutes.

Stumptown Stew

I have named this stew in Portland's honor. Stumptown was the nickname given to Portland because of the many stumps that remained in the downtown area years after the city was founded on the tree-lined banks of the meandering Willamette River. The stew is made with cubed chuck steak, cooked with the wild boletus mushroom and Pinot Noir, which makes an intensely flavorful deep brown sauce filled with tender chunks of meat. I serve the full-bodied stew accompanied by steamed new potatoes and fresh artichokes, tossed in a lemony garlic butter.

6 servings

½   ounce dried boletus (porcini) mushrooms, soaked, or additional ½ cup fresh
2   cups homemade beef stock or reduced-sodium canned beef broth
1   tablespoon corn oil
1   tablespoon mild olive oil
1   large onion, cut into eighths
½   cup flour
1   teaspoon salt
½   teaspoon freshly ground pepper
1   teaspoon dried whole thyme, crushed
2   pounds chuck steak, cut into 1-inch cubes
4   tablespoons butter or corn oil margarine
8   ounces cultivated mushrooms, cleaned and sliced lengthwise into thirds
½   cup Pinot Noir
1   pound fresh cocktail or regular-size artichokes
1   pound tiny or small-size red new potatoes
1   tablespoon fresh lemon juice
1   large garlic clove, finely minced

Preheat the oven to 350°F.

Soak dried mushrooms in ½ cup beef broth. Heat the oils in a large 5½-quart ovenproof pot and lightly brown the onion pieces. While the onions are cooking, blend the flour, salt, pepper, and thyme together and dredge the meat. Push the onions to one side and brown the meat.

Melt 2 tablespoons of butter and sauté the mushrooms just until they start to soften. Add the sautéed mushrooms, soaked dried mushrooms (if you're using them) and broth, Pinot Noir, and remaining 1½ cups beef broth to the meat. Stir to blend the ingredients and cover with a lid. Bake for 1¾ hours.

Meanwhile, trim the artichokes and remove ½ inch of the thorny tops. Cut the artichokes into fourths and remove the choke. (This is not necessary if you're using the smaller artichoke, which is entirely edible.) Put the potatoes in the bottom of a steamer and lay the artichokes on top. Cook the vegetables until they are tender, about 10 minutes for small vegetables, 25–35 minutes for larger artichokes and potatoes.

Melt the remaining 2 tablespoons butter with the lemon juice and garlic, and drizzle over the artichokes and potatoes. Serve as accompaniment to stew.

Portland Hotel Restaurant dinner menu, July 26, 1903

Portland Hotel Restaurant

PORTLAND, SUNDAY, JULY 26, 1903.

DINNER

Clams 25   Oyster Cocktail 25
Shoalwater Bay Oysters in shell 25

SOUP

Chicken, a la Castelaine 25
Consomme, Windsor 20   Consomme in Cup 15   Consomme with Nizam Pearls 25   Julienne 25
Puree of Split Peas 20   Puree of Tomato with Macaroni 25
Green Turtle, 60, ½ 35   Mock Turtle 25
Oyster Soup 25

SIDE DISHES

Radishes 10   Pickled Stuffed Mangoes, 25   Olives 15   Stuffed Olives, 50   Sardines 30
Russian Caviar 30   Chow Chow 15   Lyons Sausages 35   Pickles and Chutney 20
Green Onions 10   Anchovies on Toast 40   Pickled Walnuts 20   Pickled Beets, 20
Anchovy or Bloater Paste 40   Salted Almonds 30
Cucumbers 15

FISH

Boiled Royal Chinook Salmon, Crawfish Sauce, 50, ½ 25
Fried Flounder, Remoulade 40   Smelts Tartar 30
Fillet of Sole, Morney 40, ½ 25   Salmon Cheeks 40
Anchovies 50, ½ 30   Fried Fillet of Turbot, 40, ½ 25

JOINTS

Ham with Madeira 50, ½ 30
Corned Beef and Cabbage 50, ½ 30   Pork and Beans, 40

ENTREES

Croustade of Sweetbreads, 50, ½ 35
Croquettes of Turkey with Asparagus, 50, ½ 35
Deviled Crab, Maryland, 50, ½ 35
Oyster Patties, 50, ½ 30

ROASTS

Spring Lamb, Mint Sauce 50, ½ 35   Squab 50   Beef 50, ½ 35
Spring Chicken, Stuffed, Giblet Sauce, ½ 50

COLD

Assorted Cold Meats 50   Half Chicken 50   Lamb 60, ½ 40
Pressed Corned Beef 40, ½ 25   Beef 40   Ham 40, ½ 25   Fat Liver, Strasbourg 60, ½ 40
Goose Liver Sandwiches 40; other kinds 25, per doz. $2.50 Beef Tongue 40, ½ 25

VEGETABLES

Stuffed Tomato 30   Corn on the Cob 25   Egg Plant 25   Squash 25   New Potatoes 25
New String Beans 15   Flageolets 40   Stewed Mushrooms 50   Boiled Onions 15
Cauliflower 20; with Hollandaise 30   Stewed Tomatoes 20   French String Beans 40
Potatoes 15   Potato Souffle 40   Sarah Potatoes 20   Parisian Potatoes 20
Potato Croquettes 20   Hashed and Browned 15   Hashed in Cream 20
Mashed Potatoes 15   Macaroni, every style 20   French Peas 40
Boiled Rice 15   Spaghetti with Cheese 20
Asparagus Hollandaise 25

SALADS

Crab 40   Waldorf 50   Tomato 40   Anchovy 40   Chicken 50   Cold Slaw 25
Shrimp 40   Macedoine 25   Cress 25   Potato 25   Lettuce 25   Cucumbers 40

DESSERT

Orange Cup Custard 20   Pudding, a la Reine, Citron Sauce, 25   Glaced Chestnuts 30
Mince Pie 15   Apple Pie 15   Lemon Cream Pie 15
Cream Puffs 15   Vanilla and Chocolate Eclairs 15   Assorted Cakes 15
Madeira Jelly 20   Rum Slices 15   Charlotte Russe 25
Ice Cream—Cafe Parfait 25   "The Portland" 25   Chocolate 25   Vanilla 25
Punch or Sorbet—Roman 30   Kirsch 30   Curacao 30   Marasquino 30
Water Ice—Lemon 25   Orange 25

CHEESE

Oregon Cream 25   Edam 20   Swiss 25   American 15   Brie 25   Rocquefort 25
Neuchatel 25

FRUIT

Blackberries with Cream 25   Watermelon 25
Raspberries with Cream 25   Cantaloupe 25
Grape Fruit 25   Bar le Duc 50   Oranges 25   Stewed Prunes 20   Preserved Fruit 20
Brandy Peaches 50   Jams, all kinds 20   Nuts and Raisins 20   Preserved Figs 30
Currant Jelly 20
Black Coffee 10   Turkish Coffee 20

Half portions served to one person only.   No half portions served on the floors.
Extra service 25c.   Corkage $1 per bottle.

101

Grilled Lumberjack Steak with Black Bean Marinade

A northern California logging camp cookhouse crew

In the small lumbering town in northern California where I grew up, we would occasionally buy a "lumberjack" steak for a special dinner. It was a section of a beef loin that had not been cut into individual filet mignons and was named appropriately after its large size. It wasn't until I went away to college that I realized it was a term for a cut of beef created just for the residents of this small lumbering community.

4 servings

⅓ cup rice vinegar
3 garlic cloves, crushed
2 tablespoons black bean sauce
½ cup hoisin sauce
2 tablespoons sugar
2 pounds beef loin or fillet of beef

Put the rice vinegar, garlic, black bean sauce, hoisin sauce, and sugar in a shallow dish large enough to hold the meat. Blend the ingredients together and add the loin. Roll the meat in the marinade to coat all sides and the ends. Cover and marinate for 4 hours, turning occasionally.

Heat the grill and barbecue the meat for 20 minutes, or until done. Cut the meat into ½-inch slices and serve immediately.

East-Side Barbecued Ribs

At the turn of the century, eighty percent of Portland's population lived on the east side of the Willamette River. As the inner city swelled, residential growth sprawled in all directions, but the local Black community remained predominantly on the east side. Today there are a handful of small neighborhood restaurants in this area that serve excellent barbecued ribs, a reflection of the people's southern heritage. When I want to cook ribs at home, I use this barbecue sauce, which is also good on chicken or beef. During the summer I make large batches of the sauce and keep it in the refrigerator for impromptu dinners.

Serves 4–6

1½	teaspoons salt
1	teaspoon freshly ground pepper
4–6	pounds country-style spareribs
½	cup light or dark corn syrup
½	cup catsup
½	cup finely chopped onion
2	cloves chopped garlic
¼	cup cider vinegar
¼	cup Worcestershire sauce
2	tablespoons Dijon mustard
	A few drops liquid smoke (optional)

Rub salt and pepper into the meat and set aside. Put the remaining ingredients in a saucepan and cook over medium heat for 15 minutes. Place the ribs on the barbecue and grill for 45 minutes, turning them every 15 minutes. Brush both sides of the ribs with the sauce and cook for another 15 minutes. Brush again with the sauce just before serving.

Loggers

Loggers, hungry from the long day's labor, made short work of the fresh foods sent out from the kitchen. When a particular food was disliked it was, on occasion, found nailed to the steward's office door.

"In our mill we charged the loggers $3–$5 for three meals a day. I remember my Aunt Goldie, who was the cook, bringing out huge platters covered with mounds of steaks that were so large they hung over the edge."

—Bob Sanders, Pacific Northwest lumberman

Pork Tenderloin Stuffed with Garlic and Fennel Seed

For a Different Flavor

Toasted cumin seeds can be substituted for the fennel in this recipe, creating an entirely different flavor. Toast the seeds over medium-high heat in an ungreased cast-iron skillet until they start to turn dark brown.

The Sheridan Fruit Company, owned since 1946 by the Poelo family, is a popular Portland supermarket (and one of the oldest) located in what used to be Portland's Italian neighborhood. I go there to buy "Dave's Italian Porketta," a lean pork butt seasoned with fennel seeds and spices. It's already rolled and tied and needs only to be wrapped in foil and baked. When pork tenderloin is on sale, I like to roast it using the following similar method.

4–6 servings

4   garlic cloves, minced
1   teaspoon paprika
1   teaspoon whole fennel
½   teaspoon salt
½   teaspoon freshly ground pepper
1   3-pound pork loin

Preheat the oven to 325°F.

Mix the garlic, paprika, fennel, salt, and pepper together. Slit the loin down the center and rub with half the seasonings. Tie with string. Put it in a roasting pan and rub the remaining seasoning over the meat. Roast for 1 hour. Cover with foil and let sit for 15 minutes before carving.

Smoked Pork Chops with Potatoes and Sautéed Apple Slices

I have made this with both individual smoked pork loin fillets and smoked pork chops with the bone in. Either will work, but I prefer the flavor of the chops.

4 servings

- 1 tablespoon corn oil
- ½ pound sliced onions, ¼ inch thick (2 cups)
- 1 tablespoon plus 1 teaspoon brown sugar
- 1 pound peeled russet potatoes, sliced ¼ inch thick
- 1 pound smoked pork chops, ¾–1 inch thick, trimmed of all fat
- ½ teaspoon dry mustard
- ¼ cup dry sherry
- 1½ tablespoons butter or corn oil margarine
- 1 pound Gravenstein apples, peeled, cored, and sliced ¼–½ inch thick
- ¼ teaspoon ground cinnamon
- ¼ teaspoon ground cloves

Preheat the oven to 350°F.

Heat the oil and sauté the onions with a teaspoon of brown sugar for 8–10 minutes.

Grease a 2-quart casserole dish and arrange the potatoes on the bottom. Make a layer of onions over the potatoes followed by the pork chops.

Stir the dry mustard into the sherry and pour it over the pork chops. Cover the dish and bake for 45 minutes, or until the potatoes are tender.

Heat the butter in a skillet and sauté the apple slices for 3–4 minutes. Blend the remaining tablespoon brown sugar, cinnamon, and cloves together and sprinkle over the apples. Spread the apples over the chops and serve immediately.

A Hupa Indian woman with her burden basket full of wood

Lentils with Bratwurst and Beer

The copper brew kettle, seen in this 1906 photograph of the Weinhard Brewing Company, is still being used today.

German Sausages

When German immigrants came west they brought with them their skills for making both sausage and beer. Eugen Fetzer, a master sausage maker from Germany whose family has been making sausage since 1880, moved to Portland from Germany just ten years ago. "My biggest problem is people go to the Oktoberfest [popular in the Pacific Northwest in the fall]

In this recipe bratwurst is paired with lentils in a light yogurt-based sauce flavored with beer. The entire meal is cooked in one pan and takes less than an hour and a half to prepare.

4 servings

1	pound fresh bratwurst
3	tablespoons corn oil
¼	cup chopped onion
1	cup dried lentils, rinsed
2	cups homemade chicken stock or reduced-sodium canned chicken broth
½	teaspoon chili powder
½	teaspoon paprika
1	can beer (12 ounces)
½	teaspoon flour
½	cup low-fat yogurt or light sour cream
2	tablespoons chopped parsley

Prick the sausages with a fork and put in a heavy skillet with a lid. Pour in just enough water to cover. Turn the heat to medium-high and poach, uncovered, for 7 or 8 minutes, turning occasionally. Transfer the

sausages to a plate and discard the water.

Heat the oil in the pan and brown the chopped onion and sausages over medium heat for 8–10 minutes. Discard any fat that may have accumulated.

Add the lentils, chicken stock, chili powder, paprika, and beer and stir to blend the ingredients. Cover the pan and simmer for 45 minutes to an hour, or until the liquid has been absorbed. If the lentils are too soupy, remove the lid and cook for 10 more minutes.

Stir the flour into the yogurt (it keeps it from separating), then stir the yogurt into the lentil-sausage mixture. Just before serving sprinkle with chopped parsley.

and eat smoked sausage, then come into my shop and want to buy German sausage. There are over a thousand recipes for German sausage and they can be split up into three catagories: cured, such as salamis; ones that are cooked and processed, such as liverwurst and head cheese; and those like bratwurst which are processed raw and then cooked. The third group is the largest—there are at least 300 different sausages like franks, bologna, Thuringer, and bratwurst, to name a few."

Kegs of Henry Weinhard beer being delivered by horse-drawn wagons in Portland, Oregon, 1890

Leg of Lamb with Whole Cloves of Garlic and Yukon Gold Potatoes

I love the sweet garlic paste that results from baking whole heads of garlic. In this recipe the garlic cloves are separated and peeled before they are baked around the meat with the potatoes. The taste is the same but eating them is much simpler. They're heavenly with a crisp bite of potato or piece of meat.

4 servings

 1   *5–6-pound leg of lamb*
 1   *teaspoon salt*
 1   *teaspoon cracked pepper*
 12   *garlic cloves, peeled (about 1½ heads)*
 8   *small Yukon Gold or red new potatoes in their skins (about 1 pound)*
 1   *tablespoon chopped fresh rosemary*

Preheat the oven to 350°F.

Rub the lamb with the salt and pepper and put it in a large roasting pan, leaving room for the garlic and potatoes to cook in the lamb drippings. Put the lamb in the oven to start cooking.

Meanwhile, parboil the garlic and potatoes in a pot of boiling water for 20 minutes, or just until the potatoes start to turn tender. Drain thoroughly and arrange them around the lamb. Sprinkle the rosemary over all and continue cooking until the lamb reaches 135–140°F., about 1½ hours. Let rest 10 minutes before carving.

A Basque family in eastern Oregon's Jordan Valley

Grilled Lamb Chops with Garlic Paste

This simple and savory recipe for garlic-flavored lamb chops comes from my mother, who serves them with mint jelly. For something different, try the tangy mint sauce made from fresh mint, rice vinegar, garlic, and red pepper.

4 servings

4 garlic cloves, peeled, or 2 teaspoons prepared
    pureed garlic
½ teaspoon salt
1 tablespoon soy sauce
½ teaspoon cracked pepper
8 loin lamb chops

Mint Dipping Sauce

2 sprigs fresh mint, chopped (about 2 teaspoons)
⅓ cup rice vinegar
1 garlic clove, pressed
    Pinch of red pepper flakes

Using a fork, mash the garlic and salt together on a flat surface until the garlic breaks down into a paste. Put it into a bowl and stir in the soy sauce and cracked pepper. Spread the garlic paste on the lamb chops and let them sit at room temperature for 1 hour.

Meanwhile stir the mint, vinegar, garlic, and red pepper flakes together in a small bowl and allow the mixture to sit at room temperature for 1 hour.

Grill the chops 3 minutes a side, or until they are crusty brown on the outside and pink in the center.

Rack of Lamb with Lentil Fritters

Serving Rack of Lamb

When the lamb is done, remove the rack to a carving board and cut the meat into individual chops. Arrange the pieces on one side of a warmed serving platter and put the fritters next to them. For fancy occasions, cover the tips of the rib bones with paper frills.

A rack of lamb is a series of rib chops still connected. It's an expensive meat but simple to prepare. I season it simply with salt and freshly ground pepper before grilling it and serve the meat medium rare accompanied by cumin-flavored lentil fritters, hot from the skillet.

4 servings

¾   cup lentils
1   teaspoon salt
¼   teaspoon freshly ground pepper
4   pounds rack of lamb
2   tablespoons flour
1   egg
1   teaspoon ground cumin
2   tablespoons corn oil

Rinse lentils in cold water. Place them in a saucepan and cover with 1½ cups water. Bring the water to a boil, cover, and reduce the heat. Cook for 30 minutes until tender. Drain if necessary, and set aside.

Stir ½ teaspoon salt and pepper together and rub over the exposed surfaces of the meat. Grill the meat over medium-hot coals until a meat thermometer reads 145°F. for medium rare to 165°F. for well done. It will take about 45 minutes for a rare piece of meat and up to an hour for it to be well done. Let the meat rest for 15 minutes before carving.

While the meat is resting, blend the lentils, flour, egg, cumin, and remaining ½ teaspoon salt together in a small bowl. Heat the oil in a heavy skillet and drop several tablespoons of batter into the hot grease for 1 fritter. Repeat until all the batter is used. Quickly fry the fritters over medium-high heat, 3–4 minutes a side, until golden brown and crisp.

NOTE: The lamb can also be roasted in a 350°F. oven about 45 minutes.

Basque Lamb Shanks with Garbanzo Beans

Lamb shanks are exceptionally flavorful and have little fat. I like to cook them using this Basque method of pairing them with garbanzo beans and chopped tomatoes. I serve the lamb shanks on the side and spoon the sauce over long-grain white rice.

2–3 servings

- 2   tablespoons olive oil
- 1   cup chopped onions
- 3   pounds lamb shanks
- ½   teaspoon salt
- ½   teaspoon freshly ground pepper
- ½   teaspoon dried whole oregano, crushed
- 1   28-ounce can ready-cut and peeled tomatoes, with juice
- 2   garlic cloves, chopped
- 1   15½-ounce can reduced-sodium garbanzo beans, drained
- 3   cups cooked long-grain white rice

Preheat the oven to 350°F.

Heat the olive oil in a 3-quart ovenproof pot and sauté the onions for 3–4 minutes. Push the onions aside and brown the lamb shanks on all sides. Add the remaining ingredients except for rice, cover, and bake for 1¾ hours, or until the meat is tender and falls away from the bone. Serve with rice.

Lamb barbecue at the annual Croation-American picnic

Rotisserie Duck
with Peach-Ginger Sauce

Using Wild Duck

To use this recipe for wild duck, decrease the cooking time to take account of their smaller size. The duck is done when its juices run a rose color for medium or clear for well done.

Farm-raised duck is fattier and consequently more tender than its wild cousin and it cooks well on the rotisserie. As it turns, the fat is released, which bastes the bird as it cooks.

3–4 servings

1   *4–5-pound duckling*
½   *teaspoon salt*
½   *teaspoon dried whole thyme, crushed*
¾   *cup peach jam or Peach-Nectarine Ginger Jam (see page 242)*
¼   *teaspoon ground ginger (omit if using the Peach-Nectarine Ginger Jam)*
3   *tablespoons soy sauce*
1   *tablespoon lemon juice*
1   *garlic clove, crushed*

Light the barbecue.

Remove the neck, liver, and gizzard from the duck and discard. Rinse the cavity with cold water and pat dry with paper towels. Rub the cavity with salt and thyme and truss the bird. Prick the flesh with a metal cake tester or a fork to release the fat as it cooks. Secure the duck on the rotisserie and, with the lid of the barbecue closed, cook it over medium-hot coals. While the duck is cooking, heat the jam, ginger, soy sauce, lemon juice, and crushed garlic together over medium-low heat for 5 minutes. Strain if desired.

After the duck has cooked for 30 minutes, generously brush the skin with the glaze every 5 minutes, until it is done. The total cooking time is approximately 50 minutes. The duck is cooked when its juices run a rose color for medium or clear for well done.

Roast Chicken with Shiitake Mushrooms and Fresh Raspberries

Fresh red raspberries are a colorful addition to roast chicken, cooked to a crisp golden brown and served in its own sauce with shiitake mushrooms.

4 servings

1	*2½–3-pound whole chicken, split*
1	*teaspoon corn oil*
	Salt and pepper
1	*heaping tablespoon chopped fresh rosemary*
1	*tablespoon butter or corn oil margarine*
1	*shallot, chopped*
3	*ounces shiitake mushrooms,*
	stemmed and sliced vertically
1	*cup homemade chicken stock*
	or reduced-sodium canned chicken broth
1	*cup fresh raspberries*

Preheat the oven to 350°F.

Put the chicken, cut side down, in a shallow baking dish. Rub the exposed surfaces with the corn oil and sprinkle with salt, pepper, and chopped rosemary. Bake for 50 minutes to an hour, or until it is done. (The juices should run a clear yellow color.) Transfer the chicken to a warm dish with as much of the rosemary as possible and cover with foil. Pour the cooking juices into a small cup and discard all fat. Set aside.

Melt the butter in a sauté pan and cook the shallot and mushrooms for 5 minutes. Add the chicken stock and remaining cooking juices and turn the heat to medium-high. Cook the sauce rapidly for 2–3 minutes to reduce the liquid and intensify its flavor. Remove from the heat and add the raspberries.

Cut the chicken into quarters and place a piece on each plate. Equally divide the sauce over the chicken and serve immediately.

The Value of Wild Mushrooms

Several years ago Jerry Larson, from the Oregon Department of Agriculture, took two visiting Japanese businessmen to a mushroom show on the outskirts of Portland. The two men were dumbfounded when they saw local matsutake mushrooms being sold for $3.75 a pound, knowing that in Japan they sell for $375–$500 a pound! In disbelief, they asked if the decimal point had accidentally been put in the wrong place or if the man selling them was crazy. When they were finally convinced that the price was not a mistake, they immediately bought all thirty pounds of mushrooms and hand-carried them back to Japan the next day.

Chicken Cacciatore

Variation with Rabbit

Substitute 2 pounds jointed rabbit for the chicken.

Ida Francesconi's family emigrated to Humboldt County in northern California from Tuscany. She remembers gathering the boletus mushrooms with her family when she was a child. They would cut up the mushrooms and hang them on string to dry by the wood stove. This recipe, which Ida gave me, uses the boletus (called the porcini in Italy) but commercial mushrooms can be substituted. The cacciatore is served on top of cheese-flavored polenta; Ida accompanies it with cooked turnip greens, squeezed dry, sliced, and fried in olive oil and garlic.

4 servings

1   *tablespoon butter or corn oil margarine*
1   *tablespoon olive oil*
½   *ounce dried boletus (porcini) mushrooms
    or ½ cup fresh mushrooms, sliced*
½   *cup dry white wine*
¼   *cup flour*
1   *teaspoon salt*
¼   *teaspoon pepper*
2   *pounds boned chicken breasts, skinned*
1   *heaping teaspoon chopped fresh rosemary*
1   *teaspoon Italian seasoning*
2   *garlic cloves, peeled and minced
    Pinch sugar*
1   *15-ounce can tomato sauce (or make your own sauce
    by pureeing a 16-ounce can plum tomatoes)
    Master Polenta Recipe (page 94)*
4   *thick slices Monterey Jack cheese*

Heat the butter and olive oil and sauté the fresh mush-rooms until they are tender. Remove from the pan and set aside. If you are using dried mushrooms, soak them in the ½ cup white wine for 30 minutes, omit sautéing.

Blend the flour, salt, and pepper together and dredge the chicken. Brown the chicken pieces in the same pan. Add the mushrooms, wine, rosemary, Italian seasoning, garlic, sugar, and tomato sauce. Cover and simmer for 20 minutes; remove the lid and simmer for 20 more minutes.

Meanwhile, prepare the polenta and heat plates. To serve, place 1 slice of Monterey Jack cheese on each plate and cover the cheese with a mound of polenta. Spoon the Chicken Cacciatore over the polenta and serve immediately.

Some of the early settlers of Humboldt County in northern California used burned-out stumps of the giant redwood trees as pens for their barnyard animals. The stumps are still called "goose pens."

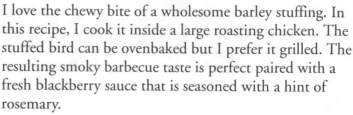

Roast Chicken with Barley-Mushroom Stuffing in Blackberry Sauce

Berry Variations

I have made this wonderful sauce with the tart-flavored loganberries and boysenberries; both were delicious.

I love the chewy bite of a wholesome barley stuffing. In this recipe, I cook it inside a large roasting chicken. The stuffed bird can be ovenbaked but I prefer it grilled. The resulting smoky barbecue taste is perfect paired with a fresh blackberry sauce that is seasoned with a hint of rosemary.

4 servings

1	*quart homemade chicken stock or reduced-sodium canned chicken broth Pinch of salt*
½	*cup pearl barley*
3	*tablespoons butter or corn oil margarine*
1	*tablespoon chopped shallot or onion*
4	*ounces fresh mushrooms, sliced (about 4–5)*
¼	*cup plain yogurt*
¼	*cup sour cream*
½	*teaspoon salt*
½	*teaspoon pepper*
1	*3–4 pound roasting chicken with neck or, if the neck is missing, cut off the tips of the wings*
1–2	*tablespoons corn oil Salt and pepper*
2	*cups fresh or frozen blackberries*
1	*sprig fresh rosemary*

Preheat grill to 350°F.

Bring 2 cups of chicken stock to a boil, add a pinch of salt, and stir in the barley. Cover and reduce the heat to simmer; cook the barley for 15 minutes or until it is tender. Turn the heat off and let the barley sit for 10 minutes. Drain if necessary.

Melt 2 tablespoons butter in a skillet and sauté the sliced shallot over medium heat for 2–3 minutes. Add the mushrooms and cook for another 10 minutes or until the mushrooms start to soften. Stir the mushroom-shallot mixture, yogurt, sour cream, ¼ teaspoon salt, and ¼ teaspoon pepper into the cooked barley.

Rinse the chicken and pat the bird dry with paper towels. Season the chicken's cavity with remaining ¼ teaspoon salt and ¼ teaspoon pepper and stuff with the barley-mushroom stuffing. Put any extra stuffing in a small baking dish to heat in the oven or microwave. Truss the bird and put it in a roasting pan. Brush the skin with corn oil, sprinkle with salt and pepper, and bake or grill the chicken for 1 hour 25 minutes or until done.

Mrs. Hahn feeding chickens

Meanwhile make the sauce by boiling the remaining 2 cups chicken stock with the chicken neck until it is reduced to 1 cup. Discard the chicken neck and set stock aside. Puree the blackberries and push the puree through a sieve to remove the seeds. Pour 1 cup of blackberry puree into the stock with the sprig of fresh rosemary and remaining tablespoon of butter. Bring the liquid to a boil and cook rapidly for 3–4 minutes until the sauce thickens slightly. Remove the rosemary and season with salt and pepper. Pour through a strainer (optional) and serve in a sauce boat to accompany the chicken.

Butterflied Grilled Chicken

*The British and
Their Curry*

*Most East Indian
food is not very well
known in the Pacific
Northwest but curry
dishes were popular
with the large British
population at the turn
of the century. One
local cookbook,* The
Portland Woman's
Exchange Cook Book, *published in Portland
in 1913, has a chapter
devoted to exotic curry
recipes.*

My grandmother spent most of her childhood on her grandparents' ranch in Sebastopol, California. Whenever she came to Portland, she always requested a chicken dinner. She called the fresh Willamette Valley fryers "real chicken," like the ones they used to raise on the ranch. Once she took two cut-up fryers home with her on the plane. We froze the chickens the night before she left and in the morning wrapped them in several layers of newspaper. When she arrived at the airport she sent the frozen bundle, tied with string, through the X-ray machine with her purse. The bones were easily visible on the screen and caused quite a commotion among the security guards. She had to unwrap the package to prove that the bones were actually from a chicken.

4 servings

1 *4-pound chicken, split down the backbone*
2 *teaspoons curry powder*
2 *teaspoons ground cumin*
2 *teaspoons salt*

Rinse the chicken and pat the bird dry with paper towels. Lay it on a flat surface, skin side up, and push on the keel (breastbone) to flatten it.

Blend the curry powder, cumin, and salt together. Rub half of the mixture over both sides of the bird. Starting at the neck opening and using a small knife or your fingers, separate the skin from the flesh. Season the flesh under the skin with the remaining seasoning. Let the bird sit for 45 minutes before grilling to absorb flavors.

Grill the chicken over hot coals until the juices run a clear yellow. Cut the chicken up before serving.

Kimmai's Vietnamese Ginger Chicken (Ga Xao Gung)

This chicken stir-fry recipe was given to me by Kimmai Hong, a Vietnamese friend.

2–3 servings

1¼ cups homemade chicken stock or reduced-sodium canned chicken broth
¼ teaspoon salt (omit if using canned broth)
1 tablespoon butter or corn oil margarine
⅔ cup long-grain white rice
2 tablespoons vegetable oil
½ pound boneless chicken, cut into bite-size pieces (8 ounces)
1 ounce shredded fresh ginger (3 tablespoons)
1 tablespoon soy sauce
1 tablespoon fish sauce (nuoc nam) (substitute approximately ½ teaspoon salt)
1 tablespoon sugar
1 tablespoon lemon grass, peeled and chopped
¼ medium onion, sliced (about ½ cup)
1 garlic clove, peeled and crushed
¼ teaspoon black pepper
2–3 cups cooked long-grain white rice

In a saucepan bring the chicken stock, salt, and butter to a boil. Stir in the rice and cover. Reduce the heat to simmer and cook for 20 minutes.

Meanwhile heat the oil to medium-hot in a frying pan and fry the chicken for 5 minutes. Add the shredded ginger, soy sauce, fish sauce, sugar, and lemon grass and cook for 5 more minutes. Add the onion and fry for 2 more minutes. Toss in the crushed garlic, sprinkle with pepper, and cook several more minutes.

Serve with hot cooked white rice.

Vietnamese Ingredients

Fish sauce, or nuoc nam, *from Thailand, is a thin, amber-colored liquid made from anchovy fish extract and salt, Lemon grass, looks like an undernourished leek both in size and color, but tastes like a lemon without any bitterness. With the recent influx of Thai and Vietnamese to the Pacific Northwest, both nuoc nam and lemon grass are now available locally. Buy them at oriental markets. Lemon grass is also available in the produce departments of most large grocery stores.*

From the Rivers and the Sea

When I cook fish I still use many of the old-fashioned cooking methods: pan-frying, baking, and broiling. They all work beautifully for seafood and fish that have short muscle fibers and need little cooking time. But I have embellished many of the recipes with new seasonings, pairing albacore with fresh rosemary and sun-dried tomatoes, cod with pickled ginger, rex sole with fresh thyme and balsamic-flavored capers, catfish with basil and Parmesan cheese, and Pacific Northwest shrimp with an Oregon Blue Cheese sauce. Freshly grated ginger, fresh herbs, balsamic vinegar, and tangy yogurt are all used to add a refreshingly new taste to many of my old-standby recipes.

When it works, I have also adapted the recipe to the microwave. Great care should be taken to cook the same size pieces of fish, so they are done in the same amount of time, and to allow for cooking time after the fish is removed from the microwave. The fish will continue cooking for another minute or so as it stands, so it needs to be slightly undercooked in the microwave.

The most important reminder is to always use very fresh fish. It should be firm, moist, and not have a strong fishy odor. I always buy fish at a fish market or at a supermarket with a reliable fish department and cook it the day I buy it.

SPRING CHINOOK WITH LEMON, CHIVES, AND CAPERS

STEAMED HOT-SMOKED SALMON WITH ONION JAM

THE SEASCAPE'S SMOKY OMELET

GRILLED WILD SALMON WITH FRESH TARRAGON BUTTER

POACHED WHOLE SALMON SERVED COLD ON A BED OF SWORD FERNS

SHIOYAKI SALMON

TROUT STUFFED WITH SMOKED SALMON

GRILLED SABLEFISH WITH PASTA, FRESH BASIL, AND RED PEPPERS

KASU HALIBUT

BAKED HALIBUT STUFFED WITH SMOKED SALMON BUTTER ON A BED OF SPINACH

BROILED PETRALE SOLE IN CORNMEAL WITH TOMATO-CAPER RELISH

REX SOLE WITH FRESH THYME AND BALSAMIC-FLAVORED CAPERS

BROILED LINGCOD WITH YOGURT-MUSTARD SAUCE

BAKED MULTNOMAH CHANNEL CATFISH

GRILLED ALBACORE WITH SUN-DRIED TOMATOES AND FRESH ROSEMARY

STIR-FRY ROCKFISH WITH GINGER AND RED PEPPER

PAN-FRIED SMELT

TERIYAKI COD WITH PICKLED GINGER

EAST-MEETS-WEST DUNGENESS CRAB

CRACKED DUNGENESS CRAB WITH HERB MAYONNAISE

PACIFIC NORTHWEST SHELLFISH TRIO

ANGEL-HAIR PASTA WITH MUSSELS AND SHRIMP IN MARINARA SAUCE

PACIFIC NORTHWEST SHRIMP IN OREGON BLUE CHEESE SAUCE

SHRIMP AND PASTA IN SWEET RED PEPPER SAUCE

FRIED RAZOR CLAMS

MASTER RECIPE FOR SMOKING FISH

Spring Chinook with Lemon, Chives, and Capers

The arrival of the spring Chinook in the Pacific Northwest has always been a time of great celebration. The
local Native Americans who lived on the banks of the
Columbia River depended on the salmon as a food
source. When the salmon came each spring it meant the
beginning of a new season when food would be plentiful.
Today we still rejoice when the fish enter the tidewater
in late February to start their migration up the river of
their birth. Their meat is high in fish oils, which give
them the energy to travel up to 700 miles to spawn. It's
this high oil content (twice as much as in the Atlantic/
Norwegian salmon) that makes them the finest-tasting
salmon in the world.

I like to prepare salmon on the grill but springtime
weather often prohibits cooking outdoors. My second
choice is to cook it in the microwave. The salmon
remains moist and tender and it is only partially cooked:
As it sits, it finishes cooking from the heat trapped inside
the steaks. Before putting the steaks in either the oven or
the microwave, I tuck the narrow side pieces up next to
the thicker part of the steak and secure them with a
toothpick to keep them from overcooking.

2–3 servings

2   salmon steaks or fillets, about 12 ounces each,
    approximately ¾ inch thick
1   tablespoon butter or corn oil margarine
    Scant ¼ teaspoon salt
⅛   teaspoon freshly ground pepper
2   tablespoons chopped chives
1   tablespoon capers, drained
3   thin slices of lemon
3   tablespoons dry white wine or fresh lemon juice

Preheat oven to 350°F.

Arrange the fish in a shallow dish with ½ tablespoon butter on each piece. Season with salt and pepper and sprinkle with the chopped chives and capers. Top each piece with a lemon slice and sprinkle the wine or lemon juice over all. Bake for 20 minutes.

Microwave Instructions:

Arrange the fish in a shallow dish with ½ tablespoon butter on each piece. Season with salt and pepper and sprinkle with the chopped chives and capers. Top each piece with a lemon slice and sprinkle the wine or lemon juice over all. Cover with microwave plastic wrap and microwave on High for 7–8 minutes. Let stand, covered, for 2 more minutes to complete the cooking.

ingeniously constructed over the rapid water. Their winter store of dried fish is stowed away in little huts of mats and branches, closely interlaced and also in caches under ground. It is often amusing to see the hungry ravens tearing and tugging at the strong twigs of the houses, in a vain attempt to reach the savory food within."

—*John Kirk Townsend,* Across the Rockies to the Columbia, July 5, 1834, *(Lincoln, Nebraska: University of Nebraska Press, 1978).*

Steamed Hot-Smoked Salmon with Onion Jam

From Lures to Little Chief Smokers

I use a Little Chief Smoker made by Luhr Jensen, Inc., in Hood River, Oregon, who also sells a large line of fishing gear and other products related to the outdoors. The late Luhr Jensen first came to the Pacific Northwest in 1912 and settled in Dee, Oregon, as a stump farmer. He paid twenty dollars for forty acres in an arrangement with the U.S. government to work the land. He cleared the acreage and grew pears, apples, and strawberries until the Depression came and destroyed the market. He then moved his family to Hood River and began selling Zenith radios and, in his spare time, handcrafted jewelry. He also began to make fishing lures with the help of a German friend who was a tool and die maker. The first lures were made out of an old Ford fender and were sold to a wholesaler in Portland. It's now a million-dollar business

Many Pacific Northwest restaurants prepare their own smoked salmon today. I have worked out a method that can be used easily at home. The fish is first soaked in a brine, then flavored with a light smoke (about 200°F.) before it is steamed. It produces delicate, buttery flakes that melt tenderly in your mouth.

4 servings

> 3   cups cold water
> 3   tablespoons salt
> 2   pounds salmon steaks or 1½ pounds salmon fillet
>   Walla Walla Sweet Onion Jam (page 254)

Pour the water into a shallow dish and stir in the salt. Immerse the salmon in the brine and soak for 2 hours, turning once at the end of 1 hour.

Put the salmon on a rack to air-dry while you are preparing the smoker.

Arrange the fish on a rack in the smoker and smoke the fish for 1½ hours, using 2 pans of alder or hickory chips. The salmon can be stored in the refrigerator at this point until it is needed.

Steam the lightly smoked fish for 10 minutes, or until it is done. Serve with onion jam.

The Seascape's Smoky Omelet

The Seascape, a small restaurant perched on the edge of the pier at Trinidad Head in northern California, has been feeding hungry fishermen at this picturesque harbor for as long as I can remember. I recently had brunch there and I can still taste the incredible flavors of their Smoky Omelet, packed full of cream cheese, smoked salmon, and chives. This is my version of their recipe, and I often serve it on nights when I want to eat "breakfast" for dinner.

2 servings

- 3 ounces whipped cream cheese
- 3 ounces smoked salmon, boneless, skinless, and crumbled
- 3 tablespoons finely chopped chives or parsley
- 1 tablespoon butter or corn oil margarine
- 4 eggs, beaten
- ¼ teaspoon salt
- ¼ teaspoon freshly ground pepper

Beat the cream cheese, salmon, and chives together and set aside.

Melt the butter over medium-high heat in a 9-inch omelet pan until the butter bubbles. Season the eggs with salt and pepper and pour them into the hot buttered pan. Gently shake the pan with one hand while stirring the eggs with a fork. When the eggs are almost set, put the filling in the center of the pan. Tilt the pan and roll the eggs over the filling. Invert the omelet onto a warmed plate and serve immediately.

and the current CEO, son Phil Jensen, is a terrific cook. One of his favorite recipes for holiday gatherings is an apple-flavored smoked turkey. His recipe calls for the 10–12-pound bird to be soaked in a special apple juice brine seasoned with herbs. Then he smokes it two hours in the electric smokehouse over apple wood chips before finishing in the oven at 325°F. Phil reports that the gravy from this recipe is "to die for."

Luhr Jensen fishing in a local stream

Grilled Wild Salmon
with Fresh Tarragon Butter

Traditional Indian Salmon Roast

Many Pacific Northwest Indians traditionally roasted fish on a leaning stake next to a smoldering fire (photo opposite). A stick about two feet long was split to three-fourths its length and a fish side was stuck on the stick. Sometimes smaller pieces of wood were horizontally woven in the fish to keep it flat as it cooked, allowing the meat to cook evenly. Clams, mussels, oysters, and barnacles were cooked in a similar fashion, never eaten raw, and were strung on buckskin or cedar bark for winter storage.

This simple method for grilling salmon is the salmon recipe most requested at our house. The grilled fish is paired with the subtle flavor of fresh tarragon and Walla Walla sweet onions that have been slowly cooked in lemon butter. We like the flavor of the fish when it is cooked directly on the grill, but it can also be cooked on a sheet of heavy-duty foil. If you use the latter method, grill the fish, skin side down, on the foil and do not turn the fish over while it is cooking. When the fish is served, the skin will stick to the foil, making it easy to serve pieces of the fillet.

4–6 servings

½   cup chopped Walla Walla sweet onion
2   tablespoons chopped parsley
8   tablespoons butter or corn oil margarine (½ cup)
2   tablespoons lemon juice
1   teaspoon fresh tarragon, minced, or ½ teaspoon whole dried tarragon, crushed
1   3-pound Chinook, silver, or sockeye salmon or steelhead fillet (see margin, page 131)
    Salt and pepper
2   lemon slices
2   sprigs fresh parsley

In a saucepan, cook the onion, parsley, butter, lemon juice, and tarragon over medium-low heat until the onions are tender, about 20 minutes. Brush the fish with a small amount of the melted butter mixture to keep it from sticking to the grill, and sprinkle it with salt and pepper. Put the fillet, skin side up, on a moderately hot grill and cook for 15 minutes. Turn the fillet over and carefully stack the onions from the tarragon butter over the fish. Cook for another 10 minutes, basting with the butter often. (The fish needs to be turned only once while cooking.) Serve the grilled fish on a warm platter garnished with slices of lemon and sprigs of fresh parsley.

A traditional salmon roast

Poached Whole Salmon Served Cold on a Bed of Sword Ferns

Potlatch

"Potlatch" is Chinook jargon for all ceremonies involving the sharing and giving of food or properties. These elaborate feasting ceremonies took place on many occasions—weddings, funerals, house buildings, name givings, passing on of territorial rights—and guests were given valuable gifts, displaying the power of the person sponsoring the potlatch and requiring the guests to eventually return the favor.

Everyone always appreciates a whole poached salmon, cloaked in a layer of Herb Mayonnaise, and served cold on a bed of freshly picked ferns. It is a wonderful dish for a festive summer occasion when salmon are plentiful and their price is at its lowest. I always poach the fish a day ahead and keep it wrapped in cheesecloth overnight in the refrigerator. I make the Herb Mayonnaise the day before, too. The next day, the fish needs only to be garnished.

16 servings

3   *quarts water*
3   *cups dry white wine*
1   *onion, peeled and quartered*
10 *peppercorns*
1   *tablespoon salt*
1   *teaspoon dried whole thyme, crushed*
1   *bay leaf, broken in half*
1   *8–10-pound salmon*
    Salt and pepper
1   *onion sliced into ¼-inch slices*
2   *lemons, sliced*
6   *fern fronds*
    Herb Mayonnaise (page 150)
2   *cucumbers, sliced*
1   *pitted black olive, cut in half horizontally*
1   *bunch Italian flat-leaf parsley*
1   *bunch fresh dill*
    Fresh flower blossoms, such as calendulas, pansies, nasturtiums, or sprigs of Oregon grape

Bring the water, wine, onion quarters, peppercorns, salt, thyme, and bay leaf to a boil in a fish poacher or large roasting pan and simmer for 1 hour. Lay the fish on a flat surface and measure its thickness with a ruler. It will need to cook 8 minutes for every inch of thickness. (Example: A fish 4 inches thick would need to be

poached a total of 32
minutes, 16 minutes a
side.) Sprinkle the fish
cavity with salt and
pepper and fill with a
layer of onion and
lemon slices. Wrap the
fish in cheesecloth or a
large cotton dish towel
and tie each end, as
close to the head and
tail as possible, with a
twistie or rubber band.
Put the fish in the

*A Depot Bay, Oregon,
fish fry*

poaching liquid, leaving the ends of the cloth out
(helpful for turning the fish), and cover the pan. Bring
the liquid to a boil, then turn the heat to simmer. Turn
the fish halfway through the cooking time. Remove the
cooked fish from the stock to cool. Store in the
refrigerator overnight.

The next day, line a large fish platter with the ferns
and set aside.

Remove the cheesecloth and scrape off all the fish skin
and grayish fatty flesh. Discard the lemon slices and
onions in the cavity. Completely coat the entire fish
(including the head but not the tail) with the Herb
Mayonnaise. Overlap the cucumbers on the top side of
the fish, starting along the backbone and ending at the
belly, to resemble fish scales. Put the olive in place for the
eye and bunch sprigs of parsley and dill under the tail. If
the tail looks too ragged, remove it completely and
replace it with the fresh herbs. Arrange the remaining
lemon slices and flower blossoms around the fish. Keep it
refrigerated until serving time. Serve any remaining Herb
Mayonnaise in a bowl next to the fish platter.

Shioyaki Salmon

Salmon Canning

The Pacific Northwest salmon industry was born on the Columbia River. The salmon canneries depended upon Chinese laborers as the main work force until the development of the (unfortunately named) "Iron Chink," at the turn of the twentieth century. The new machine (shown opposite) prepared forty-five salmon per minute for canning and the roar of its engine replaced the tonal Chinese chatter and the flash of their blades.

Shioyaki, or salt-broil, is a Japanese cooking technique that was introduced to me by Barbara and Ken Durbin. Ken, a staff biologist for the Oregon Department of Fish and Wildlife, also uses this technique for cooking steelhead. He sprinkles the fish, including the skin, with salt, then lets it sit at room temperature for one to two hours or, in his own words, "until the champagne runs out." The salt acts as a tenderizer and breaks down the tissue, including the fatty area under the skin. When the fish is broiled, juices rise to the surface and wash most of the salt away. The broiled fish is perfectly seasoned and the tender flakes melt in your mouth.

4 servings

1   *1½–2-pound fresh salmon fillet with skin on*
¾   *teaspoon salt*

Cut the salmon into 3 pieces. Arrange the fillets on a broiling pan and sprinkle all exposed surfaces of the fish with ¾ teaspoon salt. Cover with plastic wrap and let sit at room temperature for 1–2 hours.

Preheat the broiler.

Broil the fish, skin side down, 4 inches from the broiler for 4 minutes, or until the fillet starts to turn golden brown. (Ken cautions that the fish turns from pink, to brown, to black in a hurry, so watch it carefully.) Turn the fish over, skin side up, and broil until the skin starts to blister and bubble, about 1–1½ minutes.

Trout Stuffed with Smoked Salmon

I always take smoked salmon with us when we float the rivers in the summertime. It's good to eat anytime and I like to use it as a stuffing for trout or steelhead.

4 servings

 2   *tablespoons corn oil or bacon grease*
 ½   *cup all-purpose flour*
 ¼   *teaspoon salt*
6–8 *rainbow or any variety of trout, ready for cooking*
 ¼   *pound smoked salmon, cut into thin slices*
 4   *lemon wedges*

Heat the oil to medium-hot in a heavy skillet. Blend the flour and salt together. Stuff the trout with the smoked salmon and carefully dredge each side of the fish in the flour-salt mixture. Fry the fish on each side, 2–3 minutes, until it is golden brown. Serve with lemon wedges.

Steelhead Trout

The steelhead, also called a sea-run rainbow trout, is born in the river, travels to the ocean for its adolescence, and returns to the river of its birth to spawn as an adult.

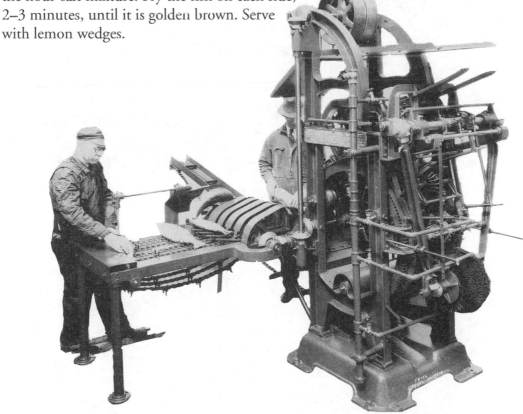

131

Grilled Sablefish with Pasta, Fresh Basil, and Red Peppers

Sablefish

Sablefish were a favorite of the Makah Indians in Washington who caught them with lines made of kelp and hemlock hooks. They preserved the catch by drying the fish in the sun or by smoking it over slow-burning green wood. Today sablefish is still popular in the Pacific Northwest as well as the Soviet Union and Japan.

Sablefish has a high oil content, which keeps it moist and tender when it's grilled. This buttery white-fleshed fish is a favorite of mine. I often add it to fresh pasta, seasoned with kalamata paste. The paste, made from ground kalamata olives and herbs, can be purchased at specialty food shops. I sometimes use this recipe as a salad, serving it at room temperature the day after it was made.

4 servings

1	*whole garlic clove, cut in half*
1	*pound sablefish fillets*
4½	*tablespoons olive oil*
	Salt and pepper
2	*garlic cloves, minced*
1	*cup chopped red pepper*
8	*ounces angel-hair pasta*
3	*heaping tablespoons kalamata paste*
½	*heaping cup chopped fresh basil*
1	*cup peeled and chopped avocado*

Turn on the grill and heat a pasta bowl.

Rub the garlic halves over the fish and brush both sides with ½ tablespoon olive oil. Grill the fillets for 8–10 minutes, or until they flake with a fork. Cut the fish into bite-size pieces. Season to taste with salt and pepper.

While the fish is cooking, heat the remaining 4 tablespoons olive oil in a small pan and add the minced garlic and red pepper. Cook for 3–4 minutes.

Meanwhile, cook the pasta in a large pot of boiling salted water until it is done. Drain and put it into the warmed pasta bowl and toss it with the hot oil, garlic, red pepper, and the kalamata paste. Sprinkle the pieces of fish over the pasta along with the basil and diced avocado. Toss one last time at the table just before serving.

Kasu Halibut

Kasu halibut is a variation of a Japanese dish that has recently become popular in the Pacific Northwest restaurants. It is traditionally made with sablefish, but when it's not available I substitute halibut. The raw fish (it's imperative that it be very fresh) is covered with a paste made from sake lees, the sediment that remains after sake is made, and mirin (rice wine). The steaks are marinated for seventy-two hours, then rinsed under cold running water and patted dry before being grilled over alder wood. I brush the pieces of fish with a store-bought teriyaki glaze just before removing them from the grill to give the steaks a lovely light golden-brown color. The tender fish melts in your mouth and has a hauntingly delicious sake flavor.

Sake Lees and Mirin

Both sake lees and mirin can be purchased in oriental markets. The sake lees resemble sticky sheets of pie pastry and come in one-pound plastic bags.

4 servings

- ¼ cup sake lees
- ½ cup mirin
- 1 teaspoon sugar
- 1 teaspoon salt
- 2 pounds halibut steaks or sablefish (black cod)
- ¼ cup commercial teriyaki sauce glaze

With a fork, blend the sake lees, mirin, sugar, and salt together. Generously rub the paste over the fish and put the steaks in a shallow dish. Cover with plastic wrap and refrigerate for 72 hours, turning the fish daily.

Rinse the paste off the steaks and pat them dry with paper towels. Grill the fish over hot coals, and 2–3 minutes before it is done, brush both sides with the teriyaki glaze. Finish grilling the fish and serve immediately.

Baked Halibut Stuffed with Smoked Salmon Butter on a Bed of Spinach

I always think of halibut as the non–fish lover's fish because its dense texture is more typical of lean meat than of fish. There's little fat in halibut so I have enhanced it with rich-tasting salmon butter, bringing both color and juiciness to this dish. It's served over a bed of chopped spinach flavored with dill, making it a pretty combination as well.

4 servings

- 4 ounces crumbled smoked salmon fillet, skin and bones removed
- 4 tablespoons soft butter or corn oil margarine (¼ cup)
- 2 pounds halibut steaks, skin removed
- ¾ teaspoon salt
- 2 cups stemmed and chopped spinach
- 1 tablespoon chopped fresh dill
- 3 tablespoons dry white wine

Preheat the oven to 350°F.

Mash the salmon and butter together with a fork and set aside. Trim the flesh away from the bone and cut the 2 fillets from each halibut steak into 4 approximately 4 x 2-inch cutlets. Sprinkle the 8 cutlets with ¼ teaspoon salt.

Cut a long, deep slit in each cutlet and stuff with a heaping tablespoon of the salmon butter.

Put the spinach, remaining ½ teaspoon salt, and fresh dill together in a baking dish and toss. Lay the cutlets on top and pour the wine over all. Cover and bake for 20 minutes.

Microwave Instructions:

Mash the salmon and butter together with a fork and set aside. Trim the flesh away from the bone and cut the 2 fillets from each halibut steak into 4, approximately 4 x 2-inch cutlets. Sprinkle the 8 cutlets with ¼ teaspoon salt.

Cut a deep slit in each cutlet and stuff with a heaping tablespoon of the salmon butter.

Put the spinach, remaining salt, and fresh dill together in a microwave-safe dish and toss. Lay the cutlets on top and pour the wine over all. Cover with microwave-safe plastic wrap and microwave on High for 3 minutes. Let stand 1 minute before serving.

Return of the halibut fishers, 1915, Puget Sound

Broiled Petrale Sole in Cornmeal with Tomato-Caper Relish

Petrale sole is a large Pacific flounder that is highly regarded for its fine flavor and texture. It can be floured and fried, stuffed and baked, or, as in this recipe, broiled and seasoned with fresh basil. When the fish is covered with the yogurt-basil mixture and popped under the broiler, the sauce glazes the fillets, giving them the same kind of satiny sour cream topping cheesecake has.

4 servings

½	cup nonfat plain yogurt
2	tablespoons chopped fresh basil leaves
¼	cup cornmeal
½	teaspoon salt
¼	teaspoon pepper
1½	pounds petrale sole, cut into 4 pieces (substitute lemon sole on the East Coast)
2	tablespoons extra-virgin olive oil
	Tomato-Caper Relish (recipe follows)

Turn the oven to broil and lightly grease a broiler pan.

Stir together the yogurt and chopped basil and set aside. Blend the cornmeal, salt, and pepper together. Brush the sole with olive oil and dredge it in the cornmeal mixture. Arrange the fillets on the broiler pan and broil them, without turning, for 4 minutes. Pull the pan out from under the broiler and spread a thick layer of the basil-yogurt mixture over the top of each piece. Put the pan back under the broiler for 30 more seconds. Serve with Tomato-Caper Relish.

Tomato-Caper Relish
Makes 1 cup

½   *pound plum tomatoes, chopped*
2   *heaping tablespoons capers, drained*
1   *teaspoon balsamic vinegar*
    Pinch of salt

Toss all the ingredients together in a bowl. Serve ¼ cup
to each person to accompany the broiled petrale sole.

*Native American oyster
pickers homeward
bound. The sail was
introduced to the Indians
by the early explorers.*

Rex Sole with Fresh Thyme and Balsamic-Flavored Capers

About Balsamic Vinegar

Balsamic vinegar, imported from Italy, is sold locally at specialty food shops. Unlike most vinegars, it is dark brown, similar in color to soy sauce, with a sweet, mellow taste. This aromatic condiment is made from the cooked juice of white grapes that is aged for several years in wood casks. The name "balsamic" comes from the late middle ages when vinegar was thought to have curative powers.

Rex sole is a fine-textured small Pacific flounder with a full flavor. These tiny fish are sold cleaned and skinned, but their central bony plate needs to be removed after cooking by scraping the meat off with a fork. It's much easier than removing the bones of a trout, since the plate is all in one piece. I serve the fish covered with the brightly colored sauce and let guests do their own boning.

4 servings

    2   tablespoons commercial capers in balsamic vinegar,
        not drained
            or
    2   tablespoons capers, drained, and 1 tablespoon balsamic
        vinegar
    2   tablespoons corn oil
    ½   cup flour
    ¼   teaspoon salt
    ⅛   teaspoon freshly ground pepper
    2   pounds rex sole (substitute lemon sole on the East Coast)
    2   tablespoons butter or corn oil margarine
    1   cup chopped scallions
    2   cups cherry tomatoes, halved,
        or 2 cups skinned chopped tomatoes
    2   teaspoons fresh thyme, stemmed

Marinate the capers in the balsamic vinegar for ½ hour. Heat the oil in a sauté pan to medium-hot. Blend the flour and seasonings together and dust the fish with it. Put the sole in the hot oil and cook for 2–3 minutes a side. Remove the fish to a warm platter and add the butter, scallions, tomatoes, thyme, and capers (including the vinegar) to the sauté pan. As soon as the butter melts and the other ingredients are hot, spoon them over the fish and serve immediately.

Broiled Lingcod
with Yogurt-Mustard Sauce

Several years ago two good friends, Michele Tennyson and Carol Ladd, were testing recipes for the West Coast Fisheries Development Foundation and invited Ginger Johnston from the *Oregonian* and me for lunch. They served four wonderful seafood dishes, but the one that has lingered in my mind is similar to the following recipe.

2–3 servings

1	tablespoon butter or corn oil margarine
¼	cup croutons
12	ounces lingcod fillets
¼	teaspoon salt
⅛	teaspoon freshly ground pepper
½	cup nonfat plain yogurt
1–2	tablespoons your favorite mustard
1	garlic clove, crushed
	Pinch of cayenne pepper

Turn the oven to broil and lightly grease a broiling pan.

Melt the butter and sauté the croutons for 2–3 minutes. Set aside.

Arrange the lingcod on the broiling pan and sprinkle the surface of the fish with salt and pepper. Broil for 4½ minutes 4 inches from the broiler.

Meanwhile, stir the yogurt, mustard, garlic, and cayenne pepper together and spread over the surface of the fish (after it has cooked for 4½ minutes). Top with the buttered croutons, and broil for another 30–45 seconds.

Lingcod

Lingcod belongs to the greenling family (not even a shirttail relative of the cods) and its raw flesh often has a slightly greenish cast to it. Once it is cooked, though, the large tender flakes of fish turn creamy white and the fish is loaded with flavor.

Baked Multnomah Channel Catfish

The First Settlers

"On the 17th, we were paddling along at day-light. On putting on shore to breakfast, four Indians on horseback joined us. The moment they alighted, one set about hobbling their horses, another to gather small sticks, a third to make a fire, and the fourth to catch fish. For this purpose, the fisher-man cut off a bit of his leather shirt, about the size of a small bean; then pulling out two or three hairs from his horse's tail for a line, tied the bit of leather to one end of it, in place of a hook or fly. Thus pre-pared, he entered the river a little way, sat down on a stone, and began throwing the small fish, three or four inches long, on shore, just as fast as he picked them up and threw them towards the fire, while the third stuck them up round it in a circle, on small sticks; and they were no sooner up than roasted. The

~~~→

The Multnomah Channel, a small arm of the Columbia River that separates Sauvie's Island from northwest Portland, is known for its great-tasting catfish. Several years ago, Frank Amato, one of the Pacific Northwest publishing barons of fishing books and magazines, took me fishing there. We motored out into the peaceful channel in a small boat and caught our share in no time at all. Frank skinned the fish back on shore by nailing their tail fins to a board and pulling the notoriously tough skin off with pliers. Afterward, he cleaned and filleted the fish and sent the day's catch home with me. Before I cooked them I removed the backbone and separated the fillets. I cooked some of the fish by simply dredging the fillets in flour and frying them in hot oil with a small amount of butter added to it. The remainder I baked as follows. Both methods produced perfectly moist and delicious fillets.

4 servings

4   *skinless catfish fillets, wild or farmed (about 1½ pounds)*
1   *tablespoon olive oil*
¾   *teaspoon salt*
1   *garlic clove, peeled*
8   *ounces nonfat plain yogurt*
1   *teaspoon all-purpose flour*
⅛   *cup packed fresh basil leaves*
¼   *cup grated Parmesan cheese*

Preheat the oven to 350°F.

Lay the fillets in a 9-inch-square baking dish. Brush them with olive oil and sprinkle with salt.

Turn on a blender or food processor and drop in the garlic clove. Add the yogurt, flour, basil leaves, and Parmesan cheese and process until the mixture is well blended. Pour on top of the fillets and bake for 15–18 minutes.

Microwave Instructions:

Lay the fillets in a 9-inch-square baking dish. Brush the fish with olive oil and sprinkle with salt.

Turn on a blender or food processor and drop in the garlic clove. Add the yogurt, flour, basil leaves, and Parmesan cheese and process until the mixture is well blended. Pour the sauce on top of the fillets and cover the dish with microwave-safe plastic wrap. Microwave on High for 6 minutes.

fellows then sitting down, swallowed them—heads, tails, bones, guts, fins and all, in no time, just as one would swallow the yolk of an egg. Now all this was but the work of a

Young Chinese man in traditional clothing squats on a floating log while fishing in the Columbia River.

141

The First Settlers, continued

~~~~>

few minutes; and before our man had his kettle ready for the fire, the Indians were already eating their breakfast. When the fish had hold of the bit of wet leather, or bait, their teeth got entangled in it, so as to give them time to jerk them on shore, which was to us a new mode of angling; fire produced by the friction of two bits of wood was also a novelty; but what surprised us most of all, was the regularity with

~~~~>

Grilled Albacore with Sun-Dried Tomatoes and Fresh Rosemary

During the summer, fresh albacore is available in Pacific Northwest fish markets. This delicate-flavored fish is the lightest and mildest of all the members of the tuna family. It is usually sold as steaks or loins and, while delicate and pink raw, once cooked it becomes creamy white and firm-textured. In this recipe I have combined the fresh albacore with sun-dried tomatoes, garlic, and fresh rosemary for a hearty summer barbecue.

4 servings

1	*lemon, cut into thin slices*
1½	*pounds fresh albacore (2 steaks, cut in half)*
4	*tablespoons olive oil*
3	*tablespoons sun-dried tomatoes (packed in olive oil)*
1	*teaspoon chopped fresh rosemary*
¼	*teaspoon salt*
⅛	*teaspoon pepper*
1	*garlic clove, peeled*

Put the lemon slices in the bottom of a baking dish and arrange the steaks on top. Mix together 2 tablespoons olive oil and 2 tablespoons oil from the tomatoes and pour it over the fish. Sprinkle the fish with the rosemary, salt, and pepper and marinate at room temperature for 1 hour.

In a food processor or blender, make a paste by pureeing the sun-dried tomatoes, garlic, and the remaining 2 tablespoons olive oil and set aside.

Heat the grill and cook the fish on the first side for 4 minutes. Brush the top side with the marinade and turn the fish over. Spread the tomato-garlic paste on what is now the top side of the fish and cook for another 2–3 minutes.

Microwave Instructions:

Put the lemon slices in the bottom of a microwave-safe dish and arrange the steaks on top. Mix together 2 tablespoons olive oil and 2 tablespoons oil from the tomatoes and pour it over the fish. Sprinkle the fish with the rosemary, salt, and pepper and let the steaks marinate at room temperature for 1 hour.

In a food processor or blender, make a paste by pureeing the sun-dried tomatoes, garlic, and remaining 2 tablespoons olive oil and set aside.

Cover the fish with plastic wrap and microwave on High 4 minutes. Uncover the fish, spread the tomato-garlic paste on top of the fish, re-cover with plastic wrap, and microwave on High 1 more minute. Let stand, covered, 1 minute before serving.

which they proceeded, and the quickness of the whole process, which actually took less time to perform, than it has taken me to note it down."

—From Alexander Ross, Adventures of the First Settlers on the Oregon or Columbia River, 1810–1813 *(Lincoln, Nebraska: University of Nebraska Press, 1986).*

Sharing the day's catch

Stir-Fry Rockfish
with Ginger and Red Pepper

Rockfish

Local rockfish or rock-cod is often marketed as sea bass in the Pacific Northwest. It is one of the most common families of fish in the Pacific Ocean and the different kinds are usually identified by color. Once I saw listed on a menu "Oregon Black Sea Bass" and deduced that it was probably black rockfish. Included in this same family are the Pacific Ocean perch and Pacific snapper. Their habitat includes clean bays and rocky areas.

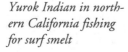

Yurok Indian in northern California fishing for surf smelt

This white-fleshed fish has large tender flakes and a mild flavor—the chicken of the ocean for cooks. It can be prepared many different ways but this method takes just minutes once the ingredients are assembled.

2–3 servings

1	teaspoon sesame oil
2	tablespoons reduced-sodium soy sauce
1	pound fillets—rockfish, perch, or red snapper, skin and bones removed and cut into bite-size pieces (1-inch cubes)
1	tablespoon corn oil
¼	medium red pepper, cut into thin strips
1	tablespoon finely slivered fresh ginger
2	scallions or green onions, trimmed and coarsely chopped
2	ounces snow peas, strings removed (about 20)
⅛	teaspoon salt
¼	cup fresh cilantro, stemmed

Blend the sesame oil and soy sauce together and set aside. Pat the fish dry with paper towels. Heat the corn oil in a wok or frying pan over medium-high heat for 30 seconds. Add the fish, red pepper, ginger, scallions, and snow peas. Gently toss and cook for 3–4 minutes. Pour the sesame oil–soy sauce mixture over all and cook for 1 more minute. Season with salt if necessary. Serve with a sprinkling of cilantro.

Pan-Fried Smelt

In the late spring the eulachons, commonly called smelt or candlefish, head up the river of their birth to spawn. Greedy sea gulls screech and soar down to the water's edge, trying to compete with the local fishermen, who scoop their dip nets into the river and dump their catch into nearby buckets, filling them in no time at all. These slender silvery fish are members of the same family as the surf (also called day smelt because they spawn during daylight) and night smelt, which are caught with nets in the pounding ocean surf. When it comes to eating, I prefer the firmer-fleshed surf and night smelt to the soft-textured eulachons. All of them are cooked the same way—simply dusted with flour and fried in hot oil. They're delicious smoked, too. Just follow the instructions for smoked fish on page 160.

Drying surf smelt, caught by the Indians near the mouth of the Smith River in northern California, are arranged in specific patterns on the beach to keep harmony with the spiritual world.

4 servings

2½–3   *pounds smelt*
¼–½   *cup corn oil*
  1   *cup flour*
  ½   *teaspoon salt*
  ¼   *teaspoon freshly ground pepper*
  4   *lemon wedges*

Rinse the fish under cold running water to remove any sand. Snip the heads off and remove the viscera.

Heat the oil in a cast-iron skillet to medium hot. Stir together the flour, salt, and freshly ground pepper. Dredge the fish in the flour mixture and fry in the hot oil until crisp and golden brown on both sides, about 5–6 minutes. Drain on paper towels and serve with lemon wedges.

Eulachons

Eulachons are also known as candlefish after the local Indian tradition of drying these oily fish and burning them for candles.

Teriyaki Cod with Pickled Ginger

As with most fish recipes, this one works well in either the conventional oven or the microwave. Before I cook the fillets, I lightly coat them with a teriyaki-butter sauce to enhance their flavor while they bake. This keeps the fish moist and provides just the right amount of seasoning, not overpowering the natural fresh taste of the fish.

Pacific Cod

The Pacific cod is closely related to the Atlantic cod and recipes can be used interchangeably. This West Coast relative is marketed as gray cod in Canada and true cod in most other regions of the Pacific Northwest. The adjective "true" is used to distinguish it from other fish, such as black cod (sablefish) and lingcod (greenling), which are not members of the cod family but use "cod" as part of their common name.

2–3 servings

1	tablespoon butter or corn oil margarine
2	tablespoons teriyaki sauce
1	tablespoon sake or dry white wine
1½	pounds true cod fillet (approximately 1 inch thick), cut into 4 servings
2	scallions or green onions, chopped
	Pinch of salt
	Pinch of pepper
4	tablespoons pickled ginger (available at oriental grocery stores)
4	lemon wedges

Preheat the oven to 350°F.

Put the butter, teriyaki sauce, and white wine in a 10-inch baking dish and heat in the oven for 5 minutes. Set aside 1 tablespoon of the teriyaki-butter sauce. Arrange the fish in the remaining sauce, turning once to thoroughly coat each side. Sprinkle the cod with the chopped scallions, salt, and pepper and cover the dish with foil. Bake for 12–15 minutes, or until the fish is done. Remove the foil and brush the fillets with the reserved teriyaki butter. Serve each piece of fish on a warmed plate accompanied by 1 tablespoon pickled ginger and a lemon wedge.

Microwave Instructions:

Put the butter, teriyaki sauce, and white wine in a 10-inch dish and microwave on High for 1½ minutes. Set aside 1 tablespoon of the teriyaki-butter sauce. Arrange the fish in the remaining sauce, turning once to thoroughly coat each side. Sprinkle the cod with the chopped scallions, salt, and pepper and cover the dish with microwave-safe plastic wrap. Microwave on High for 3½ minutes. Let rest 1 more minute and brush the fillets with the reserved teriyaki butter. Serve each piece on a warmed plate accompanied by 1 tablespoon pickled ginger and a lemon wedge.

Cod in the Northwest is associated with Norwegians. In the photograph on the opposite page Norwegian men in a Seattle waterfront factory make salted cod; below, Norwegian women prepare cod cakes at the Ballard Lutheran Church, Washington.

East-Meets-West Dungeness Crab

*Puget Sound—
the Chesapeake Bay
of the West*

*Puget Sound and the
Chesapeake Bay have
many similarities. Both
are estuaries formed
thousands of years ago
with the retreat of the
last ice age. Their tides
rise twice a day and
within their borders the
many bays, inlets,
and wetlands provide
protected areas for
hundreds of species of
seafood and shellfish.
This natural bounty
supplied Native
Americans and early
settlers in both regions
with an endless reser-
voir of food.*

*There are interesting
differences, too. The
Chesapeake Bay, the
larger of the two, is the
nation's largest estuary,
covering 3,237 square
miles, with 4,600 miles
of tidal shoreline. Its
average depth is 20 feet
and it is saltier and
warmer than the sound.
Puget Sound, on the
other hand, only covers
561 square miles,*

Several years ago in Baltimore, Maryland, Rob Kasper, a good friend who writes the syndicated "Happy Eater" column for the *Baltimore Sun*, arranged for me to have a tour of Gunning's Crab House, a lively tavern in south Baltimore known for its terrific steamed crabs. When we arrived, the manager led us to the kitchen, where his staff was filling the top part of huge steamers with layers of Chesapeake Bay blue crabs cloaked with spices. The steamers were placed on top of pots filled with beer and, as they cooked, the crabs slowly turned a deep reddish orange, the same color as the Dungeness crab. It made me wonder how Dungeness crab would taste cooked in a similar manner. When I returned to Portland, I experimented using their cooking technique on our larger West Coast crab and was thrilled with the results. I like to serve the crab hot with bowls of melted butter seasoned with the steaming spices.

3–4 servings

2   live Dungeness crabs, approximately 3½ pounds
    Enough beer or water to partially fill
    the bottom of the steamer
¼   cup Old Bay Seasoning*
1   tablespoon paprika
½   teaspoon cayenne pepper
¼   cup plus 2 tablespoons melted butter

  *Old Bay Seasoning can be found on the spice shelf at
   most grocery stores. It is a mixture of celery salt, pepper,
   dry mustard, pimiento, cloves, laurel leaves, mace,
   cardamom, ginger, cassia, and paprika.*

Place the live crabs in a large pan filled with ice. The ice numbs the crabs and helps the spices to adhere to their shell when they are cooked.

Partially fill the bottom of a steamer with beer or water and bring to a boil.

Blend the Old Bay Seasoning, paprika, and cayenne pepper together and set aside 1 teaspoon.

With tongs, place the crabs on the steaming rack and sprinkle the remaining seasoning lightly over the backs and legs. Cover and steam for 20 minutes over medium-high heat.

Melt the butter with the remaining teaspoon of spices and equally divide it among 4 small bowls.

Remove the crabs from the steamer. When they are cool enough to handle, remove the back, clean them (see page 150), and break each crab in half. Be careful not to brush off the spices from the legs.

Cover a table with plenty of old newspapers and give each person half a crab, a mallet to crack it with, a small bowl of seasoned butter, and plenty of elbow room.

has 1,800 miles of shoreline, although some of it extends as far as 200 miles inland, and a staggering average depth of 400 feet. And, because Seattle is nestled on the sound between the Cascade Mountain range on one side and the Olympic Peninsula on the other, it has a milder climate than any other American city that far north.

Cracked Dungeness Crab with Herb Mayonnaise

The Traditional Crab Feed

Crab feeds are to the Pacific Northwest what clambakes are to the Northeast. Family and friends get together for both social occasions and community fundraisers to enjoy sharing the local bounty from the sea, and in the Northwest, it's the prized Dungeness crab. This thoroughly enjoyable but messy tradition is accompanied by plenty of ice cold beer, homemade potato salad or a large green salad, and warm loaves of sourdough French bread. When we host crab feeds at our house, I cover my table with several layers of old newspapers, and the discarded crab shells are thrown in large piles in the center of the table. At the end of the meal, when all the silverware is accounted for, the newspapers are rolled up and tossed into the garbage.

Fresh crabs are most commonly sold precooked in the Pacific Northwest, but when I have time I like to buy them live and steam them myself. When they are eaten as soon as they are cooked, their meat is always succulently sweet and mild.

4 servings

- 2 live Dungeness crabs
- 4 lemon wedges
  Herb Mayonnaise or Homemade Herb Mayonaisse (recipes follow)

Use tongs to put the live crabs in a pan of ice to numb them before cooking. Steam the crabs over boiling water for 20 minutes. When the crabs are cool enough to handle, remove the backs. Discard the viscera and gills and rinse under cold water. Separate the legs from the body. Lay each leg on its edge and crack the shell by gently hitting it with a mallet. Place the crab on a platter and garnish with lemon wedges. Serve with Herb Mayonnaise.

Herb Mayonnaise

- 1 cup commercial mayonnaise
- ½ teaspoon drained capers
- 2 teaspoons chopped fresh basil
- 2 teaspoons chopped fresh dill
- 2 scallions or green onions, trimmed and chopped

Blend all the ingredients together and place in a small bowl to accompany the cracked crab.

150

Homemade Herb Mayonnaise
Makes about 2 cups

 1   *egg*
 1   *teaspoon fresh lemon juice or wine vinegar*
 ½   *teaspoon salt*
 2   *tablespoons fresh basil leaves*
 2   *tablespoons fresh dill*
1½   *cups corn oil or ¾ cup mild olive oil and ¾ cup corn oil*
 1   *tablespoon drained capers*

Put the egg, lemon juice, salt, basil, and dill in the bowl
of a food processor or blender and process for 30 seconds. Gradually add the oil until the mixture thickens.
Stir in the capers.

A Warning about
Salmonella

Due to a current out-
break of salmonellosis
on the East Coast, the
U.S. Department of
Agriculture and the fed-
eral Food and Drug
Administration recom-
mend avoiding food
containing raw eggs.

A successful day's catch
of Humboldt County
Dungeness crabs on
the rugged northern
California coast

Pacific Northwest Shellfish Trio

Clams

A line from the "Ballad of the Early Settler" reads, "When the tide is out, the table is set," and even today it's still an accurate statement. There are many varieties of shellfish harvested locally both commercially and on family outings. We used to drive to Long Beach, Washington, yearly to dig the elusive razor clam, named after its razor-sharp oblong shell. The succulently sweet meat of this bivalve is a favorite of clam connoisseurs. I like it cooked simply—dredged in flour, quick-fried in butter and oil, and served with a splash of fresh lemon juice. The geoduck (gooey-duck), also known as the king clam, is the largest American bivalve and a good portion of its huge body protrudes from both ends of its undersized shell. The tough neck is used in chowder, while the remainder of the clam is fried as steaks. I was once in a restaurant on the Olympic Peninsula in Washington and noticed a "King Clam Steak

I enjoy sipping on the rich, flavorful broth that results from cooking these three bivalves together. If there is any sand in it, strain the broth through a dish towel or cheesecloth. I serve this dish with plenty of crusty French bread—good for dunking in the flavorsome broth.

2–3 servings

1   cup water
1   cup bottled clam juice
    Large pinch of saffron threads (optional)
4   oysters, scrubbed
1   pound mussels, beards removed and scrubbed
1   pound steamer clams, scrubbed
2   tablespoons melted butter or corn oil margarine

Bring the water, clam juice, and optional saffron threads to a boil. Drop in the oysters, cover the pan, and let them cook for 2–3 minutes before adding the mussels. One minute after adding the mussels, add the clams and cook for 5–6 minutes or until all the shellfish pop open. Discard any shellfish that does not open. If the oysters have still not opened, cook them in the microwave on High for 20–30 seconds. Gently push a table knife down on the oyster hinge to release it. Pour some of the broth into 2 or 3 ramekins and serve them with the shellfish.

Pour the melted butter into 2 small sauce bowls to accompany the cooked shellfish. Place the pan with the cooked shellfish in the center of the table and let guests serve themselves.

Microwave Instructions:

Heat the water, clam juice, saffron threads, and oysters on High for 2 minutes. Add the remaining shellfish, cover with plastic wrap, and microwave on High for 2 more minutes.

Sandwich" listed on its luncheon menu.

Other clams include the gaper or horseneck, cockle, soft shell, butter, and steamer clams. I'm particularly fond of steamer clams, which I buy at the fish market, even though they, too, can be harvested locally. There are two species that are sold interchangeably—the native littleneck and the Manila clam. The latter was introduced by the Japanese along with the Japanese oyster at the turn of the century. Both clams are cooked by steaming or sautéing, but the more tender and delicately flavored Manila clam is served on the half shell as well.

Angel-Hair Pasta with Mussels and Shrimp in Marinara Sauce

Mussels

The wild blue and California mussels are easily gathered off the coastal rocks at low tide with the help of a sharp tool, such as a screw-driver. Choose small mussels, not over two to three inches in length, for the most delicate fla-vor. Mussels are also farmed in the Pacific Northwest and can often be purchased with the beard already removed. All mussels, wild or cultivated, are delicious steamed, baked, or poached.

The sharp contrast of blue-black mussel shells poking out of pasta cloaked in marinara sauce makes this a picturesque dish that tastes as good as it looks. Since the mussels are served still in their shells in the pasta, I try to buy ones that are barnacle-free and beardless. If they are not available, you will need to scrub the mussels under cold running water and cut their beards off with scissors.

4–6 servings

2	cups prepared Marinara Sauce (recipe follows)
3	quarts water
1	tablespoon olive oil
2	garlic cloves, chopped
1	pound medium shrimp, peeled
1	pound mussels, cleaned and beards removed
½	cup dry white wine
6–7	ounces angel-hair pasta
¾	cup chopped fresh basil

Heat the Marinara Sauce in a small pan.

Bring the water to a boil for the pasta.

In a sauté pan with a lid, heat the olive oil over medium heat and add the garlic, shrimp, and mussels. Toss the shellfish as they cook for 1–2 minutes. Add the wine to the shellfish and cover with a lid until the mussels pop open, about 30 seconds.

Cook the pasta in boiling salted water for 45–60 seconds, or until tender. Drain the pasta and put it in a large warmed pasta bowl. Toss the pasta with the Marinara Sauce and cooked shellfish and sprinkle with the chopped basil.

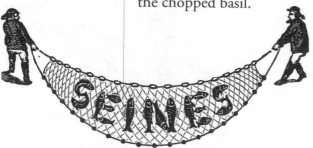

Marinara Sauce
Makes 3 cups

2   *tablespoons olive oil*
½   *cup chopped onion*
½   *teaspoon sugar*
1   *28-ounce can peeled plum tomatoes*
¼   *teaspoon whole dried oregano*
½   *teaspoon salt*
1   *garlic clove*

Heat the olive oil in a skillet and add the onion. Sprinkle the sugar over the onion and sauté until the onion starts to turn brown, about 8–10 minutes. Meanwhile, remove the seeds in the tomatoes by slicing the tomatoes in half lengthwise and scooping the seeds out with a spoon. Put the tomatoes, oregano, and salt in a food processor or blender and turn the machine on. With the machine running, add the garlic and puree for 30 seconds. Stir the tomato mixture in with the onions and cook for 30–40 minutes.

Anna, a Chetco Indian from southern Oregon, returning home from the beach near Newport. She used her sledgehammer to break the sandstone ledges to get at the burrowing Piddock clams.

155

Pacific Northwest Shrimp in Oregon Blue Cheese Sauce

Portland's Seafood

Most of the seafood sold in Portland at the turn of the century is still available in the Pacific Northwest today. Some of the species, such as salmon, oysters, and trout, are now being aquacultured. See opposite page to get an idea of the variety—and prices—in 1917.

I have combined two local shrimp with creamy Oregon Blue Cheese to create a delicate sauce that is served over mounds of lemon-flavored rice (it's also good over pasta or polenta). Because it is rich, I serve small servings in shallow soup bowls accompanied by a simple green salad and a dry white wine.

4 servings

2	*tablespoons fresh lemon juice*
¼	*teaspoon salt*
1	*tablespoon butter or corn oil margarine*
⅔	*cup long-grain white rice*
2	*peeled onion slices*
2	*tablespoons Italian flat-leaf parsley*
1	*pound medium uncooked shrimp*
1½	*cups homemade chicken stock*
	or reduced-sodium canned chicken broth
1	*cup half-and-half*
4	*tablespoons all-purpose flour*
4	*ounces Oregon Blue Cheese or Danish-style blue cheese*
8	*ounces bay shrimp (approximately 1 cup)*
4	*sprigs Italian flat-leaf parsley*

Warm 4 shallow soup bowls.

Bring 1¼ cups water, lemon juice, salt, and butter to a boil. Stir in the rice and cover. Reduce the heat to simmer and cook for 20 minutes.

Meanwhile, put 1½ cups water, the onion slices, 2 tablespoons parsley, and the uncooked shrimp in a pan and bring to a boil. Cook the shrimp until their shells turn pink and the meat is white, about 30 seconds to a minute, tossing the shrimp as they cook. Drain the shrimp and make the sauce while they cool.

Pour the chicken stock and half-and-half into a 1-quart saucepan and warm over low heat. With a fork, blend the flour and blue cheese together and whisk it into the stock–half-and-half mixture. Turn the heat to medium and continue stirring until the mixture is smooth and thickened, about 3–4 minutes. Put the peeled shrimp and the bay shrimp in the blue cheese sauce and gently heat until they are warm.

Scoop a heaping ½ cup rice out of the pot and put it in the middle of a shallow soup bowl. Ladle the sauce over all and garnish with a sprig of parsley. Repeat for the other 3 bowls.

A list of Portland fish prices from Telegram Conservation Cook Book *by Inie Gage Chapel (Aunt Prudence) (Portland Oregon: Modern Printing and Publishing Company, 1917).*

PORTLAND MARKET PRICES

Here are the prices of fish I obtained at the fish market on Saturday, October 6 (1917).

	Pounds/Cents
Salmon, Royal Chinook	20
Salmon, Silverside, by the half fish	15
Salmon, Silverside, whole, for canning	14+½
Salmon trout (Steelhead)	20
Halibut	25
Sturgeon	25
Fresh black cod, 2 lbs. for	25
Sand dabs	15
Crabs (each)	20
Shrimps	20
Smelt, 2 lbs. for	25
Bloaters (Kippered Herring)	20
Codfish	20
Boneless herring	30
Kippered salmon	30
Oysters, Eastern, per pint	65
Oysters, Western, per pint	70
Lobsters, each	35
Crawfish, per dozen	35
River trout, Grayling, lb	20

Shrimp and Pasta
in Sweet Red Pepper Sauce

Sweet roasted red peppers can be used directly from the jar for this simple recipe that takes less than 20 minutes to prepare, or roast and peel your own according to the directions on page 202.

4 servings

¾   *cup sweet roasted red peppers, drained*
2   *cups half-and-half*
   Pinch of cayenne pepper
⅛   *teaspoon salt*
8   *ounces mostaccioli or other tube-shaped pasta*
1   *tablespoon olive oil*
2   *garlic cloves, minced*
1   *pound medium shrimp, shelled*
   Pinch of salt
   Freshly ground pepper
2   *tablespoons chopped Italian flat-leaf parsley*

In a blender or food processor, puree the red peppers, half-and-half, cayenne pepper, and ⅛ teaspoon salt until smooth. Pour the sauce in a saucepan and cook over medium heat for 10 minutes.

Bring 3 quarts of salted water to a boil and cook the pasta until it is tender, about 10–13 minutes.

Heat the olive oil and sauté the garlic and shrimp for 2–3 minutes, until the shrimp turns pink on both sides. Sprinkle the shrimp with a pinch of salt and freshly ground pepper.

Drain the pasta and pour it into a heated shallow pasta bowl. Pour the sauce over the pasta and add the shrimp. Toss and sprinkle with the chopped parsley.

Fried Razor Clams

Until recently the only way to get this delicate-flavored clam was to dig for it, not an easy task since these evasive bivalves rapidly pull themselves downward through the wet sand at speeds of up to nine inches a minute! Luckily, for slow and frustrated clam diggers like myself, fresh razor clams are now being sold commercially from Alaska. The following way of cooking them is my old standby, which my family has long used.

4 servings

2   *tablespoons butter or corn oil margarine*
¼   *cup corn oil*
¾   *cup flour*
½   *teaspoon salt*
¼   *teaspoon freshly ground pepper*
2   *pounds razor clams, ready for cooking*
4   *lemon wedges*

Sam Lee, the clam digger, Seaside, Oregon

I Ieat the butter and corn oil in a large skillet until it is medium-hot. Blend the flour, salt, and pepper together and dredge the clams. Fry the clams quickly, 1–2 minutes, on each side. Serve them on a hot platter with wedges of fresh lemons.

Master Recipe for Smoking Fish

*An Indian Way of
Smoking Salmon*

*Some of the Indians
who fished on the banks
of the Columbia River
near The Dalles,
Oregon, used the strong
summer winds to help
preserve their fish. They
laid the fillets on racks
constructed over the
mouth of a dry creek
bed and built a fire on
the rocky creek bottom
downwind from the
fish. The gusty winds,
which are notorious on
this part of the river
(nearby Hood River is
one of the windsurfing
capitals of the world),
consistently blow up the
tributaries. The smoke-
filled gusts dried and
smoked the salmon at
the same time.*

Smoking food is an age-old method of food preservation that is still popular in the Pacific Northwest today. Most fishermen store their catch in the freezer and it's perfectly all right to use thawed fish for smoking if you are careful to avoid any that has been frozen too long (more than 3–4 months for fatty fish, such as Chinook; 6–7 months for lean fish). The finished product will only be as good as the quality of food being smoked.

The prepared fish is first soaked in a brine to allow salt to permeate the tissue, drawing out water and thus decreasing the chance of spoilage by harmful bacteria. The brined fish is then soaked in several changes of fresh water to remove any excess salt and placed on a rack to air-dry.

Alder, vine maple, cherry, apple, and other hardwood trees provide the best wood for smoking foods. The smoke flavors the fish and coats it with chemicals (aldehydes and ketones) that help inhibit the growth of unwanted bacteria. Wood from evergreen trees is not used because it gives off a bitter resin when burned.

I smoke fish with a hot smoke, which is also called "smoke cooking." The food is placed in a smoker with a temperature range of 120–225°F. and smoked until the internal temperature of the food reaches 165–175°F. Hot-smoked fish is still perishable and should be stored in the refrigerator or frozen, wrapped airtight in plastic wrap and foil. It will keep in the refrigerator up to 10 days and for 2 months frozen.

Makes 3 pounds

½ cup salt
1 quart water
3 pounds fish

To Prepare the Fish:

Prepare fish steaks by cutting them ½–1 inch thick.

Prepare a fish fillet by cutting it into 2 x 3-inch pieces, ½–1 inch thick.

Prepare smelt by rinsing under cold water to remove any sand. Snip the heads at the neck and eviscerate the fish. Rinse again under cold running water and leave whole.

Make the brine by stirring the salt and water together in a glass measuring cup. Put the fish in a glass 9 x 13-inch baking dish and cover with the brine. Cover with plastic wrap and allow to cure for 3–4 hours. Turn the pieces every half hour.

Pour the brine off the fish and fill the dish with fresh cold water. Repeat this process 3 or 4 times to remove excess salt. Transfer the fish to a wire rack to air-dry for an hour. Arrange the pieces, 1 inch apart on the smoking rack, skin side up. Smoke, using a hot smoke, for about 4 hours or until the fish is done to your liking. Fresh chips should be added at least 4 times during the smoking process.

Cold-Smoked Food

Cold-smoked food is smoked at temperatures below 120°F. An example is lox, smoked with a technique brought to America by the Russian-Jewish community and made with either Atlantic or Pacific salmon.

Oregon Indians drying salmon in the way of their ancestors, 1950

From the Truck Gardens
to the Markets

Today the Willamette Valley provides some of the most diversified crop land in the United States. Everything from wheat and hops to nuts and berries is grown there. Salem, in the heart of the valley, has the second largest canning plant in the nation—snap beans, corn, peas, prunes, plums, sweet cherries, caneberries, and so on.

There are many other agricultural regions in the Pacific Northwest. Oregon's Hood River Valley and The Dalles are both known for their apples, pears, and cherries; the Rogue Valley is primarily a pear-growing area. Washington's Okanogan and Wenatchee valleys also produce orchard crops, while Yakima County, farther south, is more diverse—vegetables, hops, and mint come from there in addition to fruits; the famous Walla Walla Sweet onion, wheat, and vegetables are major crops in the Walla Walla Valley. In both Washington and Idaho, the Palouse is the heartland for the Northwest's wheat, barley, lentils, and peas for drying. The Snake River Plain of Idaho is known for its famous potatoes, dry beans, sugar beets, and sweet corn; and the Okanagan Valley of British Columbia grows a large percentage of Canada's fruits—mainly peaches, pears, plums, apples, and sweet cherries.

In many areas the farmers feel strongly about their relationship with the consumer. In fact, the Pike's Place Market in Seattle was established in 1907 by the farmers so they could sell directly to the consumer. The rule was that the farmer had to sell at his table in the market at least one day a week and this is still followed. Many local farmers still sell directly to restaurants and grocery stores. Produce in the Pacific Northwest is fresh and flavorful in part because there is a short turnaround time from the field to the table.

Specialty-produce farmers are a new kind of farmer in the West. They concentrate on a variety of vegetables as well as wild greens that fashionable restaurants use these days to embellish salads. Actually wild greens and edible flowers are not such a novel idea. For centuries Pacific Northwest Indians depended on such native plants for their survival and they were expert botanists.

On a recent trip to Kah-Nee-Ta, a family resort on the Warm Springs Indian reservation in central Oregon, I took a hike with Kah-Nee-Ta's botanist, Gary Clowers, to learn more about indigenous plants used for food. We had no sooner started up the trail behind the lodge than he said, "Hey, look! There's *Lomatium canbyi;* let's have a bite." The dried seeds resemble fennel and they're known locally as "Indian candy." The root of this desert parsley, a cousin of Indian celery, was an important food for local Indians, who would boil the roots before eating them. Later on, he introduced me to a lovely and tasty edible flower, yellow bells, a member of the lily family. In the fall, when the plant has gone to seed, Gary brings schoolchildren up on the slopes and gives them handfuls of the seed to throw high into the wind to redistribute them for future generations.

I often use edible flowers from my garden to add color to a salad of mixed greens. Bright gold calendula petals, delicate pink blossoms of society garlic, a clumping perennial that also makes a lovely garden border, pansies, daylilies, violas, nasturtiums, marigolds, chrysanthemums, rose petals, and borage flowers all make colorful additions, especially if they're sprinkled on top of the salad just before it's served.

I have developed recipes in this chapter that make use of the Northwest's special produce in new and different ways—from potato dishes that feature russets and Yellow Finns to Walla Walla Sweet Onion Rings in Beer Batter and Golden Chanterelle Griddlecakes. Lentils, grown in Washington and Idaho, are paired with chicken and rice, and red Bartlett pears are stuffed with local farmstead goat cheese seasoned with toasted Willamette Valley hazelnuts. Each recipe features a local ingredient, simply prepared, to keep its own fine flavor.

SCALLOPED POTATOES WITH GRUYÈRE CHEESE AND FRESH ROSEMARY

AURORA COLONY GERMAN POTATO PANCAKES

YUKON GOLD COTTAGE FRIES

PACIFIC NORTHWEST BEANS WITH HAM HOCKS

FRED'S HONEY-BAKED BEANS

LUSTY WILD AND BROWN RICE CASSEROLE

DORRIS RANCH BARLEY-HAZELNUT CASSEROLE

GREEN BEANS WITH RED PEPPERS AND TOASTED HAZELNUTS

GOLDEN ACORN SQUASH WITH RASPBERRIES

FRESH ASPARAGUS AND POTATOES IN BASIL-MINT DRESSING

WASHINGTON ASPARAGUS WITH HAZELNUT MAYONNAISE

SLICED TOMATOES WITH HORSERADISH CREAM

GARLIC STIR-FRY SPINACH

GOLDEN CHANTERELLE GRIDDLECAKES

FRESH MORELS SIMMERED IN CREAM

STUFFED TOMATOES WITH ORZO AND FRESH CHIVES

CORN ON THE COB WITH BASIL BUTTER

STEAMED BROCCOLI WITH WASHINGTON GOUDA CHEESE

WALLA WALLA SWEET ONION RINGS IN BEER BATTER

GRILLED WALLA WALLA SWEETS WITH FRESH LEMON THYME

PUREED PARSNIPS AND POTATOES

ANGELO PELLIGRINI'S BRAISED CARDOONS

GREAT NORTHERN BEAN SALAD WITH SMOKED SALMON

PALOUSE LENTIL SALAD WITH CHICKEN AND RICE

BABY OAK-LEAF LETTUCE AND RADICCHIO SALAD WITH FRESH CRAB

TOSSED GREEN SALAD WITH OREGON BLUE CHEESE AND WALNUTS

SPINACH SALAD WITH HONEY-SESAME SEED DRESSING

SPINACH AND MUSHROOM SALAD WITH TOASTED HAZELNUTS

MIXED GREENS WITH RASPBERRY VINAIGRETTE AND CHÈVRE

SUMMER FRUIT SALAD WITH RASPBERRY-YOGURT DRESSING

RED BARTLETT PEARS STUFFED WITH CHÈVRE AND CHOPPED HAZELNUTS

CREAMY POTATO SALAD WITH OREGON BLUE CHEESE AND SCALLIONS

COUNTRY POTATO SALAD

GRILLED RED PEPPER SALAD

ANGEL-HAIR PASTA SALAD WITH SHRIMP, SUGAR SNAP PEAS, AND SESAME CHILI OIL

MCCORMICK'S HOT SEAFOOD SALAD

COUPEVILLE MUSSEL SALAD

PASTA SALAD WITH SHRIMP AND THREE PEPPERS

ARTICHOKE HEART AND SALMON SALAD WITH CAPERS

ZENON CAFÉ CAESAR SALAD

Scalloped Potatoes with Gruyère Cheese and Fresh Rosemary

The Russet Potato

The russet Burbank potato is as all-American as apple pie. Like all potatoes, it originated in South America but came to North America with the European immigrants, which explains the derivation of one of its nicknames, the Fall Irish potato. The original heirloom variety had purple flesh, but over the years breeding has changed it from purple to pink to white. Another popular name for the russet potato is Idaho potato, a marketing term for russets grown in Idaho State.

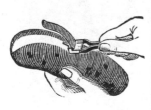

The rich volcanic soils of the Columbia basin, which extends all the way from central Washington to northern Oregon, produces the highest yield of potatoes in the United States. The majority of the crop are the rough-skinned russet Burbanks, which are commonly called Idaho or Fall Irish potatoes. In this recipe russets, known for their fine baking quality, are seasoned with fresh rosemary and baked with nutty-tasting Gruyère cheese. This is a robust dish that can stand up to the distinctive flavor of venison or lamb.

4–6 servings

2	pounds russet potatoes, peeled and cut into ¼-inch-thick slices (about 5–6 cups)
1	teaspoon chopped fresh rosemary
½	pound grated Gruyère cheese (about 1½–2 cups)
1½	cups milk (2% fat)
½	teaspoon salt
¼	teaspoon white pepper

Preheat the oven to 350°F. and grease a 2-quart au gratin or shallow dish.

In a bowl toss the potatoes, rosemary, and half the cheese together. Arrange the potatoes so that they are flat in the baking dish.

Mix the milk with the salt and pepper and pour it over the potatoes. Bake the potatoes, uncovered, for 1 hour. Sprinkle the remaining cheese over the potatoes and bake for an additional 20 minutes.

Aurora Colony German Potato Pancakes

A group of German immigrants founded the Aurora Colony on the outskirts of Portland in 1856 and historical journals always mention the fine food that was served in this small community. One of their traditional recipes was for potato pancakes made from mashed potatoes and served, covered with hot gravy, for breakfast. I especially enjoy these crisp potato pancakes because they are crusty on the outside and creamy smooth inside.

Makes 4 potato pancakes

1½	*pounds cooked Yukon Gold or new potatoes*
2	*tablespoons flour*
3	*tablespoons buttermilk*
1¼	*teaspoon salt*
½	*teaspoon freshly ground pepper*
2	*tablespoons corn oil*

Gardens have always been popular in the fertile valleys of the Pacific Northwest. This Washington garden produced giant-sized carrots.

Mash the potatoes in their skins and stir in the remaining ingredients except the oil. Shape the mixture into 4 pancakes. Heat the oil to medium-hot in a skillet and cook the pancakes for 3–4 minutes. Turn the heat to low and slowly cook the pancakes on both sides until they are golden brown.

Yukon Gold Cottage Fries

*Yukon Gold
and Yellow Finns*

*With a name like
Yukon Gold, you'd
think this yellow potato
was developed in the
Pacific Northwest but it
comes from Ontario,
Canada, where it was
released in 1980. In the
last few years it has
grown in popularity
here along with another
yellow potato, the Yel-
low Finn. The Yellow
Finn was brought to
Washington from
Finland, where, ironi-
cally enough, it was
called the Olympia,
after the Olympics held
there.*

These cottage fries are similar to the old-fashioned kind cooked over a campfire but the fire is in the pan instead of underneath it. I fry the potatoes with onions and when they turn a deep golden brown I smother them with grated cheese and chopped green chiles. The cheese melts down into the potatoes, taking the bits of chiles with it. One word of warning: You never know how hot canned chiles are going to be, so add them judiciously and taste before adding more. And be sure to buy chopped green chiles, which are mild, and not the fiery chopped jalapeño chiles for this recipe.

4–6 servings

1	tablespoon corn oil
2½	pounds Yukon Gold or Yellow Finn potatoes, cooked and cut into quarters (6 cups)
½	cup sliced green onions or scallions, including tender greens
½	teaspoon salt
¼	teaspoon freshly ground pepper
	Approximately two 4-ounce cans diced and peeled green chiles (1 cup)
½	pound grated cheddar cheese (2 cups)
¼	cup chopped cilantro

Heat the oil to medium-hot in a frying pan with a lid.
Sauté the potatoes and onions until they are golden
brown and season with salt and pepper.

Sprinkle the chiles and cheese over all and cover the
pan with a lid. (You may not want to use the full amount
of chiles called for until after you have tasted the
potatoes.) Turn the heat to simmer and cook for 5 more
minutes, or until the cheese melts and the chiles are hot.

Garnish with the cilantro and serve immediately.

Prepare Ahead

*These potatoes can be
prepared a day ahead
without the cheese. To
reheat them, cover the
pan with foil and place
it in a 325°F. oven for
15 minutes. Sprinkle
the potatoes with cheese
and heat them for 10
more minutes. To
reheat the potatoes in
the microwave, cover
the pan with plastic
wrap and microwave on
High for 4 minutes.
Sprinkle the cheese over
the potatoes and cook
for 1 more minute.*

*A Yakima Indian dig-
ging for roots, 1909*

Pacific Northwest Beans with Ham Hocks

Overnight Soak

Cover the beans with at least 6 cups of water and let sit overnight, or for 8 hours at room temperature. Drain.

Quick Soak

Put the beans in a large flameproof casserole and add enough water to cover them by 1 inch. Bring to a boil. Cover, remove from the heat, and set aside for 1 hour. Drain.

The long winters of Idaho and eastern Washington and Oregon provide plenty of opportunity to cook hardy meals, such as this one, that are nourishing to both the body and the soul. This recipe comes from my mother, Kassie Franke, who keeps ham bones in the freezer just for this dish.

8–10 servings

1	pound dried red beans, soaked (see margin)
	Water to cover beans
1½	pounds ham hocks, split, or 1 meaty ham bone
2	cups onions, peeled and chopped (about 2 onions)
3	garlic cloves, minced
2	15-ounce cans diced tomatoes with juice
2	teaspoons freshly ground pepper
1–2	cups cooked ham scraps (optional)
	Salt to taste if necessary

Put the soaked beans in a pot. Pour in enough water to cover them by 2 inches. Add all the ingredients except the salt. Bring to a boil, then reduce the heat to simmer and cook, uncovered, for 3 hours. Toss in the ham scraps, if using, and cook for another hour. Season with salt if necessary.

KETTLE

Which belonged to Mrs. Nancy Hanks Lincoln, mother of Abraham Lincoln.

She gave it to a cousin who in turn gave it to her daughter, a Mrs. Robinson who in 1895 was a resident of Mississippi.

She gave the kettle to Mrs. A. Lorenz, who brought it to Cove, Union County, Oregon and on August 22 - 1905 placed it in the custody of the Oregon Historical Society.

Fred's Honey-Baked Beans

These beans are my father-in-law's specialty. He takes a
casserole of them to weddings, christenings, and any
other occasion where a hungry crowd needs to be fed.
They are always the first dish to be emptied on the buffet
table. He bakes them in a huge cast-iron kettle ordered
out of a catalogue just for this purpose. This is my own
variation of his recipe; I find they always taste best
reheated the second day.

8–10 servings

1   *pound drained pinto beans, soaked (see page 170)*
    Water to cover beans
1   *pound meaty bacon, sliced and cut into bite-size pieces*
1   *cup diced onion*
2   *garlic cloves, peeled and minced*
1   *cup honey*
1   *teaspoon dry mustard*
1   *heaping tablespoon ground ginger*
1   *teaspoon salt*
½   *teaspoon pepper*

Cover the soaked beans with 2½ quarts fresh water.
Bring to a boil, reduce the heat to simmer, and cook
until the beans are tender, about 45 minutes. Drain the
beans and set aside the cooking liquid.

Preheat the oven to 300°F.

Put the beans in a 5½-quart casserole with a lid and
toss with the bacon, onion, and garlic. Measure 2 cups
of the reserved cooking liquid and stir in the honey,
mustard, ground ginger, salt, and pepper. Pour the liquid
over the beans and cover. Bake for 2½ hours.

Lusty Wild and Brown Rice Casserole

*Rice Farming along
the Pacific Flyway*

*If you drive to the
Pacific Northwest from
San Francisco on
Interstate 5 you'll pass
through the northern
end of the Sacramento
Valley, where many
varieties of rice are
grown. I especially enjoy
this trip in the fall and
winter, when hundreds
of geese can be seen fly-
ing in formation from
one field to another.
This rural area of
California is a neighbor
to the Pacific Northwest
and part of the continu-
ing Pacific Flyway.*

Wild rice doesn't grow in the Pacific Northwest but
nearby in the Sacramento Valley. The nutty taste and
firm texture of the rice, lightly bound by the yogurt and
sour cream, seems to be the perfect accompaniment to
the powerful flavor of fried venison or roast wild duck.

4 servings

2	tablespoons butter
½	pound fresh mushrooms, sliced
½	cup wild rice
½	cup brown rice
2½	cups water
1	teaspoon salt
¼	cup yogurt
¼	cup light sour cream
4	sprigs Italian flat-leaf parsley, chopped
½	teaspoon freshly ground pepper

Melt the butter in a saucepan and sauté the mushrooms
until soft. Stir in the rice, water, and salt and bring it to
a boil. Cover the pan and reduce the heat to simmer.
Cook for 45–50 minutes, or until done. Stir in the
yogurt, sour cream, parsley, and pepper.

*This picture was
taken when the sky
was the limit.*

Dorris Ranch Barley-Hazelnut Casserole

The Pacific Northwest, known for its large, high-quality hazelnuts, produces most of the nation's crop. This recipe comes from a small cookbook, *The Dorris Ranch Favorite Filbert Recipes*, and was contributed by Janet Van Nada.

6 servings

1	cup pearl barley
4	tablespoons butter (¼ cup)
½	cup hazelnuts, chopped
1	medium onion, finely chopped
¼	cup chopped green onion or chives
¼	teaspoon salt
¼	teaspoon pepper
3½	cups homemade chicken stock or reduced-sodium canned chicken broth (28 ounces)
3	sprigs parsley

Preheat oven to 375°F.

Rinse the barley and drain. Melt 2 tablespoons butter in a frying pan and stir in the nuts. Cook until lightly roasted, then remove from the pan and set aside.

Add the remaining 2 tablespoons butter to the pan. When it has melted stir in the onion and barley and sauté for 5–8 minutes, or until both have started to turn brown.

Stir in the nuts, green onion, salt, and pepper. Spoon into a 1½-quart casserole and pour the broth over the barley mixture. Bake for 1 hour and 20 minutes, or until the liquid is absorbed. Garnish with parsley and serve immediately.

Green Beans with Red Peppers and Toasted Hazelnuts

Beatrice Crawford Drury

Beatrice Crawford Drury is not simply a native of Salem; she was a native when Salem was in its infancy.

Drury, who was born here in 1895, recalls growing up on the family farm on Browns Island—now Minto-Brown Island Park.

This colorful dish can be served either warm, when it is first made, or the following day, but be sure to bring the refrigerated salad back to room temperature and toss the vegetables before serving.

4–6 servings

1	pound cooked whole green beans (still warm), strings removed
1½	tablespoons olive oil
¼	teaspoon salt
1	red pepper, seeded and julienned
1	tablespoon chopped and toasted hazelnuts (see margin, page 177)

Toss the beans with the oil, salt, and strips of red pepper in a shallow dish. Arrange the vegetables in horizontal rows and sprinkle with the toasted hazelnuts.

Chinese vegetable peddlers, selling produce from shoulder baskets, were a common sight in the early Pacific Northwest towns and cities.

Golden Acorn Squash
with Raspberries

Golden acorn squash are as brilliantly colored as the Yakima sun on a bright August day. When they are filled with fresh red raspberries, butter, and brown sugar they become a feast for the eye as well as the palate. If fresh raspberries are not available, frozen raspberries can be used directly from the freezer.

4 servings

 2 *golden acorn squash, cut in half and seeded*
 4 *tablespoons butter or corn oil margarine*
 4 *tablespoons brown sugar*
 1 *cup fresh or frozen red raspberries,*
    blueberries, or blackberries

Preheat the oven to 350°F.

Cut a thin slice off the bottom of the squash halves and stand them upright in a baking dish. Fill each half with 1 tablespoon butter and 1 tablespoon brown sugar. If you are using frozen raspberries, bake the squash for 35 minutes, add the berries, and bake for another 10 minutes. Fresh raspberries can be added after the squash have baked for 40 minutes. Cook them for another 5 minutes.

Microwave Instructions:

Cut each squash in half and scoop out the centers. Put the squash, cut side down, in a shallow baking dish and add 3 tablespoons water. Cover the dish with plastic wrap and bake on High for about 12 minutes, or until they are tender. Turn the squash over and cut a thin slice off the bottom. Stand the squash upright in the baking dish and fill each half with 1 tablespoon butter, 1 tablespoon brown sugar, and ¼ cup raspberries. Microwave on High for 4 more minutes for frozen raspberries and 3 more minutes for fresh berries.

Her father, Kentucky native John H. Crawford, raised vegetables on an 850-acre truck garden.

Nearby was a shanty town housing 300 Chinese, including Sam Hee, who worked for her father.

"My earliest recollection was of those Chinese, who were everywhere. Sam used to take me on the wagon when I was so little my knees wouldn't bend," she said.

Hee often would talk about children in China as he and young Beatrice traveled Salem's dirt roads selling vegetables, Drury recalled.

"I had no idea where China was. I thought it was just down the road," she said.

—From an article by Ron Cowan for The Statesman Journal, *March 24, 1991*

Fresh Asparagus and Potatoes in Basil-Mint Dressing

I have come to enjoy the combined flavors of basil and mint, which I first encountered in several of the new Thai restaurants in the Pacific Northwest. These herbs give a nice flavor to the mild taste of boiled potatoes and steamed asparagus.

4–6 servings

1	*pound white shafter or new potatoes*
1	*pound fresh asparagus*
½	*cup olive oil*
½	*cup corn oil*
4	*tablespoons fresh lemon juice*
1	*pressed garlic clove*
2	*tablespoons chopped fresh mint*
2	*tablespoons chopped fresh basil*
¾	*teaspoon salt*
¼	*teaspoon pepper*
	Butter lettuce leaves

Put the potatoes in a pot and cover them with cold water. Bring the water to a boil, then turn the heat to simmer and cook the potatoes until they are tender. Peel the potatoes while they are warm and cut them into ½-inch slices.

Break the asparagus into 2-inch pieces and cook them in boiling salted water until they are barely tender. Drain and toss the asparagus with the warm potatoes.

Whisk the olive oil, corn oil, lemon juice, garlic, mint, basil, salt, and pepper together and pour over the warm vegetables. Let stand at room temperature 1 hour. Line a shallow serving dish with lettuce leaves and arrange the potato slices and asparagus pieces in overlapping rows.

Washington Asparagus with Hazelnut Mayonnaise

Serve the asparagus hot from the steamer, or chill it and serve the cooked spears on a bed of lettuce with a dollop of nutty mayonnaise. I have included two recipes for the mayonnaise—one made from scratch and the other made with commercial mayonnaise.

4 servings

1	*pound fresh asparagus*
1	*egg*
1	*teaspoon lemon juice*
1	*teaspoon prepared mustard*
½	*teaspoon salt*
1½	*cups corn oil or ¾ cup corn oil and ¾ cup mild olive oil*
½	*cup hazelnuts, roasted, skinned, and coarsely chopped*

Prepare the asparagus by holding the base firmly and bending the stalk. It will break where it is too tough to eat. Fill the bottom half of a steamer with an inch of water and lay the asparagus in the top half. Cover and bring the water to a boil. Steam for 8–10 minutes, until tender.

While the asparagus is steaming, make the mayonnaise. (If you don't want to make the mayonnaise from scratch, add ½ cup chopped and toasted hazelnuts to 1½ cups prepared mayonnaise.)

Crack the egg into the bowl of a food processor or blender and add the lemon juice, mustard, and salt. With the machine still running slowly, add the oil, drop by drop, until the mixture thickens. Add the chopped hazelnuts and process for 3 more seconds.

Serve the cooked asparagus in a shallow dish accompanied by a bowl of hazelnut mayonnaise. Store any remaining mayonnaise in a covered jar in the refrigerator.

A Warning about Salmonella

Due to a current outbreak of salmonellosis on the East Coast, the U.S. Department of Agriculture and the federal Food and Drug Administration recommend avoiding food containing raw eggs.

Preparing the Hazelnuts

Spread shelled hazelnuts in a shallow pan and roast in a 275°F. oven for 20–30 minutes, until skins crack, or roast in the microwave. To remove skins, rub nuts while warm with a rough cloth or between your hands.

How to Microwave Hazelnuts

Place the hazelnuts in a single layer in a microwave-safe dish and microwave on High for 3–4 minutes.

Sliced Tomatoes
with Horseradish Cream

Bohemian Horseradish

In the early 1950s, Berten Hoyle was sent by the University of California at Davis to Tule Lake to develop new crops for small farms in this remote area in northeastern California. Just at that time there was a world-wide horseradish short-age and since the Tule Lake basin was at the same latitude as Silver Lake, Wisconsin, and St. Louis, Missouri, the two major horseradish regions in America, he decided to try growing it. He planted a test garden with different varieties, but soon dis-covered horseradish growing wild alongside the railroad track and in some of the sur-rounding fields. The wild horseradish had

~~~>

When I buy fresh horseradish I like to mix it with sour cream. It can be easily chopped in a blender or food processor with ice cubes. The ice keeps the hot mustard oils from forming and it can be removed afterward by straining through a colander.

4 servings

4	*butter lettuce leaves*
2	*tomatoes, cut into slices*
2	*teaspoons homemade or commercial cream-style horseradish*
¼	*teaspoon salt*
⅛	*teaspoon white pepper*
½	*cup heavy cream, whipped*

Line 4 salad plates with the lettuce leaves. Arrange 2–3 tomato slices on each plate and set aside.

Stir the horseradish, salt, and white pepper into the whipped cream. Spoon a hefty dollop of the Horseradish Cream over the sliced tomatoes. Chill until serving time.

Garlic Stir-Fry Spinach

For a quick and easy vegetable I often stir-fry tender young spinach leaves. They keep their brilliant emerald-green color and fresh flavor and need only a pinch of salt before they're served.

4 servings

  1 *tablespoon corn oil*
  1 *whole garlic clove, crushed*
 10 *ounces fresh young spinach, rinsed and
      patted dry with paper towels
      Pinch of salt
      Freshly ground pepper*

Heat the oil in a sauté pan. Add the garlic and spinach and stir over high heat until the spinach is hot and starts to wilt, about 30 seconds. Discard the garlic clove and season the spinach with salt and pepper. Serve immediately.

been brought to this community by early Czechoslovakian settlers, and this strain, planted alongside the domestic test varieties, soon proved to be the best one. He named it Tule Lake # 1 in 1953 and today this region is one of the major horse-radish-producing areas in the United States.

Shoichiro Katsuno delivering produce from his farm in Pontiac, Washington

Golden Chanterelle Griddlecakes

Jerry Larson, head of international trade with Korea for the Oregon Department of Agriculture, is called Dr. Musatake or Dr. Mushroom by the Koreans. He is one of the leading mycologists in the Pacific Northwest. He is also a professional gemologist and, in his spare time, travels around the United States with his wife competing in ballroom dancing. He graciously gave me his wife's favorite chanterelle recipe.

4 servings

2 *pounds chanterelle mushrooms,*
   cleaned and finely chopped
2 *tablespoons olive oil*
1 *egg*
½ *teaspoon salt*
¼ *cup half-and-half*

Put the mushrooms in a bowl and add 1 tablespoon oil, the egg, salt, and half-and-half and mix well. Heat the remaining tablespoon oil in a frying pan and drop the batter from a spoon, making 4 patties. Cook them 6–8 minutes on each side. Turn the heat to medium-low and cook, uncovered, for 10 minutes. Turn the griddle cakes over and cook them another 10 minutes, or until they are crisp like hash brown potatoes.

Fresh Morels Simmered in Cream

The conical-shaped morel mushrooms are indigenous to
the Pacific Northwest and start to appear in local markets
at the beginning of May. I haven't found store-bought
morels dirty, but occasionally grit can work its way into
their many convolutions. To clean them, brush the
mushrooms with a damp brush. If that doesn't work,
quickly rinse them under cold running water and blot
the mushrooms dry with paper towels. These intensely
flavored fungi are generally considered the most delect-
able of all the wild mushrooms. They have a natural
affinity for cream and can be served as a main course
over toast or as an accompaniment, spooned over grilled
beef, lamb, or sautéed venison.

4 servings

 3   *tablespoons butter*
 2   *shallots, peeled and minced*
 1   *pound fresh morels, trimmed and sliced vertically*
 1   *cup homemade beef stock*
     or reduced-sodium canned beef broth
 ½   *cup heavy cream*
 ⅛   *teaspoon salt*
     Freshly ground pepper

Heat the butter in a sauté pan and add the shallots. Sauté
for 5 minutes, until the shallots start to soften. Add the
rest of the ingredients and cook over moderately high
heat until the sauce thickens, about 10 minutes. Season
with salt and freshly ground pepper.

*A Warning
about Morels*

*Morels should never be
eaten raw, and some
people may experience
an upset stomach if they
eat morels while drink-
ing alcoholic beverages.*

Stuffed Tomatoes
with Orzo and Fresh Chives

Truck Gardens

*Truck gardens were
everywhere at the turn
of the century in the
Pacific Northwest.
Large plots of land were
used to grow vegetables
and the vegetables were
transported by truck to
the metropolitan areas.
The huge gardens were
managed by the
Chinese, Italian, and
Japanese immigrants.
Tats Yada, an onion
farmer in the Willam-
ette Valley, remembers
his father's (Jim Yada's)
truck garden and those
early-morning trips to
the wholesale market in
Portland: "The grocers
would come in and buy
right off the truck and
what was left went to
the wholesale house. A
lot of peddlers came, too,
and bought from us and
they would go from
neighborhood to neigh-*

In recent years in the Pacific Northwest, summertime restaurant menus featuring Italian cuisine have offered pasta tossed with fresh garden tomatoes and a fruity olive oil. I have done just the reverse in the following recipe by putting the pasta inside the tomatoes. I use orzo, a small pasta that resembles long-grain white rice. It can be purchased at most grocery stores and it takes only about 10 minutes to cook. It can be seasoned with any herb, but in the springtime I use the first shoots of fresh chives from my garden. This recipe will work with less-than-perfect tomatoes—just scoop out all of the pithy cavity with a serrated grapefruit spoon and increase the stuffing.

4 servings

1½   *pounds tomatoes (6 medium)*
  2   *cups homemade chicken stock
      or reduced-sodium canned chicken broth*
  2   *cups water*
 ½   *cup orzo (substitute 2 cups cooked long-grain
      white rice or a mixture of brown and wild rice
      if orzo is not available)*
  2   *tablespoons chopped fresh chives*
 ½   *teaspoon salt*
  4   *ounces mild goat cheese or light cream cheese*

Preheat the oven to 350°F.

Remove the stem end of each tomato and, holding the tomato in the palm of your hand, turn it upside down and squeeze and shake it at the same time to remove most of the seeds. Sprinkle the cavities with salt and place the tomatoes upside down on a paper towel to drain.

Heat the chicken stock and water to boiling and add the orzo. Bring the liquid back to a boil and cook for 9–10 minutes, or until the pasta is tender. Drain and let cool for 10 minutes. Put the cooked pasta in a bowl and stir in the chives and salt. Crumble 2 ounces of the goat cheese and toss it with the pasta.

Arrange the tomatoes in a shallow baking dish and equally divide the filling among them. Cut the remaining goat cheese into 6 equal pieces and place 1 slice on top of each tomato. Cover the dish with foil and bake the tomatoes for 30 minutes.

Microwave Instructions:

Cover the stuffed tomatoes with plastic wrap and microwave on High for about 2–3 minutes.

burhood, selling produce. These were Japanese, Chinese, Italian, and Caucasian truck farmers and we all worked together. At times, when we had a lot to haul to Portland, we would help one another. Before the war some of the farmers took produce to their own stall at the Yamhill Market, too, where they sold it directly to the public."

Chinese vegetable gardens at the present site of the Multnomah Athletic Club, Portland, Oregon, before 1909

Corn on the Cob with Basil Butter

Green Corn Cakes

18 ears green corn,
grated
2 cups milk
2 cups flour
1 teaspoon salt
2 teaspoons baking
powder
4 eggs

Stir all the ingredients
together and fry on a
griddle.

—The Web-Foot Cook
Book (Portland, Oregon:
W. B. Ayer and Company,
1885).

⌗

Portland Farmer's
Cooperative Market

This is a wonderful way to serve perfectly seasoned corn on the cob and the butter can be made days in advance. There is enough salt in the butter and cheese to adequately flavor the corn. You may want to add a sprinkling of freshly ground pepper at the table.

4 servings

4 tablespoons soft butter (¼ cup)
¼ cup fresh basil leaves
¼ cup grated Parmesan cheese
4 ears of corn, shucked

Combine the butter, basil leaves, and Parmesan cheese in a blender or food processor and process until well mixed. Put the corn in a pot of cold water and bring it to a boil. When the water starts to boil the corn is done. Serve the corn in individual corn-on-the-cob dishes if you have them. (They help keep the herb butter on the corn and not all over the dinner plate.) If not, put the basil butter in a small crock to accompany the corn on the cob.

Steamed Broccoli
with Washington Gouda Cheese

Fresh broccoli, harvested in the Willamette Valley from
June through December, is delicious steamed. It retains
its brilliant emerald-green color and the florets stay
perfectly crisp. I like to serve it simply, seasoned with
fresh basil and lightly covered with cheese. The cheese is
higher in protein and lower in butterfat than most
cheeses and it won't melt down into the vegetables but
forms a soft layer on top.

4 servings

4   ounces Gouda cheese, grated
¼   cup Parmesan cheese, grated
2   tablespoons fresh basil, chopped
2   tablespoons butter or corn oil margarine
1   medium bunch fresh broccoli, trimmed and
     cut into florets

Stir the Gouda cheese, Parmesan cheese, basil, and butter
together and set aside.

Bring a small amount of water to boil in the bottom
of a steamer. Put the steaming tray in and add the
broccoli. Cover and steam the florets until they are barely
tender. Remove the steaming tray with the broccoli and
set aside.

Pour the water out of the bottom of the steamer and
put it back on the burner. Turn the heat to low.

Transfer the steamed broccoli to the bottom of the
steamer. Spread the cheese mixture over the broccoli and
cover with a lid. Heat for 2–3 minutes, or until the
cheese begins to melt.

Sage Advice

The Web-Foot Cook
Book, *printed in
Oregon in 1885, was a
collection of recipes
gathered by the San
Grael Society of the
First Presbyterian
Church of Portland and
it offered this advice for
cooking fresh vegetables:*

*"Always try and secure
them as fresh as possible
and see that they are
carefully looked over
and kept in cold water
for several hours before
cooking. The water
for boiling vegetables
should always boil
before your vegetables
are put in the kettle."*

Walla Walla Sweet Onion Rings in Beer Batter

I seldom deep-fry foods, but when the Walla Walla Sweets are ripe, summer just wouldn't be the same if I didn't make onion rings at least once. Any of the sweet onions, such as the Maui onions or the Vidalias, can be substituted in this recipe. The light and airy onion rings make a perfect foil for barbecued steaks.

4 servings

1½   cups flour
 1   can beer (12 ounces)
      Pinch of salt
 2   cups corn oil
 1   pound Walla Walla Sweet onions,
      cut into ½-inch-thick rings

Make the batter by stirring 1 cup flour, the beer, and salt together. Cover the bowl with plastic wrap and let it set at room temperature for 2 hours.

Fold a piece of newspaper to fit a large platter and cover it with paper towels. Set aside.

Heat the oil to medium hot. Dredge a few rings at a time in the remaining ½ cup flour, dip them into the batter, and put them immediately into the hot oil. Fry the rings until they turn a rich golden brown, about 30 seconds. Carefully remove them from the hot grease with tongs and drain them on the prepared platter. Cover the cooked rings with paper towels to keep them warm. Serve immediately when all the rings are cooked.

Harvesting onions before automation

Grilled Walla Walla Sweets with Fresh Lemon Thyme

Grilled Walla Walla Sweets are standard fare at our cabin in the Cascade Mountains. During the summer months I keep a twenty-five-pound sack of them, hung on a nail in a dark but airy kitchen closet, for our weekend visits. The lemon thyme I planted at the base of a Douglas fir tree several years ago has usually surfaced by this time of the year and I always have olive oil and butter on hand. The secret of this recipe is not to cut the onion slices too thin or they will fall apart.

4 servings

> 2   *tablespoons mild olive oil*
> 1   *tablespoon butter or corn oil margarine, melted*
> 2   *teaspoons chopped fresh lemon thyme*
> ⅛   *teaspoon kosher salt*
> 1   *pound Walla Walla Sweet onions, or any sweet onion, peeled and cut into 1-inch horizontal slices*

Stir the olive oil, butter, chopped lemon thyme, and salt together. Brush the mixture on one side of the onions and lay them, buttered side down, on the grill. Butter the tops of the onion slices and continue cooking, and occasionally brushing with butter, until the onions are just barely tender, about 20 minutes. Don't turn them over, as they tend to fall apart.

Farmers' markets were popular throughout the Pacific Northwest in the early 1900s. Japanese Market, Tacoma, 1925.

Pureed Parsnips and Potatoes

*The Root
Festival*

*Many Pacific North-
west Indian tribes still
celebrate the arrival of
the first plants with edible roots in the spring-
time with a Root
Festival. The following
story on the origin of the
Root Festival was told
by Chief Jobe Charley,
a Wasco Indian on the
Yakima Reservation,
Washington:*

*"Long ago, our people
went up to the sky every
feasting time. There they
sang and danced and
gave thanks to the Great
Spirit for the roots and
berries on the earth.*

*"One time Speelyi,
the red fox, and Toop-
toop, his brother, went
up to the sky with the
people. All sang and
danced and prayed for
several days. Speelyi
became so tired that he
dropped down and fell
asleep. Finding him
and recognizing him,
the people threw him
down to earth, where he
belonged.*

*"His brother
Tooptoop kept on with
the thanksgiving cere-
mony. After a while he
thought of Speelyi down*

Parsnips have long been cherished as one of the most flavorful of root vegetables. They are usually boiled and served with butter. I like to cook them with potatoes, also a root (tuber), and a strip of bacon. After the vegetables are tender I puree them with the bacon, using my hand mixer, then simply season the dish with a dab of butter, salt, and freshly ground pepper.

3–4 servings

½   *pound parsnips, peeled and
     cut into 2-inch lengths (about 4 large)*
½   *pound russet potatoes, peeled
     and cut into eighths (1 large)*
1   *strip lean bacon, cut into fourths*
¼   *cup milk*
½   *teaspoon salt*
¼   *teaspoon freshly ground pepper*

Trim and scrape the parsnips and peel the potatoes. Put them in a pot with the bacon and cover with water. Cover the pan and boil until they are tender, about 10–12 minutes. Drain and put the contents in a bowl, if you are going to use a hand mixer, or in a blender or food processor. Add the milk, salt, and pepper and puree until the vegetables are just barely smooth.

Angelo Pellegrini's Braised Cardoons

The cardoons that were grown in the garden at Fort Vancouver in the 1800s were tall leafy plants, members of the same family as the artichoke; both of these vegetables are actually domesticated thistles. Only the lower portion of the cardoon, which resembles stalks of celery, is eaten. And, just like celery, it needs to be blanched to make it tender. This recipe is adapted from *Wine and the Good Life* by Angelo Pellegrini, who grows cardoons in his own garden in Seattle. They can be found in farmers' markets in the fall.

4 servings

½	*pound cardoon stalks*
2	*tablespoons olive oil*
1	*tablespoon butter*
1	*strip bacon, cut into thin slices*
3	*shallots or 3 tablespoons chopped onion*
2	*garlic cloves, minced*
	Leaf tips of 1 celery stalk, chopped
⅓	*cup tomato sauce*
⅓	*cup homemade chicken stock or beef stock, or reduced-sodium canned chicken or beef broth*
	Juice of half a lemon
2–3	*drops Tabasco sauce or 1 small chili pepper (optional)*
¼	*cup freshly grated Parmesan cheese*

Blanch ½ pound cardoon stalks in boiling water until they are tender. Drain and mince. Set aside.

Heat the olive oil and butter and sauté the bacon, shallots, garlic, and celery slowly over low heat until the onions start to brown. Add the tomato sauce and stock or broth, lemon juice, and optional Tabasco sauce. Simmer for a few minutes and add the minced cardoon. Just before serving, sprinkle with Parmesan cheese.

on the earth and went to him with some bitter-root, camas, huckle-berries, and salmon. Speelyi had a big feast.

"When he had eaten all he could eat, Speelyi raised his hand to the east and made a new law. 'My people, no more will you go up to the sky to feast and to give thanks. Many new people are coming to our land, and so we cannot do all that we are used to doing. We must share with our new friends. We must learn to bear our hardships and our sorrows as best we can.

"'I am going to put bitterroot and camas and other roots in differ-ent parts of the country. You will have feasts here every year. When you begin to dig the roots in the spring, you will sing and dance and give thanks to the Great Spirit. You need not travel up to the sky for that. And as you dig the roots, you will sing songs of thanksgiving. Your children will learn the songs from you.'"

—From Ella E. Clark, Indian Legends of the Pacific Northwest *(Berkeley, California: University of California Press, 1953).*

Great Northern Bean Salad with Smoked Salmon

I like to serve this salad in a black, shallow bowl. It shows off the white beans, accented by the colorful pieces of salmon and the bright green Italian flat-leaf parsley.

4 servings

½	*pound Great Northern beans*
4	*cups homemade chicken stock or reduced-sodium canned chicken broth*
2	*cups water*
¼	*cup olive oil*
2	*teaspoons balsamic vinegar*
1	*teaspoon lemon juice*
½	*teaspoon salt*
4	*ounces smoked salmon fillets, skin and gray fatty meat removed, diced*
½	*cup chopped green onions*
¼	*cup Italian flat-leaf parsley*
2	*heaping teaspoons capers, drained*

The favorite (Swinomish) method of preparing fresh salmon is to cut it into squares about the size of the hand, then impale it on a stick. Six to eight pieces are put on one stick. No seasoning other than a little salt is used.

Rinse the beans and cover with water. Bring them to a boil and boil for 3 minutes. Turn the heat off and let the beans stand, covered, for 1 hour. Drain and discard the soaking liquid. Add the chicken stock and 2 more cups of water. Bring the beans to a boil, reduce to simmer, and cook until the beans are tender. Drain.

Whisk the olive oil, vinegar, lemon juice, and salt together and toss with the beans while the beans are still hot.

Add the salmon, onions, parsley, and capers and carefully blend with the beans.

Palouse Lentil Salad
with Chicken and Rice

Unlike beans, lentils do not need to be soaked before cooking, so this salad is quick and easy to throw together. I find it tastes best a day or two after it is made.

6 servings

1	cup basmati rice or long-grain white rice
1	cup lentils, rinsed and drained
1	quart homemade chicken stock
	or reduced-sodium canned chicken broth
1½	cups plain low-fat yogurt
1	heaping tablespoon curry powder
½	cup chopped scallions or green onions
3	tablespoons peach chutney
¼	cup fresh cilantro, off the stem
12	ounces cooked boneless chicken breast,
	skinned and cut into bite-size pieces
	Salt to taste
¼	teaspoon pepper

Put the rice and lentils in a colander and rinse with cold water. Heat the chicken stock to boiling and add the rice and lentils. Cover and simmer for 15 minutes, or until the rice and lentils are cooked. The lentils should be slightly crunchy. Drain.

Scoop the rice-lentil mixture into a large bowl and let cool. Add the remaining ingredients, blend, and chill for several hours or overnight before serving.

Palouse

"Palouse," a French word meaning "green lawn," refers to the low, rolling hills of eastern Washington and northern Idaho which turn a brilliant pea-green in the spring. It's here, in the rich volcanic soils and crackling summer heat, that most of the lentils and dried peas in the United States are grown.

Baby Oak-Leaf Lettuce and Radicchio Salad with Fresh Crab

Local Cheese Makers

A growing number of small farmstead cheese makers produce a wide assortment of superb cow, goat, and sheep cheeses throughout the Pacific Northwest. Sally Jackson, who lives in Washington east of the Cascade Mountains, travels to Seattle every five to six weeks to sell her goat, cow, and sheep cheeses to restaurants and cheese shops. Glencorra Farm, a sheep dairy, is located on Lopez Island in Puget Sound. Recently I sampled their soft fresh farmstead cheese, which is similar in appearance and texture to chèvre but has an exceptionally mild flavor all its own. Many other rural cheese makers create an exceptional variety of farmstead cheeses that are flavored with herbs, smoked, or speckled with chiles.

New varieties of greens are constantly appearing in the market in the Pacific Northwest as well as in the rest of the nation. I am particularly fond of the colorful and delicate oak leaf lettuce, but if it is not available, substitute any tender young lettuce or spinach leaves or a mixture of both.

4 servings

1	small head oak-leaf lettuce, rinsed
1	small head radicchio
1	avocado, peeled and pitted
⅓	pound fresh crabmeat
3	tablespoons balsamic vinegar
1	tablespoon extra-virgin olive oil
½	teaspoon salt
¼	teaspoon freshly ground pepper

Tear the lettuce and radicchio into a clear glass salad bowl. Slice the avocado and add it to the salad with the fresh crab.

Whisk together the vinegar, olive oil, salt, and pepper and pour it over the salad.

Toss the greens and serve immediately.

Tossed Green Salad with Oregon Blue Cheese and Walnuts

Walnuts and locally produced Oregon Blue Cheese provide texture and flavor to a simple green salad. If you want to intensify the nutty flavor of the walnuts, toast them in a 275°F. oven for 20 minutes.

4 servings

     1   *head butter lettuce, rinsed and torn into bite-size pieces*
     4   *ounces walnuts, chopped*
     4   *ounces Oregon Blue Cheese, crumbled*
     ½   *red pepper, julienned*
     ½   *red onion, sliced into rings*
     ¼   *cup extra-virgin olive oil*
     ¼   *cup corn oil*
    3–4 *tablespoons red wine vinegar*
     ½   *teaspoon salt*
     ¼   *teaspoon freshly ground pepper*

Two Italian merchants at the Pike Place Market in Seattle after the gag rule was imposed in 1947, which forbids shouting, singing, or hollering to help sell goods

Put the greens, walnuts, cheese, red pepper, and onion in a salad bowl. Whisk the oils, vinegar, salt, and pepper together and pour over the lettuce. Toss the salad and serve immediately.

Spinach Salad with Honey–Sesame Seed Dressing

The following recipe comes from Joyce Ironsides, a friend and native Hawaiian. Although Hawaiians do not comprise a large part of the population in the Pacific Northwest, they were an integral part of its early history. Ships from the Orient often stopped in Hawaii on their way west to pick up Owyhees, or Hawaiian natives. The Owyhee River in eastern Oregon was named in 1819 after two Hawaiians who were sent by Donald McKenzie of the North West Fur Company down the river to explore it and never returned.

4 servings

6	*tablespoons corn oil*
2	*tablespoons honey*
2	*tablespoons cider vinegar*
2	*tablespoons Dijon mustard*
2	*tablespoons toasted sesame seeds*
1	*garlic clove, crushed*
½	*teaspoon salt*
¼	*teaspoon freshly ground pepper*
½	*pound young tender spinach leaves, rinsed and stemmed*
4	*scallions or green onions, trimmed and cut into small pieces*
1	*large orange, peeled and cut into ¼-inch slices*
4	*slices bacon, cooked until crisp and crumbled*

Blend the oil, honey, vinegar, mustard, sesame seeds, garlic, salt, and pepper together and set aside.

Tear the spinach into bite-size pieces in a salad bowl. Add the scallions, orange slices, and bacon and toss with the dressing.

Spinach and Mushroom Salad with Toasted Hazelnuts

Tender young spinach leaves make a refreshing change from lettuce in a salad. I marinate the mushrooms in olive oil and balsamic vinegar two to three days in advance before tossing them, and their marinade, with the spinach, which I do just before serving.

4 servings

- ¼ cup extra-virgin olive oil
  (or hazelnut oil, if you can find it)
- 1 tablespoon balsamic vinegar
- ½ teaspoon salt
- ¼ teaspoon freshly ground pepper
- ½ pound fresh commercial mushrooms, trimmed and sliced vertically into ¼-inch pieces (approximately 3 cups)
- ½ pound young tender spinach leaves, rinsed and stemmed (approximately 6 cups)
- 3 tablespoons coarsely chopped and toasted hazelnuts

Whisk the oil, vinegar, salt, and pepper together in a large bowl. Add the mushrooms and gently toss to coat each slice. Cover with plastic wrap and marinate for several hours, or overnight if possible. Tear the spinach leaves into a salad bowl and sprinkle with the toasted hazelnuts. Add the marinated mushrooms and the dressing and toss. Season with salt and pepper if necessary.

To Toast, Peel, and Chop Hazelnuts

Spread shelled hazelnuts in a shallow pan and roast in a 275°F. oven for 20–30 minutes, until the skins crack. Remove the skins by rubbing the nuts while warm with a rough cloth or between your hands. Chop the hazelnuts in a blender or food processor.

Microwave-Roasted Hazelnuts

Place the hazelnuts in a single layer in a microwave-safe dish and microwave on High for 3–4 minutes. Remove the skins by rubbing the nuts while warm with a rough cloth or between your hands. Chop the hazelnuts in a blender or food processor.

Mixed Greens with Raspberry Vinaigrette and Chèvre

Café Sport is one of my favorite Seattle restaurants. The chef, Diana Isaiou, gave me the following recipe, which combines the best of the Pacific Northwest—fresh greens, raspberries, hazelnuts, and a locally produced goat cheese. I buy the greens at the grocery store, where they are marketed as "wild greens." They are commercially grown and include wild and domestic varieties, such as watercress, dandelion greens, miner's lettuce, baby sorrel, and young lettuces.

4 servings

¼ cup mild olive oil
¼ cup corn oil
3 tablespoons raspberry vinegar
⅓ cup fresh raspberries, pureed and run through
    a sieve to remove the seeds
1 sprig fresh thyme, finely chopped
1 sprig fresh rosemary, finely chopped
½ teaspoon salt
    Coarsely ground pepper to taste
4 ounces chèvre
4 tablespoons roasted and chopped hazelnuts (see page 195)
6 cups mixed greens, such as young spinach leaves,
    butter lettuce, and green leaf lettuce
12 fresh raspberries
1 tablespoon calendula petals or 8 nasturtium flowers

Whisk the oils, raspberry vinegar, pureed raspberries, thyme, rosemary, salt, and pepper together.

Divide the chèvre into 4 equal portions. Roll each piece in the chopped hazelnuts and place them on a microwave-safe plate or baking dish. Set aside.

Arrange the greens on 4 chilled salad plates and sprinkle them with the fresh raspberries and calendula petals (or nasturtium flowers).

Microwave the nut-coated cheese for 15 seconds on High or bake for 5 minutes at 350°F. Carefully place a round of warm cheese on the side of one of the salad plates. Repeat for the other 3 salads.

Serve the salad dressing separately.

Wild Hazelnuts and Truffles

Hazelnut connoisseurs know Oregon for both its wild and domestic hazelnuts. The wild nuts, smaller than their domestic cousins, were gathered by the Native Americans and buried in a dry place to eat during the long winter months. The cultivated hazelnut tree is also being used to host the Oregon white truffle, which grows indigenously in the roots of second-growth Douglas fir trees in the Pacific Northwest.

Summer Fruit Salad
with Raspberry-Yogurt Dressing

When I put together a fruit salad I use flavorful fruits that make a pretty color combination. The low-fat dressing of yogurt and honey is flavored with rosewater.

4–6 servings

1	*pint fresh blueberries*
2	*bananas, peeled and thinly sliced*
2	*nectarines, pitted and thinly sliced*
½	*pint fresh blackberries or boysenberries*
2	*kiwi fruit, peeled and thinly sliced*
1	*pint fresh raspberries*
3	*tablespoons rosewater*
2	*tablespoons plain yogurt*
2	*teaspoons honey*
2	*sprigs fresh mint*

Layer the blueberries, bananas, nectarines, blackberries, kiwis, and all but 2 tablespoons of the raspberries in a glass bowl. Sprinkle the fruit with 2 tablespoons of rosewater.

In a small bowl, blend the remaining 2 tablespoons raspberries and rosewater with the yogurt and honey. Pour the dressing over the salad, garnish with fresh mint, and serve immediately.

Red Bartlett Pears Stuffed with Chèvre and Chopped Hazelnuts

Red Bartlett pears taste just the same as yellow pears so substitutions aren't a problem if you can't find them. Serve this salad as an accompaniment to roast pork or smoked pork chops, or cut the pears into quarters and serve them on a bed of lettuce as an appetizer.

4 servings

> 2   red Bartlett pears
> 1   thinly sliced lemon wedge
> ⅛ pound pepper-flavored chèvre
> 2   tablespoons milk
> 2   tablespoons roasted and finely chopped hazelnuts
>   (see page 195)
> 2   tablespoons chopped Italian flat-leaf parsley
> 1   tablespoon lemon juice
> 2   tablespoons olive oil
>   Pinch of salt
> 4   salad plates lined with butter lettuce

Core the pears and rub the inside of each with the lemon wedge. Stir together the chèvre, milk, hazelnuts, and chopped parsley.

Divide the mixture in half and stuff into each pear. Put the pears in the refrigerator to chill for 2–3 hours.

Make the dressing by whisking together the lemon juice, olive oil, and salt in a small bowl.

To serve, slice each pear in half with a sharp knife. Place each half, cut side up, on a lettuce leaf and ladle the dressing over the top.

Bartlett Pears

Oregon and Washington grow a third of the nation's Bartlett pears—the only summer pear because it needs two months of intense summer heat to reach maturity. Like other pears, it's picked before it is ripe and held in cold storage until its full flavor develops. The skin of the Bartlett turns yellow when ripe and the flesh is the most versatile of all the varieties. While it can be eaten fresh, poached, baked in pies, or made into preserves, it is most noted for its superb canning qualities. The firm flesh of the Bartlett enables it to retain its shape during the rigorous processing. Old cookbooks are loaded with good pear recipes and, as you can see, I use them frequently. I particularly love the preserved-pear recipe on page 237.

Creamy Potato Salad with Oregon Blue Cheese and Scallions

For this salad I use the smallest red new potatoes I can find—ideally about golf ball–size or smaller.

4 servings

1	*pound cooked red new potatoes (about 4 cups)*
1	*cup sour cream*
½	*cup plain yogurt*
½	*cup chopped green onions or scallions*
4	*ounces Oregon Blue Cheese, crumbled (½ cup)*
½–1	*teaspoon salt*
½	*teaspoon freshly ground pepper*

Toss all the ingredients together and store in the refrigerator for several hours or overnight.

Many of the Danish families who settled the Pacific Northwest started dairy farms and creameries with skills they knew from Denmark.

Country Potato Salad

White rose potatoes have a smooth, creamy texture similar to that of red new potatoes and they will become mushy if they are overcooked. I always buy potatoes that are approximately the same size so they will cook in the same amount of time.

4–6 servings

2½   *pounds cooked white rose potatoes, still warm*
2   *tablespoons corn oil*
1   *tablespoon red wine vinegar*
6   *hard-boiled eggs, peeled (discard 2 yolks) and coarsely chopped*
⅓   *cup chopped red onion*
¾   *cup commercial or Homemade Mayonnaise (recipe follows)*
½–¾   *teaspoon salt*
¼   *teaspoon pepper*
2   *tablespoons Italian flat-leaf parsley, stemmed*

As soon as the potatoes are cool enough to touch, peel and cut them into bite-size cubes. Sprinkle with the oil and vinegar and toss. Add the remaining ingredients and carefully blend the mixture together. Add more seasoning if necessary.

Homemade Mayonnaise
Makes 1½ cups

1   *egg*
1   *teaspoon red wine vinegar*
½   *teaspoon salt*
1   *cup corn oil*
½   *cup mild olive oil*

Place the egg, vinegar, and salt in the bowl of a food processor or blender and process for 30 seconds. With the machine still running, slowly add the two oils, drop by drop, until the mixture thickens.

A Warning about Salmonella

Due to a current outbreak of salmonellosis on the East Coast, the U.S. Department of Agriculture and the federal Food and Drug Administration recommend avoiding food containing raw eggs.

Grilled Red Pepper Salad

Red peppers flourish in the hot summer heat east of the Cascade Mountains. They're also known as pimientos, the Spanish name for peppers, and they're a favorite of the Basque people. Red peppers are easily charred over a grill and take on a subtle smoky flavor that seems to heighten their sweetness.

4 servings

3   large red bell peppers
¼   cup olive oil
2   garlic cloves, finely chopped
½   teaspoon whole dried oregano, crushed
    Pinch of salt
4   large lettuce leaves

Grill the red peppers on each side until they are scorched and begin to blister. (This can also be done over a gas flame in the kitchen or on a broiler rack, placed 4 inches from the broiler.) Immediately put the hot peppers in a plastic bag, seal it, and allow them to steam for 5 minutes. Peel the peppers under cold running water and remove the stem and all the seeds and membranes. Drain the peppers and slice them into 1-inch slices.

Heat the oil over low heat until it is warm. Add the garlic, peppers, oregano, and salt. Remove from heat. Let the peppers marinate for several hours.

Arrange the lettuce leaves on a dinner plate and, with a slotted spoon, transfer the peppers to the serving dish.

Angel-Hair Pasta Salad with Shrimp, Sugar Snap Peas, and Sesame Chili Oil

This recipe draws its ingredients from many cuisines—the Basque, Chinese, and Italian. All the ingredients are available at the supermarket, including the hot, spicy sesame chili oil. I use just a small amount in this dish to give the mild-tasting pasta a pleasing bite. I like to make this salad several days in advance to allow the flavors to meld.

4–6 servings

½   *pound medium-size shrimp*
3   *quarts water*
4   *ounces angel-hair pasta*
5   *colossal Spanish olives, sliced ¼ inch thick*
2   *ounces sugar snap peas*
2   *ounces red pepper, cut into thin strips*
3   *tablespoons fresh cilantro, stemmed*
¼   *cup sesame chili oil*
½   *teaspoon salt*
¼   *teaspoon freshly ground pepper*

Two Chinese boys posing for their picture at the Oregon State Fair

Put the shellfish in a saucepan and cover with water. Turn the heat to medium-high and cook the shrimp for 3–4 minutes, or until their shells turn a bright pink. Drain and shell.

Bring 3 quarts of water to a boil and cook the pasta for 45–60 seconds. Drain.

Put the shrimp, pasta, and the remaining ingredients in a large bowl and toss. Refrigerate for several hours or overnight before serving.

McCormick's Hot Seafood Salad

Scallops

Scallop lovers are blessed with a variety of scallops to choose from in the Northwest: There is the flavorful Weathervane sea scallop—the largest commercial scallop—found off the coast of Oregon all the way to Alaska; the petite Oregon bay scallop, harvested from the local coastal bays in Oregon; and the pink and spiny scallop—marketed as the "singing scallop"—which comes from the Pacific waters of Washington and British Columbia. Although the industry is small, fresh scallops are readily available at fish markets year-round unless there is a red tide. One scallop that you won't see in the fish markets, and this is a pity, is the purple-hinged rock scallop—the largest Pacific Northwest scallop, measuring up to six inches —which is not harvested commercially.

This recipe comes from McCormick's Fish House and Bar in Portland. It takes just minutes to prepare once all the ingredients are assembled and makes a complete meal in itself served with crusty French bread and a chilled bottle of white wine.

2 servings

3–4   *cups torn greens (3 parts head lettuce to 1 part romaine, green leaf, and red leaf—reserve several green leaf or red leaf leaves for garnish)*

  1   *tablespoon corn oil or 1 ounce bacon drippings*

2–3   *ounces white or yellow onion, peeled and cut into julienne strips*

3–4   *ounces zucchini, cut into julienne strips*

  4   *meaty slices bacon, cooked until crisp, drained, and crumbled*

  1   *teaspoon salt*

 ½   *teaspoon white pepper*

  3   *ounces bay or sea scallops*
      Dash of lemon juice

  1   *whole tomato, chopped*

  3   *ounces bay shrimp*

 ¼   *cup grated Parmesan cheese*

  2   *sprigs parsley*

  2   *lemon wedges*

Equally divide the torn greens between 2 dinner plates and set aside.

Heat a pan with the oil and add the onion, zucchini, and cooked bacon. Sauté for 1 minute and season with salt and white pepper. Add the scallops and sauté for another minute, sprinkling with a dash of lemon juice. Add the chopped tomato and shrimp and sauté for 20–30 seconds.

Arrange the hot seafood mixture over the torn greens. Sprinkle with Parmesan cheese and garnish with reserved lettuce leaves, sprigs of parsley, and the lemon wedges.

Pacific Northwest Indian baskets from the Oregon State Historical Society collection

Coupeville Mussel Salad

Whidbey Island

Pastoral Whidbey Island is a tranquil getaway north of Seattle and a weekend favorite for food lovers in the Pacific Northwest. Many of the restaurants and markets feature the island's fresh produce and seafood, and local smokehouses operate most of the year. From July through September there are also U-Pick farms and roadside stands that sell everything from herbs and vegetables to fresh raspberries and strawberries. At Whidbey's Greenbank Farm, Whidbey's Liqueur is made from the island's famous loganberries, and local

Coupeville, Washington, a quaint village on Whidbey Island in northern Puget Sound, is the home of the Penn Cove Mussel Farm. It is owned and operated by the Jefferd brothers, and the following recipe was inspired by a similar dish they served on a recent visit.

4 servings

2   *pounds mussels, beards removed*
3   *cups water*
½   *cup mild olive oil*
1   *tablespoon rice vinegar*
¼   *teaspoon salt*
½   *cup red bell pepper, cut into thin strips*
6   *slices red onion, peeled and with rings separated*
¼   *cup flat-leaf parsley, stemmed*

Scrub the mussels under cold running water. Pour the water into the bottom half of a steamer and place it over medium-high heat. Fill the top half of the steamer with mussels. Cover and steam until they pop open, about 3–4 minutes. Discard any mussels that do not open.

In a large mixing bowl whisk the olive oil, vinegar, and salt together. Toss the hot, cooked mussels with the dressing, red pepper strips, and onion rings. Put the salad in the refrigerator and marinate it for 3–4 hours or overnight. Sprinkle with the parsley and toss immediately before serving.

Microwave Instructions:

Microwave the mussels uncovered in a shallow dish on Medium-High for 30 seconds. Whisk the olive oil, rice vinegar, and salt together and pour over the hot mussels. Add the red pepper strips and onion rings, toss, and marinate overnight, or for 3–4 hours. Sprinkle with the parsley and toss immediately before serving.

Pasta Salad with Shrimp and Three Peppers

The terms "shrimp" and "prawns" are used interchangeably, with "prawn" usually referring to a large shrimp. I like to toss shrimp, pasta, and colorful bell peppers in a garlicky salad dressing. It makes a versatile salad that can be eaten either hot or cold, and it looks pretty when served in a glass salad bowl.

4–6 servings

½	*pound medium-size shrimp*
½	*pound rotelle pasta (3 cups)*
3	*tablespoons olive oil*
2	*teaspoons balsamic vinegar*
1	*garlic clove, crushed*
1	*teaspoon salt*
½	*teaspoon freshly ground black pepper*
¼	*red bell pepper, seeded and julienned*
¼	*yellow bell pepper, seeded and julienned*
¼	*dark purple bell pepper, seeded and julienned*
½	*cup Greek black olives*
¼	*cup fresh basil leaves, coarsely chopped*

Put the shrimp in a saucepan and cover with water. Turn the heat to medium-high and cook the shellfish for 3–4 minutes, or until their shells turn a bright pink. Drain, remove the shells, and set aside.

Bring 3 quarts of salted water to a boil in a large pot. Add the pasta, bring the water back to a boil, and cook 12–15 minutes, or until the pasta is tender. Drain.

Whisk the olive oil, balsamic vinegar, crushed garlic, salt, and pepper together. Put the pasta in a large bowl and toss with the dressing. Combine the pasta with the rest of the ingredients and chill 3–4 hours or overnight.

eateries sell slices of freshly baked loganberry pie. But Whidbey Island was not always the peaceful sanctuary it is today. In the early 1920s, Puget Sound, with its extensive shoreline and many bays and rivers, was a haven for log pirates. One of the most notorious was "High-Pockets" Peterson, who, it is rumored, used Whidbey Island as one of his hideouts.

Artichoke Heart
and Salmon Salad with Capers

This is a great way to use leftover salmon—especially if it has been grilled and has a slightly smoky taste to it.

Makes 3 cups

2 cups cooked salmon, skinned, boned,
  and broken into bite-size pieces
½ cup sweet red Italian onion, coarsely chopped
2 teaspoons capers, drained
½ cup drained and coarsely chopped
  marinated artichoke hearts
¼ cup mayonnaise
1 tablespoon fresh lemon juice
1 teaspoon fresh dill, chopped, or ½ teaspoon dried dill
  Salt and freshly ground pepper to taste

Mix all the ingredients together in a large bowl. Serve with a loaf of crusty French bread and a small bowl of sweet pickles.

Beach seining with horses was just one of the salmon fishing methods used on the Columbia River by the Indians and early settlers.

208

Zenon Café Caesar Salad

The Zenon Café in Eugene, Oregon, consistently has a creative and innovative menu. Here is their chef's version of the classic Caesar salad, Pacific Northwest–style. I serve it with tomato wedges and steamed asparagus spears. If the dressing is covered, it will keep up to two weeks in the refrigerator.

4 servings

3	*ounces smoked salmon*
1	*egg*
1	*cup grated Parmesan cheese*
1½	*teaspoons dry mustard*
2	*teaspoons black pepper*
1	*teaspoon salt*
⅓	*cup buttermilk*
2	*tablespoons lemon juice*
3	*garlic cloves, peeled*
2	*tablespoons red wine vinegar*
1	*cup olive oil*
1	*large head romaine lettuce*
1	*cup croutons*

Blend the smoked salmon, egg, ½ cup grated Parmesan cheese, dry mustard, black pepper, salt, buttermilk, lemon juice, garlic, vinegar, and olive oil together in a food processor or blender.

Tear the lettuce into a bowl and toss with enough salad dressing to coat each piece. Sprinkle with the croutons and toss again. Serve the remaining ½ cup Parmesan cheese as an accompaniment.

The Camas Lily

After dried salmon, the camas lily was the most widely traded food of the Indians. Its root was baked and eaten fresh or left to dry in the hot sun. Lewis and Clark brought Thomas Jefferson a bulb of the Columbian lily, a cousin of the camas, which can still be found growing in the flower gardens of Monticello.

Hunting: A Way of Life

Hunting has been a way of life in the Pacific Northwest since man first inhabited this wild and rugged corner of the United States. Game meant a constant supply of food, hides for shelter and clothing, and a source of sinew, used in the construction of weapons. The animals were equally important in the Indians' religion because they were considered powerful guardian spirits (see "Plain Feather," page 214).

The abundant game helped feed the wagonloads of pioneers who arrived in the Willamette Valley throughout the long, damp first winter, before crops could be planted and when domestic animals were scarce. As time passed, towns were settled and the fertile valleys of the Pacific Northwest provided the newcomers with an ample supply of fruits, vegetables, nuts, and berries. Soon herds of cattle arrived from California and man became less dependent on game for existence. But among city dwellers, hunting became a popular sport, and hunting parties, including both men and women—and often their Chinese cooks—would travel to the mountains in search of deer and elk.

The rural areas, however, at the turn of the century still depended on game as a food source. Venison was either cured by salting and smoking or processed in jars, submerged in a canning kettle, over a hot wood stove.

While most of us now store game in our freezer instead of canning it, we still cook game using the same basic methods as earlier generations. My favorite way to cook venison, for example, is to flour steaks seasoned with salt and freshly ground pepper, and fry them in hot oil until they're medium rare throughout. I have included thirteen game recipes in this chapter that I enjoy, but if I were to eat venison only once a year, I would cook it simply, as stated above.

HANDLING GAME

SAUTÉED ELK STEAKS WITH FRESH MORELS OR CHANTERELLES IN CREAM

VENISON STEAK WITH SHERRY AND BRANDY

VENISON STEW WITH HAM HOCKS AND BLACK BEANS

SAUTÉED VENISON WITH POLENTA AND HUNTSMAN CHEESE

PACIFIC NORTHWEST GAME STEW

BAKED PHEASANT WITH MORELS, PEACHES, AND CREAM

SMOKED QUAIL WITH RASPBERRY-MUSTARD SAUCE

SPINACH SALAD WITH SAUTÉED WILD DUCK AND TOASTED WALNUTS

GAME BIRDS KUNG PAO

HICKORY-FLAVORED VENISON BREAKFAST SAUSAGE

VENISON SAUSAGE WITH MORELS AND FRESH THYME

PHEASANT SAUSAGE WITH LEMON GRASS AND FRESH GINGER

HOMEMADE PEPPERED BACON

Handling Game

A Hunter's Delight

"Then we started down the hill, he with the large animal and I with the small one. In time we reached the horses, on which we lashed the carcasses. Then we led the horses to the hill, where we loaded both deer on one horse, and rode home ourselves on the other, getting home at dark. The early morning of the next day was spent in skinning and salting the meat. Then, taking two larger hams, we lost no time in riding over to father's for dinner, eager to tell and talk over our hunting exploit. We well know how much mother and father would enjoy the juicy steaks from those toothsome hams. Good coffee, hot buttermilk biscuits or corn bread and fried venison with cream gravy and potatoes, was the favorite breakfast (or any other meal) of the southern man, and

Careful handling of game in the field is essential for successful game cookery. As soon as possible after the kill, the animal is bled and eviscerated. This allows the animal to cool as quickly as possible, decreasing the chances of spoilage from harmful bacteria. Most hunters keep several clean deer bags and a spreader bar at the hunting camp. After the field-dressed deer has been packed back to the hunting camp, the spreader bar, which is attached to a rope, is inserted between the bone and tendon in each hind leg, enabling the carcass to be easily hung from a limb. The deer is skinned and enclosed in the deer bag to keep it free of dirt and insects during the ride home.

Many hunters take the animal directly to a butcher shop, where it is cut and wrapped for the freezer. The carcass is hung in a cold-storage room, held at a temperature below 40° F. for about five days to age. The hanging allows time for the animal's cells to break down, releasing enzymes into the surrounding tissue which tenderize and improve the flavor of the meat.

When the animal is butchered, removal of all the fat and bones will yield the finest-tasting meat. The fat of wild deer is unpleasant tasting and great care should be taken to trim all of it from the meat. The bones also add a strong "gamey" flavor and should be discarded.

We butcher our own deer and cut the meat up, labeling it under three different categories: steaks, cut one-half inch thick from the backstrap, hams, and shoulder; stew meat, from the neck, shank, and small pieces of ham and shoulder, cut into one-inch cubes; and scrap meat cut off the neck and ribs that I use for making sausage, mincemeat, and jerky. All the meat is double-wrapped in butcher paper in one-pound packages and stored in the freezer. Because venison is so lean, it can be frozen for at least a year or more without losing any flavor.

It's not a general practice in the Pacific Northwest to hang game birds, but if you choose to do so, hang them unplucked, drawn or undrawn, in a cool place. Hanging the birds intensifies their flavor and helps to tenderize the meat, the same as for large game animals. Game birds are drawn and picked at home (unless "home" is more than several hours away) as soon as possible after the kill. Once they're plucked the fine down is singed with a slow-burning flame from a rolled piece of newspaper. The stubborn pin feathers need to be removed, too, but they are easily pulled out with an inexpensive strawberry plucker, available at most kitchen specialty stores (buy two because when strawberry season rolls around you won't be able to find it). After the birds are completely plucked, I turn them upside down to drain on a paper towel before double-wrapping them in freezer paper. They will keep stored in the freezer for up to one year.

Many hunters prefer to simply skin or breast the birds instead of taking the time to pluck them. To protect the exposed meat, skinned birds and breast meat should be wrapped in plastic wrap before being double-wrapped in freezer paper.

a hunter's delight. My mother was a cook worthy of her name."

—From Cathy Luchetti, in collaboration with Carol Olivell, Women of the West—*excerpt from journal of Dr. Bethenia Owens-Adair (St. George, Utah: Antelope Island Press, 1982).*

Pacific Northwest hunting party with their Chinese cook

Sautéed Elk Steaks with Fresh Morels or Chanterelles in Cream

Plain Feather

"In the days of our grandfathers, a young warrior named Plain Feather lived near Mount Hood. His guardian spirit was a great elk. The great elk taught Plain Feather so well that he became the most skillful hunter in his tribe and always knew the best places to look for every kind of game."

—*From Ella Clark,* Indian Legends of the Pacific Northwest, *"The Elk Spirit of Lost Lake" (Berkeley, California: University of California Press, 1953).*

The pioneers often ate fried venison with cream gravy and biscuits for breakfast. I have developed a more sophisticated version of their simple concept by cooking morels in cream first and then serving this light brown sauce over elk steaks, which are cooked to a tender medium-rare. If you're given a package of venison, deer, or elk, and you don't know what to do with it (a comment I hear often), save it until April, when the morels are in season, or follow the same recipe and substitute chanterelle mushrooms in the fall.

4–6 servings

  2   *tablespoons butter*
 ½   *pound fresh morels or chanterelles or 2–3 ounces dried morels reconstituted, sliced, and ½ pound cultivated mushrooms, brushed clean and sliced vertically*
  1   *cup cream*
  1   *cup flour*
1¼ *teaspoons salt*
 ½   *teaspoon freshly ground pepper*
  2   *pounds elk or deer steaks*
  2   *tablespoons corn oil or mild olive oil*

Heat the butter in a skillet and sauté the morels for several minutes over medium heat. Pour in the cream and cook until the cream starts to thicken and turns a light brown, about 10 minutes.

Meanwhile, blend the flour, 1 teaspoon salt, and pepper together. Dredge the elk steaks in the flour mixture and set aside. Heat the oil to medium-hot and cook the elk steaks for 3–4 minutes on each side.

Season the morels with the remaining ¼ teaspoon of salt and serve them over the cooked elk steaks.

An Indian in the Columbia Gorge perched on a ledge with a shotgun

Venison Steak with Sherry and Brandy

Women, appropriately dressed in long dresses and hats, busily prepare a meal in this forest camp. Even today, food that is cooked outdoors still tastes better than the same food cooked inside.

The assertive flavor of venison is enhanced by this simple yet perfectly delicious sauce. The meat is cooked only until it's brown on the outside but pink in the center, taking just minutes. Because it's so simple, we often take along the ingredients for this recipe on hunting and camping trips. The meat and butter are always packed frozen and the sherry and brandy are premixed and stored in a small plastic container. The rest of the ingredients—salt, pepper, and oil—are a standard part of the camp kitchen.

4–6 servings

2 tablespoons corn oil
2 pounds venison steak or beef flank steak, sliced ½ inch thick
1 teaspoon salt
½ teaspoon freshly ground pepper
¼ cup dry sherry
2 tablespoons brandy
2 tablespoons butter

Heat the oil in a large skillet over medium-high heat. Arrange the meat in the pan and season with salt and pepper. Cook for 2 minutes on the first side, or until the juices start to accumulate on top of the meat. Turn the steaks and cook for another 2 minutes. Transfer the meat to a warm platter.

Put the pan back on the burner and add the sherry, brandy, and butter. Heat for another 1–2 minutes, scraping the bottom of the pan as the sauce cooks to loosen the caramelized juices. Pour the sauce over the meat (through a sieve first if so desired) and serve immediately.

Venison Stew with Ham Hocks and Black Beans

For those cooks who have venison stockpiled in their freezer yearly, it's always a challenge to find new ways to prepare it. This recipe pairs venison with ham hocks and the final result is a full-bodied stew that is remarkably flavorful.

6 servings

2	tablespoons corn oil
1	yellow onion, peeled and cut into eighths
1	pound meaty ham hocks, split
1½	pounds venison stew meat, cut into 1-inch cubes
2	cups cooked black beans or kidney beans
3	garlic cloves, crushed
2	teaspoons dried whole thyme, crushed
1	teaspoon salt
½	teaspoon freshly ground pepper
1	28-ounce can chopped and peeled tomatoes with juice
3	cups cooked basmati rice or long-grain white rice
½	cup sour cream
¼	cup fresh cilantro, stemmed

Preheat the oven to 350°F.

Heat the oil in a 5½-quart heavy pot. Brown the onions, ham hocks, and venison for 8–10 minutes. Stir in the beans, garlic, thyme, salt, pepper, and chopped tomatoes. Cover and bake for 2½ hours. Remove the lid and pull the meat away from the bone. Transfer the bones to a carving board and pick off any remaining meat. Discard the bone and return the meat scraps to the pot. Serve the stew over rice with a dollop of sour cream and a sprinkling of fresh cilantro leaves.

The Locomotive's Whistle

"A Siskiyou hunter, who bugled with a cow horn to disperse his 20 hounds after game, was much annoyed by the coming of the railroad, because his hounds, mistaking the locomotive's whistle for the horn, 'would wander on wild chases like the foolish after snipe.'"

—*From* Oregon: End of the Trail, *American Guide Series (Portland, Oregon: Binford & Mort, 1940).*

Sautéed Venison with Polenta and Huntsman Cheese

A weary hunter rests before packing his deer out of the woods.

Polenta, a cornmeal mush introduced to the Pacific Northwest by immigrants from northern Italy, is delicious with game. In this recipe I add crumbled Huntsman cheese to the polenta and it provides a sharp kick that is able to stand up to the robust flavor of the wild game. The venison is simply cooked and sauced with juices made from deglazing the pan with a small amount of brandy. Seasoned with salt and freshly ground pepper, it needs nothing else to enhance its fine flavor.

4 servings

	Polenta with Huntsman Cheese (see margin, page 95)
2	*tablespoons corn oil*
1½–2	*pounds venison steaks*
½	*cup flour*
¼	*teaspoon salt*
¼	*teaspoon freshly ground pepper*
¼	*cup brandy*

Make the polenta, cover, and keep warm.

Heat the oil in a heavy skillet until it is moderately hot. Flour the steaks and cook them in the hot oil, about 2 minutes a side. Season with salt and pepper while they are cooking.

Remove the cooked meat to a heated platter and add the brandy to the pan. Use a wooden spoon to loosen the caramelized juices on the bottom of the pan and stir them into the brandy. Pour over the meat (through a sieve if so desired) and serve immediately.

Variation:

Any type of fried potato goes particularly well with venison. Sometimes I cook leftover baked potatoes or steamed new potatoes, cut into thick ¼-inch slices, in a small amount of oil until the pieces are crispy on the outside and hot throughout. Another simple accompaniment is a giant potato pancake made with shredded potatoes. For this recipe it is necessary to have a large nonstick skillet. Heat a small amount of oil in the pan until it is hot and add about 3 cups shredded potatoes. Flatten the potatoes so they evenly cover the bottom of the pan and season with salt and pepper. Cook the patty for 5 minutes or until it is golden brown on the bottom. Flip the potatoes over, using two pancake turners if necessary, and cook for 5 more minutes. Cut into wedges and serve immediately.

Ralph Landon's Delux Barber Shop on opening day of deer season, 1933

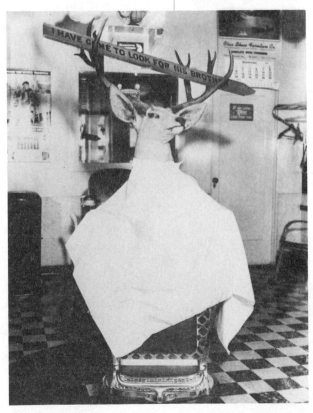

Pacific Northwest Game Stew

The French Canadians who first settled the Pacific Northwest as trappers for the Hudson's Bay Company loved to cook with dried beans. In this recipe I have paired Idaho's Great Northern beans with local game in a stew that's baked all in one dish in keeping with the French-Canadian heritage. It can be made with either wild or domestic birds, or a mixture of the two. If the birds are too large—often domestically raised geese are eight to ten pounds—I have the butcher cut them in half and I remove all the fatty skin when I get home. The skin on wild birds is removed as well, except for that of pheasant and quail. I add them last and place the pieces, skin side up, so they can brown when the lid is removed. This dish tastes even better reheated the second day.

6–8 servings

½   *pound Great Northern beans*
7   *cups homemade chicken stock or reduced-sodium canned chicken broth (three 14½-ounce cans)*
½   *pound fresh sausage, such as Polish or German (bratwurst)*
3   *large shallots, sliced (or ¼ cup chopped onion)*
     Large pinch saffron threads (optional)
1   *14½-ounce can peeled and diced tomatoes with juice*
4   *pounds fresh goose, skin and fat removed, cut up*
3   *pounds fresh duck, skin and fat removed, cut up*
1   *pound fresh pheasant, skin on, cut up*
6   *fresh whole quail, ready for cooking*

Soak the beans overnight in cold water. Discard the water and pour 6 cups of chicken stock over the beans. Bring the liquid to a boil, then reduce the heat to simmer and cook until the beans are tender, about 45 minutes to an hour. Drain the beans, reserving the cooking liquid.

Preheat the oven to 325°F.

Put the sausages in a skillet and add enough water to cover. Prick them and simmer for 6–8 minutes. Pour off the water and fry the sausages until they are brown on all sides. Drain on paper towels and cut each into 2-inch pieces.

Sauté the chopped shallots in the same pan for 3–4 minutes. Add the reserved cooking juices (about 1½ cups), remaining 1 cup chicken stock, optional crushed saffron threads, and tomatoes.

Put the beans in the bottom of a 5½-quart heavy baking dish with a lid. Lay the pieces of goose, duck, pheasant (skin side up), and sausage over the beans. Pour the shallot–chicken stock mixture over the game and cover.

Bake the stew for 2 hours. Remove the lid and arrange the quail on top of the stew. Bake, uncovered, 1 more hour.

Baked Pheasant with Morels, Peaches, and Cream

It's hard to beat this recipe for pheasant. The rosemary-flavored chicken stock keeps the bird's lean meat moist as it bakes, bringing out the best of its delicate flavor. It can be served after it's baked but I add cream and reduce it on top of the stove. Once the cream has thickened slightly, I add fresh peach slices and serve the pheasant, sauced, over brown and wild rice.

4 servings

½ cup flour
1 teaspoon salt
¼ teaspoon pepper
1 2–3-pound pheasant, cut into quarters
1 tablespoon corn oil
1 tablespoon butter
1 teaspoon chopped fresh rosemary
1½ cups homemade chicken stock or reduced-sodium canned chicken broth
3 ounces fresh or ½ ounce dried morels
1 cup cream
2 tablespoons peach brandy (optional)
2 fresh peaches, peeled, pitted, and sliced
    Lusty Wild and Brown Rice Casserole
    (see page 172, omit the sour cream and yogurt)

Preheat the oven to 350°F.

Stir the flour, salt, and pepper together and dredge the pheasant. In a 3½-quart stew pot heat the oil and butter over medium heat and put the pheasant pieces in the pan. Sprinkle with chopped rosemary and brown. Pour in the chicken stock and morels (dried morels do not need to be reconstituted) and bake, covered, for 45 minutes.

Transfer the stew to the top of the stove and turn the heat to medium. Remove the lid and pour in the cream and brandy and cook for 10 minutes. Drop in the peaches; when they are warm serve immediately over brown and wild rice.

Smoked Quail
with Raspberry-Mustard Sauce

When the hunters in my family don't bring home
enough quail, I special-order the small birds through my
butcher. They are sold four to a plastic bag and, because
they have a low fat content, they will keep in the freezer
for more than a year. They're wonderful smoked to a rich
golden brown and are served with raspberry-mustard
sauce. I often serve them in a basket lined with lettuce
leaves for informal cocktail parties.

6–8 servings

2 pounds quail (about 8)
¼ cup salt
1 quart warm water
1½ cups fresh raspberries
½ teaspoon Dijon mustard
½ teaspoon sugar

Tuck the legs of the quail up next to the body with a
toothpick. (Don't use colored ones because the
color comes off on the meat.) Blend the salt and water
together in a shallow dish. Put the quail in the brine and
soak for 2 hours. Drain and fill the dish with fresh cold
water. Let the quail sit in the fresh water for 10 minutes.
Drain and put the birds on a rack to dry. Smoke the
quail for 3 hours using alder, hickory, or cherry chips
and a hot smoke (above 120°F.).

Meanwhile, puree the raspberries and run them
through a sieve to remove the seeds. Blend ⅔ cup of the
pureed berries with the mustard and sugar.

Split the quail and serve them warm or at room temperature accompanied by a bowl of raspberry-mustard
sauce and plenty of napkins.

Game Farming

*Game farms are becom-
ing more common
throughout the Pacific
Northwest; locally
raised game can be spe-
cial-ordered at many
meat markets. For more
information, inquire at
your state Department
of Fish and Wildlife.*

Spinach Salad with Sautéed Wild Duck and Toasted Walnuts

The bright green spinach sets off the rest of the ingredients in this salad, which is a meal in itself. I serve it for dinner accompanied by French bread and a Pacific Northwest Pinot Noir. Domestic duck can be substituted for wild duck but you will need only half of the bird.

4 servings

10   ounces fresh young spinach leaves
 1   large mallard duck (substitute ½ domestic duck),
       ready for cooking
       Salt and pepper
1–2 tablespoons butter or corn oil margarine
 2   tablespoons extra-virgin olive oil
 2   tablespoons balsamic vinegar
 ½   teaspoon salt
 ½   cup toasted walnuts, pine nuts, or hazelnuts,
       coarsely chopped
 4   ounces mild goat cheese, crumbled
 8   cherry tomatoes

Preparing Domestic Duck

Skin the breast, leg, and thigh of the domestic duck. Remove all meat from the bones and add it to the salad.

Tear the spinach into bite-size pieces and put in a glass salad bowl.

Remove the leg and thigh in one piece from the bird. Pull the skin off the breast and cut the meat away from the bone. Lightly sprinkle all pieces of the duck with salt and pepper.

Heat the butter in a skillet and, when it is hot, sauté the breast meat and the 2 leg-thigh pieces until they are medium rare. Transfer the duck to a chopping board and cut the breast into thin slices. Separate the leg and thigh and set aside. Toss the sliced duck breast with the spinach.

Put the pan back over medium-high heat and add
the olive oil and balsamic vinegar. As they heat, scrape
loose any cooked particles on the bottom of the pan.
Pour the warm dressing over the spinach and toss with
salt. Sprinkle the nuts and cheese on top and toss again.
Divide the salad among 4 salad plates and garnish
each with 2 cherry tomatoes and a leg or thigh. Pass
the pepper mill around when the salad is served.

*The Pacific Flyway
covers the entire Pacific
Northwest and hunters,
whether on foot, in a
horse-drawn wagon,
or riding in the modern
automobile, always
used to shoot their limit.*

Game Birds Kung Pao

The Original Recipe

*This recipe is a modi-
fied version of Kung
Pao Chicken from the*
Sunset Chinese Cook
Book, *edited by Janeth
Johnson Nix (Menlo
Park, California: Lane
Publishing Company,
1979).*

When I asked my good friend Barbara Durbin, food
writer for the *Oregonian*, how she cooked upland game,
she replied: "When it comes to Kung Pao anything, our
twenty-one-year-old son, Chris, has a hollow leg. This is
the dish he requests most frequently. Consequently,
when I make Kung Pao for our family of four, I double
the following recipe. I've used boned pheasant, chukar
partridge, and quail. My husband, Ken, has prepared it
with ruffed grouse in hunting camp as a defense against
eating canned beef stew. No wonder he is often elected
cook. If you're short of game birds, chicken is good, as is
turkey breast. White meat stays remarkably moist with
this preparation."

4 servings

2	*tablespoons dry sherry*
1	*tablespoon plus 2 teaspoons cornstarch*
½	*teaspoon salt*
⅛	*teaspoon freshly ground pepper*
2	*pheasant, chukar partridge, or grouse breasts, skinned, boned, and cut into bite-size pieces*
4	*tablespoons peanut oil*
2	*tablespoons soy sauce*
1	*tablespoon white distilled or wine vinegar*
3	*tablespoons chicken broth*
2	*teaspoons sugar*
½	*cup dry-roasted salted peanuts*
6	*small dry hot chili peppers*
1	*teaspoon minced garlic*
1½	*tablespoons peeled, chopped fresh ginger*
6	*whole (small) scallions or green onions, trimmed and cut into 1½-inch pieces*
2–3	*cups cooked long-grain white rice*

In a bowl mix together 1 tablespoon sherry, 1 tablespoon cornstarch, salt, and pepper. Add the pheasant pieces, turning to coat them. Stir in 1 tablespoon oil, and let stand 15 minutes.

Prepare the cooking sauce by mixing the remaining 2 teaspoons cornstarch with the soy sauce, vinegar, remaining tablespoon dry sherry, chicken broth, and sugar. Set aside.

Heat a wok or frying pan over medium heat. Add 1 tablespoon oil and the peanuts and cook, stirring, for 2–3 minutes. Add the peppers and when the peppers just start to char, transfer the mixture to a paper towel and set aside.

Pour the remaining 2 tablespoons oil into the pan and increase the heat to high. Add the garlic, ginger, and pheasant and stir until the pheasant is opaque, about 4–5 minutes. Sprinkle the peanuts and chili peppers over the pheasant and stir in the cooking sauce. Continue stirring until the sauce bubbles and thickens. Add the scallions and cook for 2 more minutes, or until the scallions are hot. Serve over rice.

Two hunters rest after properly hanging their game

227

Hickory-Flavored Venison Breakfast Sausage

Last fall good friends Jerry and Barbara Boucock of Eugene, Oregon, arranged for me to visit ninety-three-year-old Jessie Wright, who had homesteaded in the Illahee area of the Umpqua National Forest in the western Cascades in 1915. I overheard Jerry telling Barbara to "follow the Umpqua River south of Roseburg and turn right at the osprey nest." Jessie, now deceased but then living in a house near her son in Glide, Oregon, greeted us at the door. Beautiful even at ninety-three, she was gracious and soft-spoken and invited us in to talk about her life as a sixteen-year-old bride, isolated in the mountains in a log cabin. She knew I was writing a cookbook, so much of our conversation centered on food. "When Perry [her husband] shot a deer and it was cold and there were no flies, we would hang it in the open woods from a branch; sheltered but so it could get air. Venison was our main meat and I always liked to can the deer he shot in the fall because it was fatter. I put a little salt down in a quart jar—a little more than a pinch—then I'd put the venison in, cover the jar with a lid, and process it for four hours. I made venison sausage by grinding the meat up in my meat grinder with bacon."

When I went home I tried making venison sausage with bacon and it was delicious. For the best flavor, it's important to use a meaty bacon, with a strong smoky flavor, such as hickory or alder. I make patties out of the sausage and serve them for breakfast with sourdough pancakes.

An Old-Fashioned Oregon Butcher Shop

"We had a German sausage maker in our butcher shop—a short stocky man who kind of looked like a sausage. He never measured anything in his life. He'd add a handful of this and a handful of that. He only added sage and pepper to our pork sausage—people liked to season it themselves. We

Makes 3 venison patties

½ pound venison, cut into 1-inch cubes
4 ounces hickory-smoked bacon, cut into 1-inch pieces
⅛ teaspoon salt
⅛ teaspoon freshly ground pepper
½ teaspoon chopped fresh thyme
1 tablespoon corn oil

Put all the ingredients except the oil in a bowl and toss. Using the ⅜-inch blade, grind the ingredients in a meat grinder. Shape into patties.

Heat the oil and fry the patties on both sides until done.

Food Processor Method:

With the steel blade intact, put all the ingredients except the oil in the workbowl of a food processor. Chop for 12–15 seconds. Shape into patties.

Heat the oil and fry the patties on both sides until done.

made minced ham in little cages and wieners. Kids that came into the shop always got a wiener. If they came in on Thursdays, they got one right out of the smokehouse."

—From Verdun Boucock, Roseburg Sanitary Market, Roseburg, Oregon, 1937 (photograph below)

Venison Sausage with Morels and Fresh Thyme

The pork shoulder in this venison sausage provides enough fat to keep the sausage moist. I shape the meat into patties, and then fry them in a small amount of oil.

Makes 4 venison patties

10	ounces venison, cut into 1-inch cubes
5	ounces fatty pork shoulder, cut into 1-inch cubes
¼	cup chopped fresh morels or 2 ounces dried morels, reconstituted, drained
1	peeled shallot or 1 tablespoon chopped onion
1	tablespoon chopped fresh thyme or 1 teaspoon dried whole thyme, crushed
1	teaspoon salt
½	teaspoon freshly ground pepper
1	tablespoon corn oil

Grind together the venison, pork, morels, and shallot using the ³/₁₆-inch blade of a meat grinder. Season with the thyme, salt, and pepper and stir until blended.

Heat the oil to medium and shape the sausages into 4 patties. Fry the sausage patties on each side until done in the center.

The uncooked venison sausage can also be double-wrapped in freezer paper and stored in the freezer.

Food Processor Method:

Using the steel blade, chop all the ingredients (except the oil) until they are coarsely ground, about 12–15 seconds.

Heat the oil to medium and shape the sausages into 4 patties. Fry the sausage patties on each side until done in the center.

The uncooked venison sausage can also be double-wrapped in freezer paper and stored in the freezer.

Pheasant Sausage with Lemon Grass and Fresh Ginger

The lean white meat of pheasant is enhanced by the addition of fresh herbs. It's also paired with pork in this recipe to give it additional fat and flavor.

Makes 4 patties

8	*ounces pheasant, skinned and boned (substitute chicken)*
4	*ounces pork shoulder, cut into 1-inch cubes*
2	*teaspoons chopped shallot or onion*
1	*inch lemon grass, outside leaves removed*
¼	*teaspoon salt*
¼	*teaspoon pepper*
1	*tablespoon stemmed cilantro*
1	*tablespoon stemmed fresh basil*
½	*teaspoon freshly grated ginger*
2	*teaspoons lemon juice*
1	*tablespoon corn oil*

In a bowl, toss the pheasant, pork, shallot, lemon grass, salt, pepper, cilantro, basil, and ginger.

Run the mixture through a meat grinder using the ³⁄₁₆-inch blade. Stir in the lemon juice and shape into 4 patties.

Heat the oil to medium and fry the patties on each side until they are done, about 4 minutes a side.

The uncooked sausage meat can be double-wrapped in freezer paper and stored in the freezer.

Food Processor Method:

Using the steel blade, chop all the ingredients (except the oil) until they are coarsely ground, about 12–15 seconds. Heat the oil to medium and shape the sausages into 4 patties. Fry the sausage patties on each side until done in the center.

The uncooked sausage can also be double-wrapped in freezer paper and stored in the freezer.

The Beaver Coin was legal tender for the Oregon Territory.

Homemade Peppered Bacon

Curing Venison

Pioneers "baconed" venison by curing the ham (round). It was left on a slanted board (for drainage) in the smoke-house to cure for two weeks before it was smoked. It was thinly sliced, the way we would serve prosciutto or Virginia ham.

The old-fashioned method of making bacon using a dry cure is not difficult. If you ask, most butchers will special-order a pork belly and a curing agent, such as Heller's Custom Cure. To cure the meat you simply rub the exposed surfaces of the belly with the curing salts and, over a two-week period, the water in the meat is gradually replaced with salt, inhibiting the growth of any harmful bacteria. Then rub the cured meat with cracked black pepper and smoke it. We cure our bacon in a hardwood box built out of alder, 10 x 20 x 24 inches deep, which has a slatted top to act as a weight on top of the meat. I recommend you find or make a similar box. The length of time it takes to cure the meat will depend on the weather. Since we don't have a walk-in refrig-erator, we make bacon during the cold winter months to lessen the chance of spoilage while it cures. It makes a nice gift to give during the holidays.

1   *meaty pork belly, 5–6 pounds*
5   *ounces Heller's Custom Cure (special-order it through your butcher or buy it at a butcher supply house)*
¼   *cup cracked black pepper*

Detailed instructions for curing meats can be found in Frank B. Ashbrook, Butchering, Processing and Preservation of Meats *(New York: Van Nostrand Reinhold Company, 1955).*

Trim the edges of the belly and the ends to make the meat rectangular. It should fit snugly inside the box and it should lie flat. Rub the entire 5 ounces of curing mixture into the pork belly and place it in the box, skin side down. Store the box in a cool place (less than 45°F.) for 14 days. (In several days, liquid will collect around the meat. This is from the action of the salts releasing liquid from the meat. If the meat is not covered with liquid within 3–4 days, add another ounce of cure to a cup of water and use just enough to cover the meat.)

At the end of the 2 weeks remove the meat from the box. Soak the bacon in warm water for 1 hour before air-drying it on a rack for 2 hours. Rub all the exposed surfaces with cracked pepper. Smoke the bacon, using a cold smoke and alder or hickory chips, for 6 hours, or until the desired bloom (color) is obtained.

The People's Market in Ballard, Washington —the Scandinavian neighborhood of Seattle —with pans of home-made bacon, sausages, and jars of pickles

Wintering-In

The earliest pioneers would gather indigenous wild fruits—Oregon grape, salal, huckleberries, wild blackberries, elderberries, and wild rose hips, to name a few—and combine them with sugar, purchased at Fort Vancouver, to make their first jams and jellies. After crops were planted and orchards and berries began to produce, there was an abundance of fruit that needed to be put up for winter's use; berries, apricots, peaches, pears, plums, cherries, applesauce, pickled fruit, and mincemeat were canned and stored in the pantry. Both herb vinegars and fruit catsups were popular pantry items in the nineteenth century, and we are seeing them again in today's menus.

Many Pacific Northwest cooks still can large quantities of fruit and vegetables at the peak of the season and a few can venison. (Recently I met a woman in a preserve class who goes hunting with her husband and cans moose right in the hunting camp!)

U-Pick farms offer the best bargains for vegetables and fruits but, of course, you have to pick the produce yourself. Most produce does not need to be canned the day it is picked, except when you are making pickles. Peaches and pears both need two to three ripening days at home after they are picked, and berries can be turned into preserves even after they have been frozen.

The following recipes make small batches and most of them can be prepared in the microwave.

PACIFIC NORTHWEST BLACKBERRY JAM

GOLDEN AUTUMN PEAR PRESERVES

FRENCH PRAIRIE RASPBERRY-CHERRY SAUCE

SCARLET STRAWBERRY-BLUEBERRY FREEZER JAM

APRICOT-NECTARINE SPOON MARMALADE WITH CINNAMON

PEACH-NECTARINE GINGER JAM

TRISH'S RASPBERRY—EARLY ITALIAN PRUNE PLUM JAM

GOLDEN PEACH BUTTER WITH CARDAMOM

ROSE GERANIUM HONEY

CRANBERRY-QUINCE PRESERVES WITH GOLDEN RAISINS

CLOVE-STUDDED SECKEL PEARS WITH PEAR BRANDY

PEPPERED LADY APPLES IN MADEIRA AND PORT

PERFECT PICKLED FIGS

LINGONBERRY-HORSERADISH SAUCE

CRIMSON RHUBARB SAUCE

PIONEER BLUEBERRY CATSUP

RASPBERRY VINEGAR WITH FRESH ROSEMARY

WALLA WALLA SWEET ONION JAM

WALLOWA COUNTY MINCEMEAT

GREEN TOMATO MINCEMEAT

SUN-DRIED TOMATOES

Pacific Northwest Blackberry Jam

Every region of the United States has its own variety of blackberries. In the Pacific Northwest, where there are many to choose from, I like to combine them. It makes a full-flavored jam that seems to bring out the best in all the berries. You can use one or two local varieties or half cultivated and half wild—the flavor won't be the same but it'll still be delicious.

Makes 6½ cups

    1 *heaping cup boysenberries*
    1 *heaping cup Marion blackberries*
    1 *heaping cup Kotata or Waldo blackberries*
  5¼ *cups sugar*
    1 *2-ounce box powdered pectin*
   ¾ *cup water*

Put the berries in a bowl and lightly mash half of them. Measure 3 cups crushed-and-whole berries and put them in a large bowl. Stir the sugar into the fruit and let stand for 10 minutes.

In a very large pan, stir the powdered pectin into the water and bring the mixture to a full rolling boil, stirring constantly. Continue boiling for 1 minute. Add the pectin mixture to the berries and stir constantly for 3 minutes, or until all the sugar is dissolved.

Fill plastic containers to within ½ inch of tops. Cover and let stand at room temperature for 24 hours before storing in the freezer.

Golden Autumn Pear Preserves

Make this preserve in the fall when there's a chill in the air and the leaves are flying. The lingering aroma of freshly cooked pears and ginger is a welcome respite from the cold outdoors.

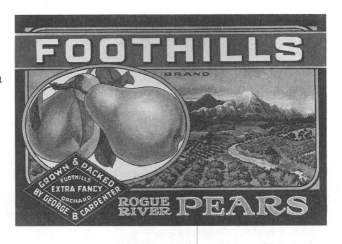

Makes 2 cups

2½   pounds pears, cored, peeled, and cut into eighths
 2   cups sugar
 3   tablespoons lemon juice and pulp
 ½   cup crystallized ginger, cut into ½-inch pieces
 ¼   cup pear brandy

Put the pears, sugar, and lemon juice with pulp in a heavy pot and bring it to a boil. Adjust the heat to medium and simmer for 1 hour until the mixture turns a deep golden brown and thickens. Remove from the heat and stir in the crystallized ginger and brandy.

Pour into a jar or plastic container and let cool. Cover and store in the freezer.

Wild Ginger

Wild ginger, though not related to tropical ginger, thrives in the moist coniferous forests of the Pacific Northwest. Pioneers dried and ground the stems and used it as a seasoning, while the Upper Skagit Indians in northwestern Washington made a tonic tea out of its heart-shaped leaves. I picked it once near our cabin in the Cascade Mountains and let it dry by the wood stove. When I crushed the dried stems, I found it had a tangy, unfamiliar flavor.

French Prairie Raspberry-Cherry Sauce

The French Prairie

Nestled in the heart of the Willamette Valley is the French Prairie, a diversified growing area where I annually pick cherries. It's named for the French Canadians who retired there after leaving the Hudson's Bay Company. Edith Belleque married the son of French-Canadian descendants and has lived in the French Prairie for seventy-seven years. She remembers her mother-in-law telling her about those early days: "When they left the Hudson's Bay Company in Vancouver and settled in the prairie, Father McLoughlin* gave them grains and seeds to start with. They had to sell their crops back to him and that worked out well. They raised oats, wheat, and a little barley. My husband doesn't like to talk about it much because those were difficult times."

*I questioned Edith about why she called John McLoughlin "Father," and she said it was his common name because he took care of so many people.

High-quality cherries can now be purchased at the grocery store, pitted and frozen in one-pound bags. In this recipe all of the cherries and half of the raspberries are cooked with the sugar and lemon juice. At the end of the cooking time the uncooked raspberries are stirred in along with the raspberry liqueur and a dash of cinnamon. The result is a deep ruby-red sauce loaded with bite-size chunks of flavorful fruit. Serve it warm over vanilla ice cream or vanilla-flavored yogurt. Since this recipe has a low sugar content, it will not keep more than a couple of weeks in the refrigerator.

Makes about 3 cups

2   cups pitted dark sweet cherries, fresh or frozen, thawed
2   cups raspberries, fresh or frozen, thawed
½   cup sugar
1   tablespoon lemon juice
1   tablespoon raspberry liqueur
¼   teaspoon ground cinnamon

Heat the cherries, 1 cup raspberries, the sugar, and the lemon juice until the mixture starts to boil. Reduce the heat to simmer and cook for 20 minutes, or until the cherries start to soften. Remove from the heat and gently stir in the remaining 1 cup raspberries, the raspberry liqueur, and the cinnamon. Let cool and store in a covered jar in the refrigerator.

Microwave Instructions:

Put the cherries, 1 cup raspberries, the sugar, and lemon juice in a microwave-safe bowl. Microwave on High for 5–8 minutes. Remove from the oven and gently stir in the remaining 1 cup raspberries, the raspberry liqueur, and the cinnamon. Let cool and store in a covered jar in the refrigerator.

The Bing Cherry Tree

In 1847 Henderson Luelling brought 700 fruit trees from Iowa over the Oregon Trail to the Oregon Territory. He settled in Milwaukie, a suburb of Portland, and thus began the Pacific Northwest fruit industry. Henderson packed up and moved on to California, but his brother, Seth, arrived in Milwaukie in 1851. He was experienced in grafting and developed the Black Republican and Bing cherry trees. The latter was named after his Manchurian foreman. Both Seth and Bing had a row of grafted cherry trees and the Bing cherry grew in Bing's row and consequently was given his name.

Original Bing cherry tree in Milwaukie, Oregon

Scarlet Strawberry-Blueberry Freezer Jam

It took me a few tries before I figured out how to make this jam without having all the blueberries float to the top. I found that if I froze some of the berries they would stay toward the bottom while the fresh ones surfaced. Then, once the jam starts to set up, I just poke down any of the remaining blueberries with a spoon.

Makes approximately 4 half-pints

3½ cups pureed strawberries (about 2 quarts whole berries)
 ¼ cup lemon juice
 1 2-ounce package powdered pectin
 1 cup frozen blueberries
 1 cup fresh blueberries
 1 cup light corn syrup
4½ cups sugar

Put the pureed strawberries in a large pan and blend with the lemon juice. Slowly stir in the pectin and set aside for 30 minutes, stirring occasionally.

Drop ¼ cup frozen blueberries in the bottom of each container. Lay ¼ cup fresh blueberries over the frozen berries.

Stir the corn syrup into the berry-pectin mixture. When it is well mixed, gradually add the sugar, stirring constantly until it is completely dissolved. If it is a cool day, place the jam over low heat and warm it to 100°F. to hasten the dissolving. Pour the warm jam over the berries and seal. Once the jam starts to set up, poke down any berries that have floated to the surface. Freeze.

Apricot-Nectarine Spoon Marmalade with Cinnamon

Both apricots and nectarines are grown in the Pacific Northwest and I like the flavor that results from cooking them together. The fruit cooks down into a thick, deep golden jam that is loaded with bite-size chunks of tender fruit; the hint of cinnamon comes as a pleasing aftertaste.

Makes about 2½ cups

1½	*pounds apricots, halved and pitted (about 4 cups)*
3	*nectarines, pitted and diced, skin on (12 ounces)*
3	*cups sugar*
¼	*cup lemon juice*
1	*teaspoon ground cinnamon*
3	*cinnamon sticks*

In a pan, combine the apricot halves, nectarine pieces, sugar, and lemon juice over medium-high heat, stirring until the sugar dissolves. Continue cooking until the jam thickens, about 30–35 minutes.

Remove the jam from the heat and stir in the cinnamon. Pour the jam into plastic freezer containers and poke a cinnamon stick in the center of each. Let stand until cool. Cover the jam and store in the freezer.

keeps them from holding well when shipped. Though the luscious bright red Hood is by far the sweetest berry—and the standard for measuring all strawberries—it is unfortunately being plagued by virus problems, and, like the Marshall, which also used to be exceptionally popular, it is becoming difficult to find. The leading commercial varieties of strawberries include the Totem, Benton, Olympus, Hood, and Shuksan. In recent comparative tastings, I rated the Benton after the Hood as my favorites.

Peach-Nectarine Ginger Jam

Nectarines

Nectarines are a variety of peach with a smooth skin and no down. These sweet and aromatic fruits are not a major crop in the Pacific Northwest but they are grown here, mostly east of the Cascades where the summer heat is most intense.

I like the way freezer jam retains the natural taste of fresh fruit and it's especially true with peaches and nectarines. I leave the skin on the nectarines to add a bit of texture. The jam is a deep sun-gold color, dotted with red flecks of nectarine. It's seasoned with ground ginger, which leaves a pleasant, lingering aftertaste.

Makes seven 8-ounce jars

2½ *cups fresh peaches, sliced and peeled (1 pound)*
    (see margin, page 244)
2½ *cups fresh nectarines, sliced, pitted,*
    and not peeled (1 pound)
 ½ *cup lemon juice*
 1 *2-ounce package powdered pectin*
 1 *cup light corn syrup*
4½ *cups sugar*
 2 *teaspoons ground ginger*

Puree the peach and nectarine slices until smooth in a food processor or blender. Pour the fruit into a large pan and blend with the lemon juice. Slowly stir in the pectin and set aside for 30 minutes, stirring occasionally.

Pour the corn syrup into the fruit and stir until blended. Gradually add the sugar, stirring constantly until it is completely dissolved. If it is a cool day, place the jam over low heat and warm it to 100°F. to hasten the dissolving. Stir in the ginger. Pour into jars and seal. Freeze.

Trish's Raspberry–Early Italian Prune Plum Jam

Every year my sister-in-law picks the early Italian prune plums and fresh raspberries that are raised commercially near her home in Salem, Oregon.

She makes this wonderful ruby-red jam, interspersed with bits of tart prune plum skin, which counteracts the sweetness of the sugar—giving it a sweet-and-sour flavor.

Makes about 5½ pints

2½ *pounds fresh early Italian prune plums, pitted*
1¾ *cups whole red raspberries*
 1 *2-ounce box powdered pectin*
 ¼ *cup lemon juice*
 1 *cup light corn syrup*
4½ *cups sugar*

Grind the plums through the coarse blade of a meat grinder or finely chop by pulsing in a food processor.

Measure 1½ cups plum pulp and put it in a large pan with the raspberries. Stir in the pectin and lemon juice and let the mixture sit for 30 minutes.

Stir in the corn syrup and blend. Gradually add the sugar. Heat to 100°F., or until the sugar dissolves. Pour into plastic containers, seal, and freeze.

Italian Prunes

An Italian prune is a variety of plum noted for its high sugar content.

243

Golden Peach Butter with Cardamom

Packing peaches in Yakima, Washington

The recipe for Blackberry Butter (see page 67) uses fresh blackberries combined with butter, while this recipe uses just the fruit embellished with sugar and spices. It is an old-fashioned method of preserving fruit that is too ripe for canning. The ingredients are slow-cooked until they turn into a buttery-smooth preserve. Keep it in a covered jar in the refrigerator.

Makes about 1 cup

1 pound ripe peaches, peeled, pitted, and sliced
   (about 2½ cups)
2 tablespoons lemon juice
½ cup sugar
¼ teaspoon ground cardamom
⅛ teaspoon freshly grated nutmeg or ground nutmeg

Put the sliced peaches in a heavy saucepan and sprinkle with the lemon juice. Add the sugar, cardamom, and nutmeg and stir to mix. Cook over medium heat for 20 minutes, or until the peach butter thickens. Store in a covered jar in the refrigerator.

Microwave Instructions:

Toss all the ingredients together in a small bowl and microwave on High, uncovered, for 10 minutes. Stir and store in a covered jar in the refrigerator.

How to Remove Peach Skins

Dip peaches in boiling water, then in cold water. Remove the skins and cut into slices.

Rose Geranium Honey

I love the intense perfume of the rose geranium and always plant at least one of them in my herb garden. It's an annual in the Pacific Northwest and, besides adding a splash of color to my summer yard, it has rose-scented leaves that I like to use in the kitchen. In this recipe I infuse honey with the fragrant leaves to add a delicate rose flavor to it.

Makes four 8-ounce jars

2   cups clover honey
4   rose geranium leaves
4   rose geranium blossoms

Gently heat the honey in a small saucepan with the geranium leaves. When it is barely warm, pour the honey into glass jars and let it come to room temperature. Poke a flower blossom down into the honey and cover the jars with lids. Store the honey at room temperature and let it stand 2 weeks before using.

Try a Bit of Lavender

For a different flavor and color put a flowering lavender stem in each jar instead of the geraniums.

245

Cranberry-Quince Preserves with Golden Raisins

Wild Cranberries

The Native Americans and pioneers in the Pacific Northwest harvested the wild cranberry which grew in coastal bogs and in the grassy meadows of the Cascade Mountains. The Quinault Indians of Washington called them "prairie berries" and the Lower Chinook Indians traded them with the "whites." When the Finns settled along the Washington coast, they pioneered the commercial cranberry industry.

Washington cranberry harvest before automation

The microwave makes this preserve in less time than it takes to peel the apples and quinces. Occasionally I add a splash of Grand Marnier after it is cooked and match it with the rich flavor of wild duck or goose.

Makes about 1½ pints

1½ pounds quinces, peeled, cored, and cubed (5 cups)
2 pounds apples, peeled, cored, and cubed (5½ cups)
1 pound fresh cranberries (4 cups)
3 cups sugar
1 cup golden raisins

Bring all the ingredients to a boil in a large, heavy pot. Turn the heat to simmer and cook for 45 minutes, or until the fruit is tender and the mixture has thickened. Store in jars in the refrigerator.

Microwave Instructions:

Put all the ingredients in a microwave-safe dish and cover with plastic wrap. Microwave on High for 8–10 minutes, or until the fruit is tender and the mixture has thickened.

Clove-Studded Seckel Pears
with Pear Brandy

Seckel pears are the smallest of the pear varieties and are
easily identifiable by their tiny size and dark green color.
These diminutive pears are pleasingly sweet from an
abundance of sugar, which has given them the nickname
"sugar pears." They are most commonly canned whole,
embellished with fragrant spices. In this recipe, I have
added locally made pear brandy to intensify their flavor.

Makes 6 pints

> About 100 cloves
> 18   whole Seckel pears, peeled but not cored
>   (about 2½ pounds)
> 6   cups water
> 3   cups sugar
> 1   cup pear brandy

Stick 5 or 6 cloves into each pear. Wash 6 pint jars and
lids; keep hot. Bring the water and sugar to a boil, reduce
the heat, and cook the syrup for 5 minutes. Add the
pears and simmer gently for another 20 minutes. Turn
the heat off and stir in the pear brandy.

Carefully pack 3 pears in each hot jar and fill with the
brandied sugar syrup, leaving ¼ inch head space. Adjust
caps and process 20 minutes in a boiling water bath.

Fruit Brandies

*There are only a hand-
ful of distilleries producing fruit brandy in
North America, and
one of them, Clear
Creek Distilleries, is
located in Portland,
Oregon. It is owned
and operated by
Stephen McCarthy, who
buys Bartlett pears from
his brother's pear
orchard nestled against
the sun-kissed slopes of
Mt. Hood. He trans-
ports the pears to his dis-
tillery in downtown
Portland, where they
are distilled into 80-
proof brandy in copper
pot stills imported from
Germany. The popular
imported pear brandy,
Williams Eau De Vie,
is made from the
Williams pear—the
European name for the
Bartlett.*

Peppered Lady Apples in Madeira and Port

Lady Apples

The petite Lady apple is a favorite apple of mine to can and it can be used whole as a condiment during the holidays. The apples are grown as a small specialty crop and are found only in some supermarkets around holiday time.

These miniature apples are the size of large apricots and appear in local markets around Thanksgiving. They retain their shape and firmness when canned, and when they are infused with the complex flavors of Madeira, port, and bruised peppercorns, are a lovely foil for game or smoked fowl. I like to serve them in a clear glass bowl to show off their perfectly preserved shape.

Makes 1 pint

1½ teaspoons ascorbic acid (such as Fruit Fresh)
1   quart water (4 cups)
11 ounces whole Lady apples, peeled and cored (about 10 apples)
½   cup sugar
¼   cup Madeira
¼   cup port
10 bruised peppercorns

Mix the ascorbic acid and 2 cups of water together in a large bowl. As soon as each apple is peeled and cored drop it into the ascorbic acid to keep it from turning brown.

Make a syrup by boiling the sugar and the remaining 2 cups of water together for 5 minutes. Remove the syrup from the heat.

Drain the apples and add them to the hot sugar syrup. Place the pan back on the burner and bring the apples to a boil. Reduce the heat to simmer and cook for 30 minutes. Turn the heat off and let the apples cool in the syrup.

Place the apples, without the syrup, in a pint jar. Heat the syrup until it boils, pour ¾ cup syrup, Madeira, and port into the jar, leaving ¼ inch head space. Add the peppercorns and adjust cap. Invert the jar several times to blend the liquids. Refrigerate the apples 1 month before using.

Perfect Pickled Figs

The pioneers planted fig trees, and although the fruit is not as popular now as it was then, I still like the old-fashioned method of preserving them by pickling. They retain their shape and go beautifully with game or poultry.

Makes 1 pint

1	cup sugar
1¼	cups water
⅓	cup vinegar
7	whole cloves
1	pound fresh figs

Bring the sugar and water to a boil over high heat until the sugar dissolves. Reduce the heat to medium and add the vinegar, whole cloves, and figs. Simmer over medium heat for 45 minutes. The figs will become soft with clear flesh underneath the skin. Pack the figs into a jar and store in the refrigerator.

Microwave Instructions:

Pour the sugar and water into a microwave-safe bowl and microwave on High for 6 minutes. Add the vinegar, whole cloves, and figs. Cover with plastic wrap and microwave on High for 6 more minutes.

Pack the figs into a jar and store in the refrigerator.

Lingonberry-Horseradish Sauce

Lingonberries

In North America the lingonberry, a cousin of the huckleberry, cranberry, and blueberry, is native to Alaska and Canada and is known as the lowbush cranberry, partridgeberry, and wild cranberry. It grows in Alpine meadows and on tundra slopes, low to the ground, about three to four inches high, and spreads out three to six feet. It is rare to find lingonberries fresh in American markets. That may change in years to come.

I first read about Karin Arfsten Koal and her husband, Ralph, in Viking, *a monthly magazine produced by the Sons of Norway. Karin had written an article about their lingonberry farm in Washington, a business venture they started in 1983:*

"We were living on ten acres, overgrown by Douglas fir, alder, cascara, cedar, blackberries, foxglove, trillium, daisies, and inhabited

The combination of slightly sweet with tangy-hot goes nicely with smoked game or with the slightly sweet meat of antelope.

Makes ½ cup

2 tablespoons Horseradish Cream (*see page 178*)
½ cup wild lingonberries in sugar
   (*available in specialty food shops*)

Stir the horseradish into the lingonberries.

For fresh lingonberries, combine 1 cup berries, ½ cup sugar, and 1 tablespoon water over medium heat for 15 minutes. Stir in 2 tablespoons Horseradish Cream.

Huckleberry feast

Crimson Rhubarb Sauce

Fresh rhubarb can be found in local Pacific Northwest markets from April to September. I recently discovered how easy it is to prepare rhubarb in the microwave. It needs only to be sprinkled with a little sugar before being cooked down into a thick, tangy sauce. If you don't have a microwave, it can easily be cooked on top of the stove—it will just take a few minutes longer. Try serving this lovely crimson sauce (instead of applesauce) with smoked pork chops.

Makes about 2 cups

2   cups diced rhubarb (1 pound)
½   cup sugar
¼   cup water
    Dash of ground cinnamon or ground nutmeg (optional)

Heat the rhubarb, sugar, and water in a saucepan over medium heat until the mixture thickens, about 7–8 minutes. Season the sauce with cinnamon or nutmeg and serve warm or cold. I like it both ways.

Microwave Instructions:

Put the rhubarb and sugar in a bowl and microwave on High until the mixture thickens, about 4–5 minutes. Season the sauce with cinnamon or nutmeg and serve warm or let it cool to room temperature.

by deer, rabbit, mountain beaver, grouse, birds, and an occasional bear. We had cleared just enough to build our house, a small lawn, and garden.

"Ralph and I decided to take up the challenge as the first and only lingonberry farmers in the United States, growing them for berry harvest in the marketplace. We did not feel overly guilty when we cleared some of our land because the trees would be replaced with another wild treasure of Nature—the lingonberry."

They planted seedlings from Norway, Sweden, Finland, Germany, and Alaska and it took five years for these slow-growing plants to mature. Then the yield was only about two cups for six plants. But an unexpected bonus has been a biannual harvest, once during the end of July and once at the end of November. They feel that it's because of Washington's location on the southern edge of native lingonberry country combined with a mild and long growing season.

Pioneer Blueberry Catsup

While fruit catsups seem to be part of the trendy food scene of the nineties, they were not strangers to the pioneers. The following recipe is a variation of a grape catsup from *The Experience Cook Book* published in 1899 by the Ladies' Aid Society of the Methodist Episcopal Church in Roseburg, Oregon. It's not overly sweet and its spicy flavor makes it a nice condiment to serve with poultry, rabbit, or smoked game.

Makes 1½ cups

2 pints blueberries, fresh* or frozen (If you are using frozen blueberries it is not necessary to thaw them first.)
½ cup sugar
½ teaspoon salt
1 teaspoon ground allspice
1 teaspoon ground cinnamon
¼ teaspoon ground cloves
¼ teaspoon ground nutmeg
⅛ teaspoon cayenne pepper

   **Add ½ cup water for fresh blueberries.*

Bring all the ingredients to a boil in a heavy pan. Reduce the heat to simmer and cook the catsup for 30 minutes. Let cool and store in a covered jar in the refrigerator.

Microwave Instructions:

Put all the ingredients in a microwave-safe dish and microwave on High for about 10 minutes. Let cool and store in a covered jar in the refrigerator.

Raspberry Vinegar
with Fresh Rosemary

Although fruit-flavored vinegars have recently become
popular, they were actually a favorite of the early settlers
in the Pacific Northwest. I like to make them with rice
vinegar, which is slightly less acid than regular vinegar;
I use a little of the vinegar to deglaze the pan after I have
sautéed mild-tasting fish, such as sole, or as a dressing
for fresh tomatoes with a fruity olive oil.

Makes 1 pint

3	cups red raspberries, fresh or frozen
1½	cups rice vinegar
1	sprig fresh rosemary

Put the raspberries in a bowl and
add vinegar. Cover and let stand
for 3 weeks at room temperature. Strain the raspberry
vinegar through a cheese-
cloth and pour it into a
clean bottle containing a
sprig of fresh rosemary.
Seal with a cork or lid. Use
this same recipe to make other
berry vinegars, such as blackberry or
blueberry.

Walla Walla Sweet Onion Jam

*Walla Walla
Sweet Onions*

*When Peter Pieri emi-
grated to the Walla
Walla Valley in eastern
Washington from
Corsica, he brought
with him the seeds of his
favorite sweet onion.
Local farmers bred the
Italian onion with a
regional variety, and
the Walla Walla Sweet
onion industry was born
more than eighty years
ago. These juicy onions
are mild and sweet, and
can weigh several
pounds at maturity.
They are similar in fla-
vor and sweetness to the
Vidalia onion of
Georgia and the Maui
onion of Hawaii.*

I like to buy Walla Walla Sweets in the late spring, when
the fields are thinned. The culled onions resemble a leek
with a golf ball–size bulb and their juicy flesh is sweet
and mild—a welcome change from the strong dry onions
held over from the previous summer.

Makes scant 1 cup

3   tablespoons mild olive oil
1   pound Walla Walla Sweet onions or any sweet onions,
    peeled and sliced ¼ inch thick
2   tablespoons packed brown sugar
    Pinch of salt
2   tablespoons balsamic vinegar

Heat the oil and sauté the onions for 8–10 minutes.
Toss them with the sugar, salt, and balsamic vinegar and
cook the onions until they turn a deep golden brown.
Serve the onion jam hot or at room temperature as a
condiment with grilled salmon or beef.

*Local preserves
were a special
part of Astoria's
Centennial
Exhibition held
in 1911.*

Wallowa County Mincemeat

I was given this recipe by Jerry Begley, whose family from Missouri homesteaded in Payette, Idaho. She moved to Wallowa County in eastern Oregon in 1933 and has lived there most of her married life—almost sixty years. When I tried the recipe, I was surprised at how flavorful it was without first cooking the mincemeat. Jerry included a note with the recipe which said, "Freeze my mincemeat uncooked in quart jars—it's better without cooking. I have made this for fifty years."

Makes approximately 8 pints

5	*cups cooked ground venison*
2½	*cups suet or 24 tablespoons corn oil margarine (1½ cups)*
7½	*cups chopped apples (approximately 2½ pounds)*
3	*cups cider*
½	*cup vinegar*
1	*cup molasses*
5	*cups sugar*
1	*cup pitted and chopped pie cherries*
2½	*cups raisins (1 pound)*
½	*cup currants*
	Juice of 2 lemons (⅓ cup)
	Juice of 2 oranges (⅔ cup)
1	*teaspoon ground mace*
1	*teaspoon ground cloves*
1	*teaspoon ground nutmeg*
2	*teaspoons ground cinnamon*
2	*teaspoons ground allspice*
1	*tablespoon lemon extract*
1	*tablespoon almond extract*
3	*cups homemade beef stock or reduced-sodium canned beef broth*

Blend all the ingredients together and freeze in plastic containers.

Mincemeat

Mincemeat, traditionally served during the Christmas holidays, is delicious when it is homemade (I never liked it until I made my own.). This old British method of preserving was popular before the advent of electricity. Old recipes called for a mixture of cooked chopped meat, spices, and alcohol, which was sealed with wax and stored in a cool place.

Green Tomato Mincemeat

The old nickname for Bonners Ferry, Idaho, was "Swede Island" because of the many families that emigrated from Sweden to work in the town's lumber mill. This recipe belonged to Lina Johnson, who spent several years cooking in the mill's cookhouse after arriving in Idaho from her native Sweden in 1906. She made mincemeat every fall and substituted green tomatoes for venison when deer was not available.

Makes approximately 10 pints

 2 *quarts small green tomatoes (approximately 23)*
 2 *quarts tart apples, peeled, cored, and cut into quarters (approximately 20)*
 1 *pound raisins (2½ cups)*
 1 *pound currants (3¼ cups)*
1¼ *cups cold suet or butter (20 tablespoons)*
1½ *cups white sugar*
1½ *cups brown sugar*
 1 *tablespoon ground nutmeg*
 1 *tablespoon salt*
 1 *tablespoon ground cinnamon*
 1 *cup vinegar*

Grind the tomatoes using the coarse blade of a meat grinder and drain them in a colander. Put the ground tomatoes in a pot with a small amount of water and bring them to a boil. Discard the water and repeat this process 2 more times.

Put the apple quarters, raisins, currants, and suet through the coarse blade of a meat grinder or coarsely chop in a food processor. (If you are using butter, melt it in the last step when all the ingredients are combined and cooked.)

Combine all the ingredients over medium-high heat and cook rapidly for 1 hour. Pour into hot sterilized 1-pint jars, leaving ½-inch head space. Process in a boiling water bath for 25 minutes.

Sun-Dried Tomatoes

This recipe captures the sweet flavor of sun-ripened tomatoes by only partially dehydrating them. I prefer to make
them in the microwave, but they can also be slow-cooked
in the oven. I use these intensely flavored tomatoes in
salads, pastas, on pizzas, and occasionally, I open the
refrigerator and eat one or two just because I love them.

Makes 2 cups

 1   *pound fresh plum tomatoes, ends trimmed
     and cut into ½-inch horizontal slices*
 ½   *teaspoon salt*
 2   *cups extra-virgin olive oil*
 1   *garlic clove, peeled and split*
 1   *sprig fresh basil*

Preheat the oven to 250°F.
    Lay the tomatoes on a lightly greased flat dish and
sprinkle them with salt. Bake them for 2 hours, 15
minutes. They should be wrinkled and dry around the
edges but the centers will be slightly soft and pulled away
from the skin. Remove them with a spatula and drop
them into the oil. Add the garlic and basil leaves. Poke all
the slices down into the oil until they are completely
covered. When they are cool, seal and store in the
refrigerator up to three weeks.

Microwave Instructions:

Lay the tomatoes on a lightly greased flat dish and
sprinkle with salt. Microwave the slices on Medium,
uncovered, for 35 minutes. The edges of the tomatoes
will be wrinkled and dry but the centers will be slightly
soft and pulled away from the skin.
    Pour the olive oil in a jar and add the tomato slices,
one by one. Drop in the garlic clove and immerse the
basil in the oil. Cover and store in the refrigerator.

*Storing Sun-Dried
Tomatoes*

*Once they are de-
hydrated I store them
in a glass jar in the
refrigerator completely
submerged in oil. I dis-
card the garlic clove
after the first night. If
the oil solidifies, leave
the jar at room temper-
ature for 1 hour and the
oil will liquefy again.*

Old-Fashioned Desserts
with a New Touch

When the pioneers arrived in the Pacific Northwest they planted seeds and rootstock in the fertile valley soils. Before the orchards bore fruit, wild fruits and nuts were gathered to supplement their diet. Cows that survived the arduous journey over the Oregon Trail provided milk, and eggs, flour, and sugar could be purchased at Fort Vancouver. From these basic supplies the settlers made simple custards, puddings, and dumplings to serve at the end of a meal.

The mild climate and rich, cocoa-brown alluvial soils quickly produced an abundance of fruits and nuts with superior flavor from the exceptionally long days found this far north during the summer. It was these fruits that the pioneers who traveled to the Oregon Territory had dreamed about.

With the wood stove fired up, the sweet, sun-drenched fruit was turned into plump dumplings, deep-dish pies, and sugar-topped coffee cakes. Buttermilk biscuits, hot from the oven, were buttered and covered with mashed berries, then buried in a pile of whipped cream. Cobblers were, and still are, made by two different methods. Either sweetened stewed fruit is baked with a biscuit topping, giving it a "cobbled" effect, or the fresh berries are tossed with sugar and baked, covered by a sugar-coated pie crust. These old-fashioned desserts are a traditional part of our heritage, and fortunately they're just as popular today as they were a hundred years ago.

BUTTERMILK POUND CAKE WITH ROSE GERANIUM–FLAVORED STRAWBERRIES

BLUEBERRY-RASPBERRY UPSIDE-DOWN CAKE

WILLAMETTE VALLEY BLUEBERRY TART

THE BLACKBERRY COBBLER DUO

BLACKBERRY COBBLER FROM THE HERITAGE TREE RESTAURANT

BLACKBERRY CREAM TART

LOGANBERRY PIE WITH BAKED SOUR CREAM TOPPING

BOYSENBERRY SWIRL CHEESECAKE WITH A HAZELNUT CRUST

CASCADE MOUNTAIN HUCKLEBERRY TARTS

STRAWBERRY SORBET WITH ROSE WATER

ELDERBERRY DUMPLINGS

FRESH RASPBERRY PIE WITH CHOCOLATE CRUMB CRUST

THREE-LAYER CAKE WITH WHIPPED CREAM, BERRIES, AND PEACHES

FRESH RASPBERRY CAKE

FRESH RASPBERRY SHORTCAKE

FLAMING RASPBERRY SOUFFLÉ

INDIVIDUAL CHERRY COBBLERS

CHERRIES IN AMARETTO SOUR CREAM AND HAZELNUT SUGAR

MOIST PRUNE CAKE WITH GINGER–CREAM CHEESE FROSTING

BAKED PEARS WITH CARAMELIZED ALMONDS

TAPIOCA CARAMEL WITH FRESH PEACHES

MCINTOSH APPLE TART

BETTY LOU'S APPLE CRISP

OREGON HAZELNUT CHOCOLATE MOUSSE

BASQUE WALNUT PUDDING

FORT VANCOUVER GINGER BISCUITS

SAMOA COOKHOUSE COOKIES

BUTTERY HAZELNUT TEA COOKIES

BASIC PIE CRUST RECIPE

FAVORITE TART PASTRY

Buttermilk Pound Cake with Rose Geranium–Flavored Strawberries

Pound cake was a good standby for the pioneers because they had all the ingredients on hand. This particular recipe belonged to my great-grandmother, a native of Germany. I always make it in June to celebrate the first picking of strawberries, which I flavor with rose geranium leaves from my garden.

Makes 1 pound cake

Wild Strawberries

At least three varieties of wild strawberries grow in the Pacific Northwest, all belonging to the rose family. The fruit is tiny and has an intense strawberry flavor. The trouble is it takes patience to pick them.

The first year we owned our cabin in the Cascade Mountains, my daughter and her friend, who were fourth-graders at the time, eagerly went out to the grassy opening surrounding our cabin to pick wild strawberries for a Fourth of July strawberry shortcake. The girls picked the berries for over an hour without gathering

~~~>

Cake

8	*tablespoons butter, softened (½ cup)*
1	*cup sugar*
2	*eggs*
1½	*cups all-purpose flour*
¼	*teaspoon baking soda*
¼	*teaspoon baking powder*
¼	*teaspoon salt*
½	*cup buttermilk*
½	*teaspoon vanilla*
	Zest of 1 lemon, chopped

Sauce

3	*cups fresh strawberries, stemmed and sliced*
¼–½	*cup sugar*
4	*rose geranium leaves, halved*
	Rose geranium flowers for garnish

Preheat the oven to 350°F. and grease an 8 x 5½ x 3-inch loaf pan.

Cream the butter, sugar, and eggs together for 3–5 minutes, or until the mixture becomes fluffy.

Blend the flour, baking soda, baking powder, and salt together and add alternately with the buttermilk to the creamed mixture. Stir in the vanilla and lemon zest.

Pour the batter into the greased pan and bake for 1 hour, 10 minutes, or until the cake is done. Let the cake cool for 5 minutes before removing from the pan.

While the cake is baking, blend the strawberries, sugar, and geranium leaves. Just before serving, discard the leaves.

Cut the cake into thick slices and serve it with a bowl of flavored strawberries garnished with the geranium flowers.

enough to cover the bottoms of their buckets. They decided to forget the shortcake and instead folded the delicate berries into buttermilk biscuits, which they baked in my wood stove while I fried chicken and made potato salad. Since then, we have left the berries for the deer that come to graze on them in the early-morning hours.

Early Pacific Northwest strawberry pickers

Blueberry-Raspberry Upside-Down Cake

Blueberries

Blueberries belong to the same family as the rhododendron and azalea and thrive in open, acid soils. They flourish in the mild climate of the coastal regions and inland valleys west of the Cascades. Most of the blueberries sold in the grocery store or at U-Pick fields are "high-bush blueberries," named for the large shrub they grow on. Just like peaches, blueberry varieties can be categorized as to the time of summer they ripen, such as the early-ripening (late June to early July) Bluetta, the midseason (mid-July to mid-August) Bluecrop, and the late-ripening (early August to mid-August) Jersey. Once they reach maturity they can last about a week on the bush without deteriorating in quality. Frank Lolich, an ex–New York Met who owns Lolich Farms on the outskirts of Portland, recently confided that his biggest

I bake this wonderfully moist cake in my 9-inch cast-iron frying pan—the heavy pan keeps the butter from burning and the handle makes it easy to flip the cake upside down when it is done. It can be served warm from the oven for dessert or as a coffee cake for a brunch, but once it has cooled, the cake needs to be tightly wrapped in plastic wrap—it will get more moist the longer it sits.

8 servings

7	*tablespoons butter*
1	*cup brown sugar*
2	*eggs*
1	*cup sugar*
½	*cup milk*
¼	*teaspoon salt*
1	*cup all-purpose flour*
1	*teaspoon baking powder*
1	*pint fresh raspberries*
1	*pint fresh blueberries*
1	*pint heavy cream (2 cups)*
¼	*cup powdered sugar*
1	*teaspoon vanilla*

Preheat the oven to 375°F.

Melt 5 tablespoons butter in a heavy skillet and stir in the brown sugar. Cook over medium heat until the sugar dissolves. Keep warm over low heat.

Beat the eggs and sugar together until they are light, about 4 minutes.

Melt the remaining 2 tablespoons butter in the milk over low heat or in the microwave, on High, for 1 minute.

Sift together the salt, flour, and baking powder. Add the dry ingredients and the warm milk to the beaten eggs and sugar.

Stir the brown sugar and butter mixture in a cast-iron skillet and sprinkle the raspberries and blueberries over it. Pour the batter over the berries and bake the cake for 45 minutes, or until a toothpick stuck in the center of the cake comes out clean.

As soon as it is done, carefully turn the cake upside down onto a large platter with a lip, to catch the juices.

Whip the cream with the powdered sugar and vanilla. Serve the cake warm with a dollop of whipped cream.

problem is that the consumer is demanding more and more early blueberry varieties. "They are used to seeing blueberries in the grocery store in June and expect to be able to pick local blueberries at the same time. Blueberries need long cool summers like grapes to fully develop their flavor. The peak of the season is really mid-August to September. A lot of my berries go to the birds because people think the season is over with."

Willamette Valley Blueberry Tart

*Introducing
Commercial Blueberries*

*Commercial blueberries
were introduced in
Oregon by ninety-five-
year-old Beatrice
Crawford Drury, a
native of Salem, and
her husband, Professor
James Drury, of New
York University, in the
late 1930s. They spent
their summers in Salem
and acquired the first
plants from a widow
who lived nearby, upon
the death of her hus-
band. The two Rubel
blueberry bushes had
come from New Jersey
and were cultivated by
pioneer nurserywoman
Elizabeth White and
Dr. Frederick V.
Coville, a USDA plant
breeder. These two hor-
ticulturist were the first
to take wild blueberries
and crossbreed them*

Every bite of this glorious tart is delicious since you get
the intense flavor of the cooked blueberries combined
with the juicy natural sweetness of fresh berries.

8 servings

¾	cup sugar
2	tablespoons cornstarch
¼	teaspoon salt
⅔	cup water
3	cups fresh blueberries, rinsed and stems removed
2	tablespoons butter
2	tablespoons lemon juice
1	baked 11-inch tart shell
	(see Favorite Tart Pastry, page 301)
4	nasturtium flowers, stems removed
½	pint heavy cream (1 cup)
2–3	tablespoons powdered sugar
1	teaspoon vanilla

Stir the sugar, cornstarch, and salt together in a small
pan and whisk in the water. Add 1 cup berries and bring
to a boil. Boil for 1 minute, stirring constantly, until the
mixture thickens.

Remove the pan from the heat and stir in the
remaining 2 cups blueberries, the butter, and the lemon
juice. Pour the blueberry filling into the cooked tart shell
and chill until set, about 2 hours.

Arrange 4 nasturtium flowers in the center of the tart.
Whip the cream with the powdered sugar and vanilla until
it thickens and serve it in a bowl to accompany the tart.

The Blackberry Cobbler Duo

There are many varieties of blackberries grown commercially in the Pacific Northwest and each one has its own unique characteristics. In this recipe I have combined two of them: the Marion berry, known for its sweetness and excellent flavor, and the refreshingly tart loganberry. The combination produces a deep-maroon-colored tart that is intensely flavorful.

6 servings

  3   cups loganberries
  3   cups Marion blackberries
  ⅔   cup plus 1 tablespoon sugar
  3   tablespoons all-purpose flour
  2   tablespoons corn oil margarine or butter
       Pastry for one 8-inch pie
       (see Basic Pie Crust Recipe, page 300)
  2   tablespoons milk or heavy cream

Preheat the oven to 400°F.

Place the berries in a shallow 8-inch baking dish. Blend the ⅔ cup sugar and all of the flour together and sprinkle over the berries. Dot with margarine or butter.

Make the pastry and roll it out to ¼-inch thickness. Place over the top of the berries, covering the berries completely and leaving ½ inch of dough over the edge of the baking dish. Gently push the dough down into the pan and roll it back ¼ inch to create a border along the outside edge of the dish. Brush the top of the pastry with milk or cream.

Sprinkle the remaining 1 tablespoon sugar over all and bake the cobbler for 45 minutes, or until the crust is a golden brown. Serve it warm, topped with frozen vanilla yogurt or vanilla ice cream.

commercially. More plants were sent for and, as Mrs. Drury recalled, "we thought they would only grow at the coast but we soon discovered that with a little sawdust and peat moss they would grow anyplace. We sold them to the Union Pacific dining cars and they were really something. The Portland Rose went from Portland to Chicago and the blueberries were kept on ice for the entire round trip."

Blackberry Cobbler from the Heritage Tree Restaurant

Wild Blackberries

One of life's simple pleasures is the fruity aroma of a ripe black-berry patch on a hot summer day. Most northwesterners are familiar with this fra-grant smell since black-berries thrive in our mild climate and grow profusely all the way from the coast to the slopes of the Cascade Mountains.

In the lush redwood country of northern California where I grew up, "blackberryin'" was just part of our daily summer routine. We always picked bucketfuls of what we called "wild blackberries." The berries were a mixture of Himalayan Giants and the evergreen black-berry—two native European immigrants that have become naturalized in most regions of the Pacific Northwest. They both have large, seedy fruit and their thick and aggressive brambles grow so rampantly they can be a terrible nuisance if they are not kept under control.

The Heritage Tree Restaurant in Salem, Oregon, is just a few blocks away from the state Capitol. It is to Salem what the Old Ebbit Grill is to Washington, D.C.—an unofficial gathering place for legislators and their staffs to enjoy fine regional food. The proprietors, Jeanette Steinmetz and her brother John Miniken, restored this lovely 1913 bungalow and named it after the huge black walnut tree in the backyard, designated a "Heritage Tree" by the city of Salem. The tree grew from a nut brought to the Pacific Northwest by the LaFollette family in their covered wagon in the mid-1800s.

12 servings

14 cups fresh or frozen blackberries, thawed
 1 cup plus 2 tablespoons sugar
⅓ cup quick-cooking tapioca
 3 cups all-purpose flour
 1 teaspoon salt (optional)
 1 cup vegetable shortening
3–4 tablespoons cold water
 1 tablespoon milk
 1 pint heavy cream (2 cups)
¼ cup powdered sugar
 1 teaspoon vanilla

Preheat oven to 400°F. and adjust the rack to the middle.

Put the berries in a 9 x 13-inch pan and sprinkle with 1 cup sugar and the tapioca.

Lightly flour a pastry cloth. Measure the flour and salt into a mixing bowl and cut in the shortening with a pastry cutter until it resembles cornmeal. Add 3–4 tablespoons water and form the mixture into a smooth ball.

Place the dough on the pastry cloth and roll out from the center to the shape of the pan, turning it over once. Place the pastry over the berries and trim the edges to fit inside the pan. Brush the milk over the pastry. Cut several vents in the dough and sprinkle on the remaining 2 tablespoons sugar. Bake for 40 minutes, or until the crust is golden brown.

Whip the cream with the powdered sugar and vanilla until thickened.

Serve the cobbler while it is still warm with dollops of sweetened whipped cream.

The true native wild blackberry, the Pacific blackberry, has small dime-size fruit loaded with intense blackberry flavor. It grows in areas rich in decaying matter, such as old orchards, barnyards, and logged-over areas. Jessie Wright, an Oregon homesteader (see page 86), commented that when she and her husband lived in the mountains "wild blackberry vines were everywhere, but they didn't produce much fruit. After logging came the ground was stirred— wild blackberries came by the wagonloads."

We often find the scraggly native Pacific blackberry trailing beneath the upright wild black raspberry bush (also known as the blackcap) when we hike in the Cascade Mountains. The wild black raspberry is also small and flavorful but it's loaded with seeds—I always make it into jelly, as I do the Himalayas and the evergreen blackberry.

Blackberry Cream Tart

I found this intriguingly simple recipe while I was looking through old cookbooks at the Oregon Historical Society in Portland. It's from *The Neighborhood Cookbook,* published in Portland in 1914 by the National Council of Jewish Women, and was written to raise money for the Neighborhood House, the precursor to the current Portland Jewish Community Center. I used their basic pie recipe but baked it in a tart pan with the buttery Favorite Tart Pastry recipe on page 301. The thin tart was the perfect balance between sweet and rich with the gloriously intense flavor of the blackberries.

A 1914 Portland cooking class at the Neighborhood House

Makes one 11-inch tart

    Favorite Tart Pastry (see page 301)
2½ *cups fresh or frozen blackberries, thawed on a paper towel*
  1 *cup heavy cream*
  1 *beaten egg*
  1 *cup sugar*

Preheat the oven to 350°F.

Roll out the pastry and fit it into the tart pan. Sprinkle the blackberries over the crust and set aside. Blend the cream, egg, and sugar together and pour over the berries. Bake for 1 hour and 10 minutes.

Loganberry Pie with Baked Sour Cream Topping

Loganberries, a variety of blackberry grown commercially in the Pacific Northwest, are a cross between a raspberry and a wild blackberry. Their intense berry flavor and slight tartness make them perfect candidates for pies and preserves. Most of the commercial loganberries grown here are used for wine production and for commercial pie fillings.

8 servings

    Crust for one 10-inch pie (see Basic Pie Crust Recipe, page 300)
- 4 *cups loganberries*
- 1 *cup sugar*
- ¼ *cup all-purpose flour*
- 1½ *cups sour cream*
- 3 *tablespoons sugar*
- 1 *teaspoon vanilla*

Preheat the oven to 400°F.

    Roll the crust out on a floured board and fit the dough into the pie pan. Blend the loganberries, 1 cup sugar, and flour together and pour the filling into the prepared crust. Put the pie in the oven to bake 30 minutes.

    Blend the sour cream, remaining 3 tablespoons of sugar, and vanilla. At the end of the 30 minutes carefully spoon the topping over the berries, completely covering them. Turn the oven to 500°F. and bake for 3–4 more minutes. Let the pie cool. If necessary spread a thin layer of sour cream on the pie just before serving to hide any discoloration or cracks in the topping.

Commercial Blackberries

Many of the commercial blackberry products made in the United States—such as jam, pies, pie fillings, and wine—come from berries grown in Oregon, the world's largest producer of commercial blackberries. The two main varieties are the Marion blackberry, developed in Oregon and named after Marion County, and the thornless evergreen, a mutation of an old variety of evergreen; both of them are sold generically as blackberries. The Marion berry can be found in local markets from early July to mid-August, while the late-ripening thornless evergreen is available from mid-August to mid-September.

Boysenberry Swirl Cheesecake
with a Hazelnut Crust

Hazelnut Farming

*When George Dorris
ordered fifty hazelnut
trees from a French
nurseryman in Calif-
ornia in 1903, he had
them shipped to Oregon
by boat. He planted the
saplings on his ranch
near the meandering
McKenzie River in
Springfield, Oregon.
The trees thrived in the
mild climate of the fer-
tile Willamette Valley
and the ranch eventu-
ally became the first
commercial hazelnut
orchard in the United
States. Pioneer hazelnut
groves such as this one
were planted with trees
just nine feet apart,
which makes it easy to
identify the older
orchards—the trees look
as if they are covered by
one huge leafy canopy.
Today most hazelnut
trees are planted at a
distance of eighteen to
twenty feet and are
often interspersed with
crops of raspberries or
wheat. Michael Dollan,
owner of Burnt Ridge
Nursery, thirty minutes
west of Mt. St. Helens
in Onalaska, Washing-*

Many pioneers of Irish and British descent settled in the Pacific Northwest and cheesecake recipes were part of their heritage. It was natural for them to make use of indigenous nuts and berries; this recipe reflects that kind of adaptation. In this recipe I use the intensely flavorful boysenberry—the commercial blackberry I consider number one for flavor. It's a cross between a wild blackberry, raspberry, and loganberry and features the best of each berry.

8–10 servings

Crust

8 tablespoons butter, softened (½ cup)
1 cup all-purpose flour
½ cup finely ground and roasted hazelnuts (see page 195)
½ cup sugar

Put all the ingredients for the crust in a bowl and blend with a fork or pulse 8–10 times in a food processor. Put the mixture in an 11-inch springform pan and pat the crust into the bottom and sides of the pan. Chill the crust in the refrigerator while preparing the filling.

Filling

3 8-ounce packages cream cheese, softened
2 cups sugar
3 eggs
1½ cups fresh or frozen boysenberries (or any variety of blackberry or raspberry), thawed and drained

Preheat the oven to 375°F.

Using a mixer, blend the cream cheese, sugar, and eggs together until smooth.

Run the berries through a food mill or puree them in a blender or food processor and push them through a sieve to remove the seeds.

Layer half of the cheese mixture over the crust, then spread on all of the pureed berries. Carefully add the remaining cheese filling over the berries and cut through the batter with a knife, using a circular motion, to create the swirls.

Bake the cheesecake for 45–50 minutes. Remove the cake from the oven and let it cool to room temperature. Chill in the refrigerator for 3–4 hours before serving.

ton, predicts that "soon you'll start to see an explosion of new hazelnut varieties that are suitable for different purposes—such as those grown just for flavor, or to grind into flour, or smaller nuts good for candy making." His good friend Bill Schildgen of the Okanogan Valley in Washington has crossed a Turkish tree hazel with a European filbert and calls it a "trazel." He has been working on this project for thirty years and so far has over twenty different varieties. The tree has a high yield and produces an elongated nut without a pellicle (skin). If it's resistant to the eastern filbert blight, it may have a big future in the Pacific Northwest but it's too early to tell.

Cascade Mountain Huckleberry Tarts

*Huckleberries
and Wild Blueberries*

In the Pacific Northwest, Labor Day weekend is traditionally the time to head for the mountains to pick huckleberries. There are at least twelve varieties as well as one wild species of blueberry that thrive in the volcanic soil of the Cascades. They are all members of the same family and often grow in close proximity to one another.

In the fall the Cascade blueberry bush is the easiest to find—its leaves turn a deep reddish orange, often carpeting whole hillsides. The small plant is only two to eighteen inches tall but has flavorful deep-blue berries that are always covered with a heavy waxy bloom.

Recently my mother-in-law showed me the quick way her parents used for cleaning huckleberries. She wrapped a small lightweight chopping board in a terry-cloth towel with a high nap and rested the bottom of it in a colander. With the board tilted at a forty-five degree angle, she poured the berries down it. The small leaves and twigs stuck in the towel, leaving the berries free to fall into the colander at the bottom of the board. She then put the colander in the sink and briefly rinsed the berries under cold running water.

Makes 12 individual tarts

½ recipe for Favorite Tart Pastry (see page 301)
8 tablespoons butter, softened (½ cup)
⅓ cup sugar
2 egg yolks
3 tablespoons fresh lemon juice
½ pint cream (1 cup)
¼ cup powdered sugar
1 teaspoon vanilla
½ pint fresh huckleberries or wild blueberries

Preheat the oven to 400°F.

Roll out the pastry and line twelve 2-inch tart tins. Put the tins on a cookie sheet and bake them for 10–12 minutes, or until they are golden brown. Remove them from the oven and let them cool.

Whisk the butter, sugar, egg yolks, and lemon juice together in a saucepan. Turn the heat to medium and stir until the butter melts and the mixture thickens. Remove from the heat and let cool. Whip the cream, sugar, and vanilla together until the cream thickens.

Put 1 heaping tablespoon of the lemon filling in each tart shell and cover with a smooth layer of whipped cream. Top with as many individual berries as will fit on each tart. Refrigerate the tarts when all the shells are filled. Remove the tarts from their tins just before serving.

A local Native American making huckleberry pies

Huckleberries, on the other hand, grow on large shrubs, one to six feet tall, and, depending on the variety, have red, black, or blue berries. The black huckleberry was the most important indigenous fruit to the local Native Americans, who successfully burned large areas to encourage its growth. In the late summer whole villages would move to the mountain meadows to pick the wild berries and hold festivities, with dancing, gambling, and horse racing. Several years ago we hiked into one of the most famous gathering spots, Indian Racetrack, near Mt. Adams in southern Washington. After six miles, mostly uphill, we reached a broad meadow and the well-worn race-track was easily visible even though it was last used around the turn of the century. In the mountain stillness it was easy to imagine the Indian men wildly rac-ing their horses around the track, and the wo-men, with their baskets strapped to their waists, gathering the ripe huck-leberries from the bushes bordering the meadow.

Strawberry Sorbet with Rose Water

The Portland Rose Garden is one of the oldest rose test gardens in the United States.

Making Rose Water

Imported rose water is made by distillation, but I have found a simple way to make my own. Gather ½ cup wild-rose petals and put them in a shallow bowl. Bruise the petals and cover with 2 cups hot water. Let stand 2 hours. Strain and store in a covered bottle.

Portland, Oregon, also known as the "Rose City," has a terraced rose garden with 10,000 rose bushes. When they're in bloom, it's a lovely summer picnic spot. The following recipe for strawberry sorbet uses rose water, which can be purchased at the grocery store or liquor store. This fragrant water is imported from France, where it's made by distillation, in a process similar to that of making perfume. Its seductive flavor brings out the best in these succulently sweet strawberries, which are usually ripe just when the first roses start to bloom.

Makes 1 quart

1¾ cups water
 2 cups sugar
 1 pound strawberries (4–5 cups)
 2 teaspoons commercial rose water

Heat the water and sugar together in a saucepan until the sugar dissolves.

Puree the strawberries in small batches in a food processor or blender until smooth. If necessary, add some of the sugar syrup to facilitate the pureeing.

Blend the pureed strawberries, the remainder of the sugar syrup, and the rose water together until well blended. Freeze in an ice cream machine according to the manufacturer's instructions.

Elderberry Dumplings

Before fruits and berries planted by the pioneers could bear, wild berries were used to make preserves and desserts. Elderberries were plentiful and used frequently to make these dumplings. Other berries can be substituted.

4 servings

Sauce

2 cups washed and stemmed blue elderberries
  (or other berries)
¾ cup sugar
1 tablespoon flour
1 cup water

Put elderberries in kettle. Mix sugar and flour and sprinkle over berries. Add water, bring to a boil, and reduce heat just to keep berries hot.

Dumplings

¾ cup sifted flour
1½ teaspoons baking powder
¼ teaspoon salt
¼ cup sugar
¼ cup milk
1 egg

Preheat the oven to 400°F.

Sift flour with baking powder and salt and add the sugar. Combine the milk and egg and stir into dry ingredients just until blended. Do not overbeat. Pour elderberries into an 8-inch-square baking pan and drop dumpling batter into sauce by tablespoonfuls. Bake until the dumplings turn a golden brown.

The Gardens at Fort Vancouver

"…And what a delightful place this. What a contrast this to the barren sand plains through which we had so recently passed. Here we find fruit of every description. Apples, peaches, grapes, pear plum & every kind of vegetable, too numerous to be mentioned. Every part is very neat & tastefully arranged fine walks, each side lined with strawberry vines. On the opposite end of the garden is a good Summer house covered with grape vines. Here I must mention the origin of these Apples & grapes. A gentleman twelve years ago, while at a party in London, put the seeds of the grapes & apples he ate in his vest pocket & soon after took a voyage to this country and left them here. Now they are greatly multiplied…"

—From My Journal, 1836, *Narcissia Whitman (Fairfield, Washington: Ye Galleon Press, 1836).*

Fresh Raspberry Pie
with Chocolate Crumb Crust

Raspberries

*The moderate climate
and well-nourished soil
in the western Pacific
Northwest is known
worldwide for produc-
ing superior raspberries.
They require mild win-
ters, cool summers, and
a rain-free harvest sea-
son. The leading com-
mercial variety is the
all-purpose Willamette,
a lovely large, round,
dark-red berry that is
delicious eaten fresh,
frozen, or made into
pies or preserves. (The
Meeker is the other
commercial variety
grown—it is not as
flavorful and is a paler
color.) Almost all of the
commercial raspberries
grown in North America
(ninety-four percent)
come from Oregon,
Washington, and
British Columbia, and
most of them are sold to
processors for freezing.
The remainder are sold
fresh around the world.
Luckily for local resi-*

~~~>

The combination of fresh raspberries, chocolate, and brandy creates a dessert that looks just as wonderful as it tastes.

Makes one 8-inch pie

Crust

   3   *cups finely crushed chocolate wafers (one and a half
        8½-ounce packages)*
   8   *tablespoons butter, melted (½ cup)*
   2   *tablespoons brandy*

Filling

   ½   *cup sugar*
   2   *tablespoons cornstarch*
   ¼   *cup water*
   4   *cups fresh raspberries or two 12-ounce packages frozen
        berries*

Topping

   ½   *pint heavy cream (1 cup)*
   ½   *cup powdered sugar*
   3   *tablespoons brandy*

Combine the crushed cookies with the melted butter and brandy; set aside 1 heaping tablespoon of the crust for garnishing the whipped cream. Press the remaining mixture onto the bottom and sides of an 8-inch pie pan.

Blend the sugar and cornstarch together in a small saucepan. Stir in the water and raspberries. Bring the fruit mixture to a boil, stirring constantly, and cook until the filling thickens. Pour the filling into the crust and chill until set.

Whip the cream, powdered sugar, and brandy together until the mixture thickens. Pipe or spread the whipped cream on top of the filling and sprinkle with the reserved chocolate crumbs.

dents, there are loads of U-Pick farms scattered throughout the region, and I always pick three or four flats and store the berries in half-pint and one-quart freezer bags in my freezer. They freeze quite well for up to a year; I regularly use the thawed berries for fruit butters, jams, and pureed in sauces. All raspberries should be picked in the cool morning hours when they are still firm. Care should be taken not to overfill containers, which will crush the berries. They can be purchased fresh at local supermarkets, roadside stands, and farmers' markets, too. If they are kept in the refrigerator—unrinsed so they do not become soggy—the luscious berries will keep for up to two weeks.

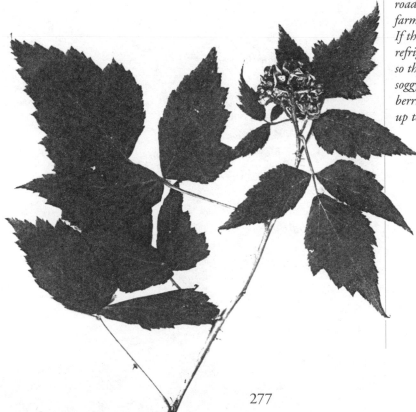

Three-Layer Cake with Whipped Cream, Berries, and Peaches

In an 1850 copy of the *Oregon Spectator,* I noticed an advertisement for layer cake pans imported from England. Cake pans were in great demand because it was the custom when you invited someone for dessert to make a cake in proportion to the guest's social status—the more important he or she might be, the greater the number of layers. I particularly like this luscious cake the day after it is made, when the whipped cream, fruit, and cake lose their separate identities and become one.

Makes one 10-inch cake

5	eggs, separated
½	cup ice water
1½	teaspoons almond extract
1½	cups sugar
1½	cups cake flour
½	teaspoon baking powder
¼	teaspoon salt
¾	teaspoon cream of tartar
1	pint heavy cream (2 cups)
¼	cup powdered sugar
¼	cup peach schnapps or light rum
2	peaches, peeled (see margin, page 244), pitted, and cut into thin slices
1	tablespoon lemon juice
1	cup blackberries
1	cup blueberries
15	borage flowers or any small fresh flowers, stemmed

Homemade Raspberry Liqueur

Barbara Boucock is one of my friends who always inspires me with new recipes. Last Christmas she gave me a bottle of her homemade raspberry liqueur and I was surprised to learn how simple it is to make. According to Barbara you need to fill a 1-gallon glass jar full of raspberries and pour in one fifth of vodka (or until the jar is full), leaving 1 inch head space. Sprinkle 4 cups of sugar over the raspberries and stir. Cover and leave in a cool place (about 50°F.) for 4–6 weeks, stirring occasionally. Strain and store in the refrigerator.

Preheat the oven to 325°F.

Beat the egg yolks until thick and lemon-colored, about 45 seconds. Add the ice water and ½ teaspoon almond extract and beat until the mixture turns pale yellow and is foamy on top. With the mixer still running, gradually add the sugar and continue beating until the sugar is dissolved.

Sift the cake flour, baking powder, and salt together and fold them into the yolk mixture.

Beat the egg whites with the cream of tartar until stiff but not dry. Gently fold the whites into the yolk mixture.

Carefully pour the batter into an ungreased angel food cake pan. Bake for 1 hour, or until done. Invert the pan over a bottle with a long neck to cool.

Whip the cream with the powdered sugar and the remaining 1 teaspoon almond flavoring until thick.

Cut the cake into 3 layers. Put the bottom layer on a cake platter, cut side up, and generously brush with ⅓ of the peach schnapps. Spread with a generous amount of whipped cream.

Sprinkle the peach slices with lemon juice. Arrange ⅓ of the blackberries, blueberries, and peaches over the whipped cream, alternating the fruit as you work. Repeat for the other 2 layers, ending with a layer of fruit on top.

Use the remaining whipped cream to frost the sides of the cake. Decorate the border along the top outside edge of the cake with the flowers.

A Famous Cake

Dorothy Johansen, a distinguished professor emeritus of history from Reed College, told me about how she was invited many years ago to the home of Mrs. Mary Failing, a member of a prominent early Portland family, to sample her famous cake. "When I went out to her rural mansion in Dunthorpe, the pièce de résistance was the fourteen-layer cake the maid brought out. Well, I'm not sure if it was exactly fourteen layers; it towered but it didn't lean. They were very thin layers filled with raspberry jelly and the whole cake was covered with chocolate icing."

Fresh Raspberry Cake

When Using Frozen Raspberries

Thaw frozen raspberries on paper towels for three hours before putting them on top of the cake batter.

This smashing recipe is from a local Girl Scout troop's collection of "Grandmothers' Recipes." It makes a moist one-layer cake that is topped with fresh raspberries and cloaked with a light dusting of granulated sugar. The cake makes a stunning presentation since the raspberries keep their shape as the cake bakes. I serve it as both a coffee cake and a dessert.

8 servings

4	tablespoons butter (¼ cup)
1	cup sugar
1	egg
2	cups sifted all-purpose flour
½	teaspoon baking powder
1	teaspoon baking soda
⅛	teaspoon salt
1	cup buttermilk
2	cups fresh raspberries or one 12-ounce package frozen raspberries

Topping

1	pint heavy cream
¼	cup powdered sugar
2	teaspoons raspberry liqueur or 1 teaspoon vanilla

Preheat the oven to 350°F. and grease a 9 x 9-inch pan.

Cream the butter and ¾ cup sugar. Add the egg and beat well. Mix the flour, baking powder, soda, and salt together and add alternately to the creamed mixture with the buttermilk. Pour into the greased pan and cover with the raspberries. Sprinkle with the remaining ¼ cup sugar and bake for 45–50 minutes, or until done.

Whip the cream, powdered sugar, and liqueur or vanilla together until the cream is thick. Serve the cake from the pan with a dollop of whipped cream.

Fresh Raspberry Shortcake

Fresh raspberries are crushed and sweetened with a little sugar before being spooned over freshly baked cream biscuits in this recipe. Then the berry-soaked biscuits are topped with whipped cream and a sprinkling of whole berries just before they are served, garnished with fresh mint leaves and pansy blossoms.

4 servings

½	*Cream Biscuits recipe (see page 71)*
⅛–¼	*cup raspberry liqueur or light rum (optional)*
1½	*pints fresh raspberries*
¼	*cup sugar*
1	*pint whipping cream*
4	*mint leaves*
4	*purple pansy flowers, stemmed*

Cut the biscuits in half and lay them, cut side up, on separate dessert plates. Sprinkle each half biscuit liberally with liqueur.

Crush 2 cups raspberries with 2 tablespoons sugar. Equally divide the pureed raspberries over the biscuits. Top with the remaining biscuit half and set aside.

Whip the cream with the remaining 2 tablespoons sugar and divide among the 4 shortcakes. Sprinkle the remaining whole raspberries over the whipped cream. Garnish each dish with a mint leaf and pansy blossom.

Heritage, Fallgold, and Black Raspberries

Last September at the "Taste of Washington," an event sponsored by local farmers at the Seattle Pike's Place Market to allow the public to sample local produce, I tried two fall-bearing raspberries, the Heritage and a wonderful sweet yellow variety, Fallgold. Both are known for their winter hardiness and are grown most successfully east of the Cascades. West of the mountains, the season starts in late June and lasts from four to six weeks or longer.

Black raspberries are also grown in the Pacific Northwest, and in the Willamette Valley, fifteen acres produce enough black raspberries to make all the organic dye used for stamping USDA grades on meat in the United States.

Flaming Raspberry Soufflé

Cyrus Walker

"The mansion at Port Ludlow was not only Cyrus Walker's home; it also served as an advertisement for the firm of Pope & Talbot. The company's fleet of eighty-nine vessels was carrying Puget Sound lumber all over the world, and to Cyrus Walker's mansion in the deep woods came lumber buyers and brokers, politicians, shipping officials, timber barons, and railroad kings. The food was sumptuous. The cellar was suave, stocked with everything from Medford rum for old sea captains to marque champagne for the delicate but often thirsty ladies of lumber buyers. The service was cared for by a long line of Chinese—father, son, and grandson who cooked dishes that would have amazed the folks in Cyrus Walker's native Skowhegan."

—From Stewart H. Holbrook, Holy Old Mackinaw *(New York: Macmillan, 1938).*

This is the type of dessert that might have been served in Cyrus Walker's mansion at Port Ludlow, Washington (see margin).

4 servings

2   cups fresh raspberries
5   tablespoons plus 1 teaspoon sugar
2   tablespoons plus 1 teaspoon dark rum
2   eggs, separated
2   tablespoons 151-proof rum (for flaming only)

Just Before Dinner:

Preheat the oven to 500°F. Adjust the rack to one notch above center.

Put the raspberries in an 11 x 8 x 2-inch-deep au gratin dish. Sprinkle the berries with 2 generous teaspoons sugar and 2 tablespoons dark rum. Set aside.

After Dinner:

Whisk the yolks with 2 tablespoons of sugar and the remaining teaspoon dark rum until they are smooth, about 30 seconds.

Beat the whites until they start to foam, then gradually add remaining 2 tablespoons sugar and continue beating until barely stiff.

Gently fold the yolk mixture into the whites and spread it on top of the berries, completely covering them.

Sprinkle the remaining 2 teaspoons sugar over the beaten egg topping. Bake the soufflé 6–7 minutes, or until it is lightly browned on top.

While the soufflé is baking, warm 2 tablespoons 151-proof rum over very low heat. Don't boil the rum or it will burn off all the alcohol, which makes it flame.

Remove the soufflé from the oven when it has doubled in height and is golden brown. Put it on a trivet with a plate underneath and carefully pour 2 tablespoons warm rum over the top. Quickly touch the surface of the soufflé with a lit match and when the flame has burned out, serve the dessert.

*Transporting berries
from the field*

Individual Cherry Cobblers

*Pacific Northwest
Cherries*

*During the summer I
always look forward to
July's warm summer
days and the first crop
of local Northwest cher-
ries. They are grown on
both sides of the
Cascades and thrive in
the hot summer heat of
the Yakima, Wenatchee,
and Hood River valleys.
The cooler Willamette
Valley also produces a
large crop of cherries. I
always enjoy the ride
through the lovely pas-
toral countryside to a
large U-Pick orchard
south of Portland. Once
you leave the freeway,
it's a ten-minute drive
on a narrow rural road
bordered on both sides
by waving fields of
golden wheat. The
turnoff to the orchard is
well marked, and the
long driveway brings
you to an old-fashioned
rambling farmhouse
and barn, shaded by a
row of sprawling white
oak trees so typical of
this part of the Willam-
ette Valley. The empty
buckets are weighed at*

Fresh cherries make a delicious cobbler when flavored
with just a few drops of almond flavoring. I make this
recipe in individual ramekins, but if you don't have
them, bake the cobbler in an 8-inch-square baking pan
for 20 minutes.

6 servings

1   cup water
2   tablespoons cornstarch
1   pound fresh cherries, pitted (about 2 cups)
1   teaspoon grated lemon peel
¼   cup plus 1 tablespoon sugar
¼   teaspoon plus a pinch salt
½   teaspoon almond flavoring
½   cup all-purpose flour
¾   teaspoon baking powder
2   tablespoons softened butter
1   egg
2   tablespoons milk
1   cup heavy cream, whipped,
      or the Amaretto Sour Cream (see opposite page)

Preheat the oven to 375°F. and grease six 12-ounce
ramekins.

In a 2-quart saucepan stir together the water and
cornstarch. Add the cherries, lemon peel, ¼ cup sugar,
and ¼ teaspoon salt. Cook the mixture over medium
heat until it thickens and becomes clear (about 5
minutes). Remove from the heat and stir in the almond
flavoring. Divide the mixture among the ramekins and
set aside.

In a small bowl or food processor blend the flour,
1 tablespoon of sugar, baking powder, pinch of salt, butter, egg, and milk until just blended. Spoon the batter
over the cherries and bake for 20 minutes or until the
crust is golden brown. Serve warm with a dollop of
whipped cream or Amaretto Sour Cream on top of each.

Cherries in Amaretto Sour Cream and Hazelnut Sugar

This is the most delicious way I know to serve cherries for dessert without pitting them. I buy fresh sweet cherries with their stems on and put them in a large colorful dish accompanied by bowls of amaretto-flavored sour cream and hazelnut sugar. The juicy fruit is held by the stem and dunked first in the flavored sour cream, then in the sugar.

4 servings

1½ pounds fresh Bing cherries
½ pint light sour cream
3–4 tablespoons amaretto liqueur
¼ cup powdered sugar
2 tablespoons hazelnuts, chopped and lightly
   toasted (see margin, page 195)

Rinse the cherries and place them in a shallow bowl. Blend the sour cream and amaretto together and set aside. Stir the powdered sugar and nuts together and put in a small bowl. Serve the cherries accompanied by the sour cream and hazelnut sugar. Give guests individual plates and let them prepare their own.

the barn, but it's necessary to get back in the car and drive out behind the house to reach the cherry orchard. The first tree of each row is tied with a different color of ribbon to designate the variety of cherry. One year I picked cherries from each of the rows and found the yellow Royal Ann—also called Napoleon, which is used for commercial candy making and maraschino cherries—juicy and mildly flavorful; the Black Republican small, dense, and packed full of flavor; the Hoskin and Viola of average size and flavor; and my favorite, the plump Bing, firm, juicy, and packed full of flavor. Bings are the leading commercial variety of cherries in the Northwest, followed by the Lambert, Van, and superior yellow-skinned Rainier. The latter originated in Washington in 1960 and is delicious canned or eaten fresh, with clear juice and flesh.

Moist Prune Cake with Ginger–Cream Cheese Frosting

Pacific Northwest Prunes

With the exception of Michigan, the nation's plum and prune production is concentrated in Oregon, Washington, and Idaho. Local prunes have gained national recognition for their flavorful, sweet flesh and tender skin, and they are shipped throughout the United States by mail-order packing houses such as Harry and David in southern Oregon.

High-quality prunes are available throughout the Pacific Northwest. In Oregon there are four varieties grown in the Willamette Valley—the Parson Sweet, Brooks, Italian, and Moyer; most of them are exported to Austria and Germany. The most popular is the Parson Sweet, pure black with an especially tender skin and the sweetest of the four. The Italian prune is put up fresh and marketed as "canned purple plum." Traditionally, a prune cake is similar to a spice cake: It's flavored with allspice, nutmeg, and cinnamon, but in addition to the spices, chopped prunes are added to the batter, making it an exceptionally moist cake.

8–10 servings

2	cups all-purpose flour
2	cups sugar
2	teaspoons baking soda
1	teaspoon ground cinnamon
1	teaspoon ground nutmeg
2	teaspoons ground ginger
½	teaspoon salt
1½	cups corn oil
4	eggs
1½	cups cooked dried prunes, drained, pitted, and coarsely chopped or pulsed in a food processor 8–10 times

Preheat the oven to 350°F. and grease a 12-cup Bundt pan.

Place all the ingredients in a large mixing bowl and beat at medium speed for 3–4 minutes. Pour into the pan and bake for 50 minutes. When the cake is done, let it set at room temperature for 3–4 minutes before inverting onto a cake rack.

Ginger–Cream Cheese Frosting

    8   ounces softened cream cheese
    1   cup unsalted butter, at room temperature
    4   cups powdered sugar
 1¼   teaspoons ground ginger
    ½   cup finely chopped cooked prunes
    2   tablespoons buttermilk
    2   teaspoons vanilla
    1   tablespoon lemon juice

Beat all the ingredients together until the mixture is
well blended, about 4 minutes. Spread on the cake
when it is cool.

*Coffee houses were a
part of the early Pacific
Northwest cities—an
influence from the large
Scandinavian popula-
tion—and the tradition
of fine coffee continues
to this day. City corners
and parks have vendors
selling freshly ground
beans, brewed into
bone-warming cups of
hot coffee.*

Baked Pears with Caramelized Almonds

Winter Pears

Winter pears ripen in the fall and ninety-five percent of the nation's crop comes from Oregon and Washington. The most important varieties are the Anjou, Bosc, Comice, Nelis, Forelle, and Seckel pears. The Anjou is the leading commercial winter pear, but I prefer the fragrant Bosc, distinguished by its russet skin and long graceful neck and stem. The firm texture of the Bosc makes it the ideal baking pear, but if it's allowed to soften, the firm flesh becomes buttery tender, sweet, and full of flavor. Two of the less-well-known winter pears are the Nelis and Forelle. The Nelis is a medium-small pear with russet over golden-yellow skin and it's good eaten either fresh or canned. The smaller Forelle is distinguished by red freckles which form a lovely crimson blush over its yellow skin when the pear is ripe. This sweet and juicy pear is available only from October to February.

Bosc pears are intensely flavorful and hold their shape when baked. Try to buy pears that still have a stem on them—they will look prettier that way.

4 servings

> 4   *Bosc pears, peeled with a swivel peeler, cut in half, and cored**
> 4   *tablespoons sugar*
> 1¼ *cups cream*
> ½   *cup sliced almonds*
> 3   *tablespoons powdered sugar*
> 3   *tablespoons pear brandy*
>
> * *I cut the pears in half first and then core each half with an apple corer to give them a uniform appearance.*

Preheat the oven to 350°F. and butter a 9 x 13-inch baking dish.

Lay the pears, cut side down, in the dish and sprinkle them with 2 tablespoons sugar. Bake for 30 minutes.

Leave the pears in the oven and carefully pour ¾ cup cream into the baking dish. Bake the pears for another 15–20 minutes, or until the cream turns a light golden color and thickens slightly. Remove from oven.

Turn the oven to broil and adjust the rack 4 inches from the broiler.

Spread the almonds on a cookie sheet and sprinkle them with the remaining 2 tablespoons sugar. Put the nuts under the broiler for 10–15 seconds, shaking the pan if necessary, until the sugar begins to melt and the almonds turn brown. They burn easily, so watch them carefully.

Whip the remaining ½ cup cream with the powdered sugar and pear brandy. Place 2 pear halves on a dessert plate and top with a dollop of whipped cream and a sprinkling of caramelized almonds.

Tapioca Caramel
with Fresh Peaches

Recently I read an inspiring recipe from *The Portland Woman's Exchange Cook Book*, published in 1913 to raise money for the unemployed. This particular recipe gave instructions for baking tapioca with brown sugar, and the author, who identified herself only by the initials M.L.P., called it Tapioca Caramel. It brought back fond memories of my mother's homemade tapioca pudding, infused with fresh fruit, and I have created a combination of the two.

4 servings

   3   *tablespoons quick-cooking tapioca*
2¾ *cups milk*
   1   *egg*
  ½ *cup plus 2 tablespoons sugar*
   1   *teaspoon almond flavoring*
       Pinch of salt
   2   *ripe peaches, skinned (see margin, page 244) and pitted*
   1   *teaspoon lemon juice*

Whisk the tapioca, milk, and egg together in a small pot and set aside for 5 minutes.

Sprinkle ½ cup sugar over the bottom of a heavy skillet. Turn the heat to medium and slowly melt the sugar. Leave it over the heat until it caramelizes—it will become thick and golden brown.

Add the caramel to the pot with the tapioca, milk, and egg. It will harden when it touches the cold milk but the caramelized sugar will dissolve once the mixture is heated. Place the mixture over medium heat and bring it to a full boil. Remove the pot from the heat and stir in the almond flavoring and a pinch of salt. Pour the pudding into a bowl and chill until thickened.

Slice the peaches into a bowl and toss with the remaining 2 tablespoons sugar and a teaspoon of lemon juice.

Serve the pudding in individual bowls topped with a spoonful of sliced peaches.

McIntosh Apple Tart

When I really want to show off the blue-ribbon fruit of the Pacific Northwest I make a tart. For this simple dessert I use a Pacific Northwest favorite, the flavorful McIntosh, one of the main apple varieties grown in the western valleys of British Columbia.* This simple recipe has perfectly sliced apples flavored with cinnamon and freshly ground nutmeg and arranged in concentric circles. Halfway through the cooking time they are covered with cream that seeps down into the crust and, as the tart cooks, changes the color of the apples to a beautiful golden brown.

Apples

Apples are big business in the Pacific Northwest—Washington alone grows 60 percent of the nation's commercial fresh apple crop. The industry started in the mild climate west of the Cascade Mountains, but as new technology developed in the late nineteenth century, such as irrigation and cold storage, and the railroad was completed to make transportation easy, the apple industry blossomed in the intense summer heat east of the mountains. These two growing regions, east and west—each with its own distinct climate— provide the consumer with a multitude of apple varieties to choose from.

8 servings

Pastry

1 11-inch unbaked pastry shell (see page 301 for *Favorite Tart Pastry*)

Filling

3 pounds McIntosh or Golden Delicious apples, cored, peeled, and cut into slices ¼–⅛-inch thick
1 cup plus 2 tablespoons sugar
1 teaspoon ground cinnamon
1 teaspoon freshly ground nutmeg
¼ pint whipping cream (½ cup)

　I do not favor the Red Delicious apple for this recipe; it lacks character and often has a mushy texture.

Put the pastry shell in the refrigerator to chill while preparing the filling.

Preheat the oven to 400°F.

Toss the apples with 1 cup sugar, the cinnamon, and the nutmeg. Starting in the center of the pastry, make a small circle of apple slices. Make another circle around it and continue until the bottom of the pastry shell is evenly covered. Repeat this process for a second layer, using all of the apple slices.

Bake the tart for 30 minutes. Leave it in the oven but slide the rack out and pour the cream over the apples. Sprinkle the tart with the remaining 2 tablespoons sugar and bake it for an additional 30 minutes.

The leading varieties grown east of the mountains are Red Delicious, an apple sold fresh around the world, and Golden Delicious, known for its tender skin and delicate, sweet flavor. The Golden Delicious is the apple I use for making applesauce, but it's good eaten fresh as well if you enjoy eating a sweeter apple

A Washington apple picker at harvest time

Betty Lou's Apple Crisp

Apples, continued

that is not firm. I prefer the deliciously tart and crisp Newton-Pippons, grown in this area.

West of the mountains, in Washington's Skagit Valley—an hour from the Canadian border—the apple industry is being revived with the help of Dr. Bob Norton, a horticultural researcher at the Washington State University Experiment Station in Mt. Vernon. Major varieties include the Gravenstein, Spartan, Melrose, and the popular Jonagold. When Dr. Norton asked twenty-four international apple-variety experts to rate the ten best apples in the world, they placed Jonagold first. It is a cross between a Jonathan and a Golden Delicious, with a full flavor that is completely balanced between acidity and sweetness. The Jonagold was developed in New York in 1943, but it thrives in the damp, mild coastal climate of the western Pacific Northwest. It's tasty cooked in pies and applesauce or baked whole.

I always look forward to an evening of good food and interesting conversation when we are invited to the home of Portlanders Betty Lou and Ty Hutchens. This is one of Betty's recipes that is an often-requested dessert at our house. She bakes tart Newtown-Pippin apple slices under a thick layer of brown sugar, butter, cinnamon, flour, and four-grain cereal (available at most supermarkets). As it cooks, the not-too-sweet topping becomes delicately crisp and sinks down into the apple slices. Serve the crisp warm with vanilla yogurt.

6 servings

5	cups Newton-Pippins, cored, peeled, and cut into slices ¼ inch thick
¾	cup butter or corn oil margarine
¼	cup flour
1	teaspoon cinnamon
½	cup brown sugar
¾	cup four-grain cereal

Preheat the oven to 350°F. and grease a 1½-quart shallow baking dish.

Arrange the apple slices in a baking dish. With two knives, or a food processor, cut the butter into the flour, cinnamon, and sugar. Stir in the cereal and sprinkle the mixture evenly over the apples. Bake for 30 minutes, or until the apples are tender.

Oregon Hazelnut Chocolate Mousse

Hazelnuts are not used as much here as they are in Europe, where you'll find them in all kinds of pastries. This rich and intense chocolate dessert is from the Oregon Hazelnut Marketing Board. I make it with imported Callebaut bittersweet chocolate from Belgium and cream cheese without preservatives. Both of these products can be purchased at most specialty food stores.

8 servings

7	*ounces bittersweet chocolate*
5	*tablespoons water*
2	*teaspoons vanilla*
1¼	*cups sugar*
8	*ounces cream cheese, softened*
1	*cup hazelnuts, toasted and chopped (see margin, page 195)*
⅓	*cup hazelnut liqueur or light rum*
1	*pint heavy cream*
8	*candied violets*
16	*fresh mint leaves*

Slowly melt the chocolate in a heavy saucepan. Gradually stir in 2 tablespoons water until it becomes a paste.

Blend the vanilla, 3 tablespoons water, and the sugar in a separate bowl. Stir the mixture into the chocolate paste and bring it to a boil over low heat. Remove from the heat and fold in the cream cheese, hazelnuts, and liqueur; set aside to cool.

Whip the cream until it is stiff and fold it into the chocolate mixture.

Divide the mousse among 8 small bowls and chill for several hours. Before serving, decorate each bowl with a candied violet and 2 fresh mint leaves.

Cookhouse Store

"When I was growing up my father ran the company store at Camp 20 (logging camp) near Arcata, California. He did a rousing good business in vanilla. The loggers couldn't buy liquor so they drank vanilla instead and that's where I learned all those delicious swear words."

—Lynette Hibler, author's mother-in-law

Basque Walnut Pudding

The Basque Museum and Cultural Center in Boise, Idaho, published a collection of recipes from the local Basque community. This recipe is from their book, *Basque Recipes,* and was submitted by Marie Galdos Landeen. "My mother, Josefa, served this during the holidays and it is a very popular Basque dessert and was served in all Basque boarding houses at holiday time."

6 servings

1   *quart whole milk*
1   *cup sugar*
1   *cup finely ground walnuts*
1   *cup finely ground bread crumbs*

Many ethnic groups in the Pacific Northwest traditionally hold festivals featuring the food, music, and dancing of their homelands, like these Basque dancers at the Sheepherders' Ball.

Combine all of the above ingredients in a medium pot and bring to a boil over low heat, stirring constantly until it thickens. This will scorch if not stirred.

Pour into a serving bowl and chill.

Fort Vancouver Ginger Biscuits

Imagine a buttery ginger cookie that's so tender it melts in your mouth and you'll know what lies ahead when you make these delightful "biscuits," a British term for cookies that can be sweet or savory. The recipe comes from Rick Edwards, park ranger at Fort Vancouver, Washington, who developed it from the list of ingredients recorded in the original Hudson's Bay Company records of the fort.

Makes 2 dozen cookies

3	*cups unbleached flour*
2	*teaspoons baking powder*
1	*teaspoon ground cinnamon*
4	*teaspoons ground ginger (1 tablespoon plus 1 teaspoon)*
24	*tablespoons butter, softened (1½ cups)*
1½	*cups sugar*
½	*cup molasses*

Preheat the oven to 375°F. and lightly grease a cookie sheet.

Blend the flour, baking powder, cinnamon, and ginger together and set aside. In a large bowl mix the softened butter, sugar, and molasses together and stir in the dry ingredients.

Roll out on a lightly floured board to ½ inch thick. Cut with a 2-inch cookie cutter and place ½ inch apart on the cookie sheet. Bake for 6–8 minutes. Do not overbake.

Samoa Cookhouse Cookies

I have changed this recipe only slightly from the original version. I use a little less flour, double the vanilla, and use half butter instead of all oil. The cookies are fluffy and tender, but they will become crispy if they are baked the full 10 minutes.

Makes seventy-four 3-inch cookies

8	tablespoons butter (½ cup)
½	cup corn oil
2¼	cups sugar
2	eggs, beaten
1	cup milk
2	teaspoons vanilla
7	cups all-purpose flour
2½	teaspoons baking powder
1	teaspoon baking soda
1	teaspoon ground cinnamon

Preheat oven to 375°F.

Cream together the butter, oil, and 2 cups sugar. Add the eggs, milk, and vanilla and beat for 1 minute. Measure the flour, baking powder, and baking soda into the mixing bowl and beat for 2 more minutes.

Blend the remaining ¼ cup sugar with the cinnamon in a small bowl. Take a walnut-size piece of dough, roll it into a ball, and put it on an ungreased cookie sheet. Dip the bottom of a glass into the sugar and cinnamon and press it down on top of the cookie. Repeat until the cookie sheet is full. Bake for 7–10 minutes. Repeat for the remaining dough.

Original Samoa Cookhouse Cookies

2	cups sugar
2½	teaspoons baking powder
1	teaspoon baking soda
7½–8	cups flour
1	cup Wesson oil
2	beaten eggs
1	cup milk
1	teaspoon lemon or vanilla flavoring
	Sugar (optional)

Sift dry ingredients. Mix all liquids together and stir into dry mixture. Roll (not too thin) and bake in moderate oven. Sugar may be sprinkled on top if desired before baking. Cookies are usually about 4 inches in diameter.

Samoa Cookhouse crew taking a break

Buttery Hazelnut Tea Cookies

Buying and Storing Hazelnuts

All of the hazelnuts in the western hemisphere are grown in Oregon, Washington, and British Columbia. Most come from Oregon's Willamette Valley, where the crop is har- vested in October. The most economical way to buy hazelnuts is at local roadside stands. They are put up in eight- to ten-pound sacks with the shells lightly cracked. After I shell the nuts, and it doesn't take long, I store them in freezer bags and keep them in my freezer until I need them. You can also buy them shelled at health food stores.

I serve these delicate butter cookies on a small doily- lined platter to accompany a pot of hot tea on rainy afternoons or, in the evening, I use them as a simple and elegant dessert accompanied by a glass of Pacific Northwest Late Harvest Riesling.

Makes 2 dozen

16	tablespoons butter, at room temperature (1 cup)
¼	cup sugar
1	egg yolk
2	cups all-purpose flour
½	teaspoon ground allspice
1	egg white, lightly beaten
½	cup hazelnuts, roasted and chopped (see margin, page 195)

Preheat the oven to 275°F.

Using an electric mixer, cream the butter and sugar together. Add the egg yolk, flour, and allspice and blend until well mixed.

Pat the dough into a 10½ x 10½-inch square on an ungreased cookie sheet. Brush with egg white and sprinkle with the toasted hazelnuts. Bake for 1 hour, 20 minutes, or until the cookies are a light golden brown. Cut them into approximately 1½-inch squares while they are still warm.

Food Processor Method:

Process the butter, sugar, and egg yolk for 15 seconds. Stir the flour and allspice together and add the dry ingredients to the workbowl. Pulse until the ingredients adhere.

Pat the dough into a 10½ x 10½-inch square on an ungreased cookie sheet. Brush with egg white and sprinkle with the toasted hazelnuts. Bake for 1 hour, 20 minutes, or until the cookies are a light golden brown. Cut them into approximately 1½-inch squares while they are still warm.

Two young Chinese girls taking tea in Portland

Basic Pie Crust Recipe

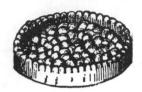

This unusual pie crust is very popular in the Pacific Northwest. It has vinegar in it, which entertains the old-fashioned notion of adding an acid to tenderize the crust. One recipe makes enough dough for two double-crusted pies and one single-crust pie, and the unused dough will keep in the refrigerator for several weeks. During the summer months, when there is a constant supply of berries and fresh fruit readily available, I wouldn't be caught without it.

Makes enough for 2 double-crusted pies plus 1 single crust

  5 *cups all-purpose flour*
2½ *cups shortening*
  2 *teaspoons baking powder*
  2 *teaspoons salt*
  1 *egg*
  1 *tablespoon white vinegar*
      A little less than 1 cup water

In the bowl of an electric mixer place the flour, shortening, baking powder, and salt. Break the egg in a 1-cup measuring cup and add the vinegar. Beat with a fork to break up the egg. Fill with cold water not quite to the top and stir. With the mixer at low speed, slowly pour in the liquid and blend the ingredients until they form a ball. As your recipe requires, roll out enough dough for 1 or 2 crusts on a floured board and store the remaining dough tightly wrapped in plastic wrap or a plastic bag in the refrigerator.

Food Processor Method:

Put the flour, shortening, baking powder, and salt in a food processor bowl and pulse 10 times. Break the egg in a 1-cup measuring cup and add the vinegar. Fill with cold water not quite to the top. With the machine running, gradually pour in the liquid until the dough just starts to form a ball. Add more flour if necessary.

Favorite Tart Pastry

I use this recipe for sweet tarts when I want a rich, short crust. It can be made by hand, but I prefer to make it in my food processor.

Makes one 11-inch pastry shell

   2   cups all-purpose flour
  16   tablespoons chilled butter, cut into ½-inch pieces (1 cup)
   1   egg
   1   tablespoon heavy cream
   1   tablespoon lemon juice
   1   teaspoon sugar
   ¼   teaspoon salt

Preheat the oven to 375°F.

Cream the flour and butter. Add the egg, cream, lemon juice, sugar, and salt and mix well.

Place the dough on a floured surface and roll out to a 12-inch circle, ⅛ inch thick. Carefully fold the dough over the rolling pin and transfer to the tart pan. Push the dough into the corners with your fingers. Trim off the excess dough by running the rolling pin over the top of the tart pan. Prick the bottom and sides of the pastry with a fork and bake it for 8–10 minutes.

Food Processor Method:

Using the metal blade, process all the ingredients in a food processor until the dough starts to form a ball. Place the dough on a floured surface and roll out to a 12-inch circle, ⅛ inch thick. Carefully fold the dough over the rolling pin and transfer to the tart pan. Push the dough into the corners with your fingers. Trim off the excess dough by running the rolling pin over the top of the tart pan. Prick the bottom and sides with a fork and bake for 8–10 minutes.

A Pacific Northwest Legend

This recipe is a variation of Very Short Pastry from New Recipes for the Cuisinart, *compiled by James Beard and Carl Jerome in 1978. About the time this small booklet was published, I took a cooking class in Portland from James Beard on American cookery. It was exciting to watch him work the pastry with his skillful hands and listen to his enthusiasm about the local indigenous food. He knew firsthand of the bountiful Pacific Northwest since he was born and raised in Portland, where his mother once owned and operated the Gladstone Hotel. He left Portland in his early twenties to pursue a career in acting, but his life's work would eventually revolve around the kitchen. Throughout his life he traveled often to the Pacific Northwest and for many years taught cooking classes in Gearhart, on the beautiful Oregon coast. Although he lived in New York, he always considered the Pacific Northwest his home.*

A Country of Beauty

"I can't hope to explain to you how happy we all were. Father and Mother and all eight children had crossed the plains in good health. We children were particularly happy, for, instead of having to strike out each morning and walk barefooted in the dust, where we stubbed our toes, stepped on cactus and watched that we didn't step on any rattlesnakes, we were in a country where the grass was belly-deep for the cattle and when the sea breeze made it wave it looked like waves of changeable green silk. We didn't have to worry about the Indians running off our stock. No longer did we have to eat bacon, beans, and camp bread, and not get as much of them as we wanted, for here we had found a country of beauty, where we could have all the vegetables we wanted, where the hills were full of deer, and the streams full of trout, where, when we looked to the westward, instead of seeing nothing but a long winding train of prairie schooners with a cloud of dust hanging over all, we saw waving grass and vividly green fir trees. We looked up at a blue sky with white clouds and to the eastward we could see Mount Hood, clean and clear and beautiful and so wonderful that it almost took your breath."

—*Catherine Thomas Morris,* Conversations with
Pioneer Women *by Fred Lockley, compiled and edited by
Mike Helm (Eugene, Oregon: Rainy Day Press, 1981).*

SOURCE LIST

SELECTED BIBLIOGRAPHY

INDEX

PHOTOGRAPHIC ACKNOWLEDGMENTS

303

SOURCE LIST

For a directory of Pacific Northwest food products and farm commodities contact the following:

Alaska Seafood Marketing Institute
    P.O. Box D
    Juneau, Alaska 99811
    1-907-586-2902
    (seafood and fish only)

Honorable Larry Chalmers
    Minister of Agriculture,
        Fisheries, and Food
    Parliament Building
    Victoria, British Columbia V8V-1Y4

Idaho State Department of Agriculture
    P.O. Box 790
    Boise, Idaho 83701

Oregon State Department of Agriculture
    121 Southwest Salmon Street,
        Suite 240
    Portland, Oregon 97204-2987
    1-503-229-6113

Washington State Department of
Agriculture
    Market Development Division
    406 General Administration
        Building, AX-41
    Olympia, Washington 98504
    1-206-753-5063

Local suppliers include the following:

Bandon Foods, Inc.
    P.O. Box 1668
    Bandon, Oregon 97411
    1-503-347-2456
    (cheese)

Cascade Mushrooms
    530 Northwest 112th Avenue
    Portland, Oregon 97229
    1-503-294-1550
    (wild mushrooms)

The Creamery/Ferdinand's
    Washington State University
    Pullman, Washington 99164-4418
    1-509-335-4014
    (Cougar Gold cheese)

Cypress Grove Chèvre
    4600 Dows Prairie Road
    McKinleyville, California 95521
    1-707-839-3168
    (goat cheese)

Glencorra Farm
    Rt. 1, Box 1408
    Lopez Island, Washington 98261
    1-206-468-3848
    (sheep's milk cheese)

Harry and David
    23518 South Pacific Highway
    P.O. Box 712
    Medford, Oregon 97501
    1-503-776-2121, Extension 2180
    (fresh fruit, prunes)

Hurst's Berry Farm
  23301 Southwest McKibben Road
  Sheridan, Oregon 97378
  1-503-843-3185
  (gooseberries, currants, berries)

Jake's Famous Products
  4252 Southeast International Way,
    Suite G
  Milwaukie, Oregon 97222
  1-800-777-7179
  (Dungeness crab, salmon, crawfish)

Josephson's Smokehouse and Dock
  106 Marine Drive
  P.O. Box 412
  Astoria, Oregon 97103
  1-503-325-2190
  *(canned, cured, pickled, and smoked
  seafood, fresh caviar)*

Loleta Cheese Factory
  252 Loleta Drive
  Loleta, California 95551
  1-707-733-5470
  (cheese—cheddar with smoked salmon)

Oregon Prune Exchange
  1840 B Street
  Forest Grove, Oregon 97116
  1-503-357-6800
  (hazelnuts, walnuts, prunes)

Rogue Gold Dairy, Inc.
  234 Southwest Fifth Street
  Grants Pass, Oregon 97526
  1-503-476-7786
  (cheese)

Rogue River Valley Creamery
  P.O. Box 3606
  Central Point, Oregon 97502
  1-503-664-2233
  (cheese)

Rollingstone Chèvre
  27349 Shelton Road
  Parma, Idaho 83660
  1-208-722-6460
  (goat cheese)

Sally Jackson Cheese
  Star Rt. 1, Box 106
  Oroville, Washington 98844
  1-509-738-2011
  (cow, goat, and sheep's milk cheese)

Specific Forest Products
  2680 Roosevelt Boulevard
  Eugene, Oregon 97402
  1-503-688-5645
  (wild mushrooms, huckleberries)

Stringer's Orchard
  Highway 395
  New Pinecreek, California 97635
  1-916-946-4112
  (wild plum jelly)

Walla Walla Gardners' Association
  210 North 11th Street
  Walla Walla, Washington 99362
  1-800-553-5014
  (Walla Walla Sweets)

Whidbey's Liqueur
  Whidbey's Greenbank Farm
  Whidbey Island, Washington 98253
  1-206-678-7700
  (loganberry liqueur)

Yakima Cheese Company
  P.O. Box 814
  Sunnyside, Washington 98944
  1-509-837-6005
  (Gouda cheese)

SELECTED BIBLIOGRAPHY

Clark, Ella E. *Indian Legends of the Pacific Northwest.* Berkeley, California: University of California Press, 1953.

Collins, Dean. *The Chedder Box.* Portland, Oregon: *The Oregon Journal,* 1933.

Flaherty, David C., and Sue Ellen Harvey. *Fruits and Berries of the Pacific Northwest.* Edmonds, Washington: Alaska Northwest Publishing Company, 1988.

Gunther, Erna. *Ethnobotany of Western Washington.* Seattle, Washington: University of Washington Publications in Anthropology, 1945.

Hatton, Raymond R. *Oregon's Big Country: A Portrait of Southeastern Oregon.* Bend, Oregon: Maverick Publications, 1988.

Hildebrand, Lorraine Barker. *Straw Hats, Sandal and Steel: The Chinese in Washington State.* Tacoma, Washington: The Washington State Historical Society, 1977.

Howe, Carrol B. *Ancient Tribes of the Klamath Country.* Portland, Oregon: Binford & Mort, 1968.

Jackman, E. R., and R. A. Long. *The Oregon Desert.* Caldwell, Idaho: The Caxton Printers, Ltd., 1964.

Johansen, Dorothy O., and Charles M. Gates. *Empire of the Columbia.* New York: Harper & Row, 1957.

Kimerling, Jon A., and Philip L. Jackson, editors. *Atlas of the Pacific Northwest.* Corvallis, Oregon: Oregon State University Press, 1985.

Ladies' Aid Society of the Methodist Episcopal Church, Roseburg, Oregon. *The Experience Cook Book.* Roseburg, Oregon: *The Umpqua Valley News,* 1899.

Ladies of the Christian Church, Eureka California. *The Ladies' Cook Book.* Eureka, California: La Marrt & McKrehan, Printers, 1898.

Ladies of the Congregational Church, Olympia, Washington. *The Capital City Cook Book.* Olympia, Washington: Recorder Press, 1914.

Lavender, David. *Westward Vision, The Story of the Oregon Trail.* Lincoln, Nebraska: University of Nebraska Press, 1973.

Lockley, Fred. *Conversations with Pioneer Women.* Compiled and edited by Mike Helm. Eugene, Oregon: Rainy Day Press, 1981.

Luchetti, Cathy, in collaboration with Carol Olivell. *Women of the West.* St. George, Utah: Antelope Island Press, 1982.

Maser, Chris. *Forest Primeval, The Natural History of an Ancient Forest.* San Francisco, California: Sierra Club Books, 1989.

Mathews, Daniel. *Cascade-Olympic Natural History.* Portland, Oregon: Raven Editions in conjunction with the Portland Audubon Society, 1988.

Morgan, Murray. *Skid Road, Seattle: Her First 125 Years.* Sausalito, California: Comstock Editions, Inc., 1951.

National Council of Jewish Women, Portland, Oregon, Chapter. *The Neighborhood Cookbook.* Portland, Oregon: National Council of Jewish Women, 1914.

Newson, David. *David Newson: The Western Observer, 1805-1992.* Portland, Oregon: The Oregon Historical Society, 1972.

O'Donnell, Terence, and Thomas Vaughan. *Portland, A Historical Sketch and Guide.* Portland, Oregon: Oregon Historical Society, 1976.

Olson, Joan and Gene. *Oregon, Times and Trails.* Merlin, Oregon: Windyridge Press, 1965.

Orr, Elizabeth and William. *Rivers of the West: A Guide to the Geology and History.* Salem, Oregon: Eagle Web Press, 1985.

Pelligrini, Angelo. *Wine and the Good Life.* New York: Alfred A. Knopf, 1965.

The Portland Woman's Exchange Cook Book 1913. Contemporary edition. Portland, Oregon: Oregon Historical Society Press, 1973.

Root, Waverly, and Richard de Rochemont. *Eating in America.* New York: Morrow, 1976.

Ross, Alexander. *Adventures of the First Settlers on the Oregon or Columbia River, 1810–1813.* Lincoln, Nebraska: University of Nebraska Press, 1986.

Ruby, Robert H., and John A. Brown. *Indians of the Pacific Northwest, A History.* Norman, Oklahoma: University of Oklahoma Press, 1981.

San Grael Society of the First Presbyterian Church, Portland, Oregon. *The Web-Foot Cook Book.* Portland, Oregon: W. B. Ayer and Company, 1885.

Schwantes, Carlos A. *The Pacific Northwest: An Interpretive History.* Lincoln, Nebraska: University of Nebraska Press, 1989.

Strong, Emory. *Stone Age on the Columbia River.* Portland, Oregon: Binford & Mort, 1959.

Townsend, John Kirk. *Across the Rockies to the Columbia.* Lincoln, Nebraska: University of Nebraska Press, 1978. (Originally published: *Narrative of a Journey Across the Rocky Mountains to the Columbia River.* Philadelphia: H. Perkins, 1839.)

White, Sid, and S. E. Solberg, editors. *Peoples of Washington.* Pullman, Washington: Washington State University Press, 1989.

Whitman, Narcissa. *My Journal, 1836.* Fairfield, Washington: Ye Galleon Press, 1986.

Wright, Jessie Louetta. *How High the Bounty.* Roseburg, Oregon: Friends of the Douglas County Museum, 1982.

Zucker, Jeff, Kay Hummel, and Bob Hogfoss. *Oregon Indians, Culture, History & Current Affairs.* Portland, Oregon: Oregon Historical Press, 1983.

INDEX

N

PHOTOGRAPHIC ACKNOWLEDGMENTS

The photographs reproduced in this book were provided with the permission of the following:

Oregon Historical Society: 3(negative: Lot 369-A-1984), 19(ORHI 002639), 23(ORHI 001154), 25(ORHI 67789), 29(CN 001341), 32(CN 001479), 39(ORHI 57215), 40(CN 018866), 51(ORHI 38157), 53(CN 022698), 54(ORI II 4048), 55(ORHI 11984), 61(ORHI 84041), 67(ORHI 5662), 71(ORHI 27409), 81(ORHI 78226), 83(ORHI 84104), 87(ORHI 84100), 89(Finley A1604), 90(ORHI 84101), 93(ORHI 086086), 101(ORHI 46145), 102(ORHI 85590), 103(ORHI 64474), 106 top(ORHI 50642), 106 bottom(ORHI 70849), 107(ORHI 11983-A), 108(ORHI 38052), 111(CN 022347), 117(CN 022635), 123(ORHI 85278), 127(CN 077248), 130(ORHI 85374), 133(ORHI 55764), 135(ORHI 78261), 137(ORHI 36647), 141(CN 016278), 144(ORHI 85583), 155(ORHI 57080), 159(ORHI 45703), 161(ORHI 60409), 169(ORHI 85584), 170(ORHI 74735), 172(ORHI 85585), 183(ORHI 12176), 184(ORHI 46342), 186(ORHI 85589), 198(ORHI 86396), 203(CN 015381), 205(ORHI 55643), 208(CN 008057), 209(ORHI 47480), 213(ORHI 85582), 214(ORHI 23917), 215(ORHI 12592), 216(ORHI 4366), 218(ORHI 82627), 219(ORHI 85581), 225(ORHI 38151), 227(ORHI 4368), 228(ORHI 537), 231(ORHI 857), 237(ORHI 86395), 239(ORHI 11285), 243(CN 015185), 244(ORHI 22054), 249(ORHI 60451), 250(CN 015228), 254(Lot 741-20), 260(ORHI 37785), 261(ORHI 85586), 263(0181G071), 272(CN 011495), 273(CN 012618), 274(ORHI 43224), 278(ORHI 58963), 283(ORHI 85588), 287(ORHI 62614), 294(CN 022699), 299(ORHI 70380)

Nordic Heritage Museum, Seattle, Washington: 16, 69, 91, 146, 147, 200, 233
Humbolt County Historical Society: 21, 174
Wescott Bay Sea Farms: 35, 59
Pike Place Market Archives: 44
The Seattle Times Co.: 47, 193
The Collection of Peter E. Palmquist, Arcata, California: 57, 77, 115, 151, 224
Nippon Kan Heritage Association Photo Exhibit, Seattle, Washington: 63, 179
Idaho Sheep Industry: 82
Smithsonian Institution National Anthropological Archives, Bureau of American Ethnology Collection: 94(75-16174), 105(79-8490), 143(55403), 190(55405), 221(75-16203)
Lhur Jensen, Inc.: 125
Washington State Historical Society, Tacoma: 131, 167, 187, 246, 291
Humboldt State University Foundation Library: 145
Verdun Boucock Family: 229
Jewish Historical Society of Oregon: 268(CN 23271)
Washington Apple Commission: 290
Evelyn McCormick, Arcata, California: 297

A NOTE ABOUT THE AUTHOR

Janie Hibler grew up in Arcata, a small coastal town in the lush redwoods of
northern California, 120 miles south of the Oregon border. She graduated
from Dominican College of San Rafael and worked as a medical technol-
ogist for eight years. After several years of teaching cooking classes as a
hobby, she became director of the Kitchen Kaboodle Cooking School in
Portland in 1978 and, later, the director of the Discriminating Palate, a
small cooking school in Strohecker's, a third-generation specialty food store
in Portland. Mrs. Hibler has written a column on seafood for *The
Oregonian,* as well as articles for *Good Food, Cuisine, Oregon Magazine,
Salmon–Trout Steelheader,* and *Gourmet.* She and her husband live in
Portland but spend time frequently at their cabin in the Washington
Cascades.

A NOTE ON THE TYPE

The text of this book was set in Garamond, a modern rendering of the type
first cut by Claude Garamond (c. 1480–1561). Garamond was a pupil of
Geoffroy Tory and is believed to have based his letters on the Venetian
models, although he introduced a number of important differences, and it is
to him we owe the letter which we know as "old style." He gave to his
letters a certain elegance and a feeling of movement that won for their
creator an immediate reputation and the patronage of Francis I of France.

PRINTED AND BOUND BY THE COURIER COMPANIES, INC.
WESTFORD, MASSACHUSETTS

COMPOSED BY DONNA DAVID
NEW YORK, NEW YORK

DESIGNED BY BARBARA BALCH